Korean-English Bilingualism in Early Childhood

BILINGUAL EDUCATION & BILINGUALISM

Series Editors: **Nancy H. Hornberger** *(University of Pennsylvania, USA)* and **Wayne E. Wright** *(Purdue University, USA)*

Bilingual Education and Bilingualism is an international, multidisciplinary series publishing research on the philosophy, politics, policy, provision and practice of language planning, Indigenous and minority language education, multilingualism, multiculturalism, biliteracy, bilingualism and bilingual education. The series aims to mirror current debates and discussions. New proposals for single-authored, multiple-authored, or edited books in the series are warmly welcomed, in any of the following categories or others authors may propose: overview or introductory texts; course readers or general reference texts; focus books on particular multilingual education program types; school-based case studies; national case studies; collected cases with a clear programmatic or conceptual theme; and professional education manuals.

All books in this series are externally peer-reviewed.

Full details of all the books in this series and of all our other publications can be found on http://www.multilingual-matters.com, or by writing to Multilingual Matters, St Nicholas House, 31-34 High Street, Bristol, BS1 2AW, UK.

BILINGUAL EDUCATION & BILINGUALISM: 142

Korean-English Bilingualism in Early Childhood

A Longitudinal Investigation of Development

Sunny K. Park-Johnson

MULTILINGUAL MATTERS
Bristol • Jackson

DOI https://doi.org/10.21832/PARK2897
Library of Congress Cataloging in Publication Data
A catalog record for this book is available from the Library of Congress.
Names: Park-Johnson, Sunny K., author.
Title: Korean-English Bilingualism in Early Childhood: A Longitudinal
   Investigation of Development/Sunny K. Park-Johnson.
Description: Bristol; Jackson: Multilingual Matters, [2024] | Series:
   Bilingual Education & Bilingualism: 142 | Includes bibliographical
   references and index. | Summary: "This overview of the linguistic
   development of Korean-English bilingual children in the US focuses on
   morphology and syntax acquisition in early childhood, a time when
   language dominance is shifting rapidly. It expands our understanding of
   heritage language acquisition and furthers bilingualism research on
   typologically distinct language pairings"—Provided by publisher.
Identifiers: LCCN 2023042974 (print) | LCCN 2023042975 (ebook) | ISBN
   9781800412897 (hbk) | ISBN 9781800410374 (pbk) | ISBN 9781800412903
   (pdf) | ISBN 9781800412910 (epub)
Subjects: LCSH: Bilingualism in children—United States. | Korean American
   children—Language. | Second language acquisition. | Heritage language
   speakers—United States.
Classification: LCC P115.2 .P37 2024 (print) | LCC P115.2 (ebook) | DDC
   495.7/04221—dc23/eng/20231114
LC record available at https://lccn.loc.gov/2023042974
LC ebook record available at https://lccn.loc.gov/2023042975

British Library Cataloguing in Publication Data
A catalogue entry for this book is available from the British Library.

ISBN-13: 978-1-80041-289-7 (hbk)
ISBN-13: 978-1-80041-037-4 (pbk)

Multilingual Matters
UK: St Nicholas House, 31-34 High Street, Bristol, BS1 2AW, UK.
USA: Ingram, Jackson, TN, USA.

Website: www.multilingual-matters.com
Twitter: Multi_Ling_Mat
Facebook: https://www.facebook.com/multilingualmatters
Blog: www.channelviewpublications.wordpress.com

Copyright © 2024 Sunny K. Park-Johnson.

All rights reserved. No part of this work may be reproduced in any form or by any means without permission in writing from the publisher.

The policy of Multilingual Matters/Channel View Publications is to use papers that are natural, renewable and recyclable products, made from wood grown in sustainable forests. In the manufacturing process of our books, and to further support our policy, preference is given to printers that have FSC and PEFC Chain of Custody certification. The FSC and/or PEFC logos will appear on those books where full certification has been granted to the printer concerned.

Typeset by Deanta Global Publishing Services, Chennai, India.

To Aurelia Eunsu and Vincent Sungwoo

Contents

	Tables and Figures	ix
	Acknowledgements	xiii
1	Introduction	1
	1.1 Introduction	1
	1.2 Theoretical Framework	2
	1.3 Definitions	4
	1.4 Heritage Speakers	9
	1.5 Theoretical and Practical Implications of Studying Bilingual Children	14
2	Source of Data and Language Overview	18
	2.1 Introduction	18
	2.2 Participants	19
	2.3 Data Collection	22
	2.4 Language Overview: Korean	24
	2.5 Language Overview: English	28
	2.6 Chapter Summary	29
3	Korean Morphology	30
	3.1 Introduction	30
	3.2 Case Markers and Case Ellipsis	31
	3.3 Classifiers	37
	3.4 Transitivity Markers	40
	3.5 Sentence Final Markers	43
	3.6 Chapter Summary	46
4	Korean Syntax	48
	4.1 Introduction	48
	4.2 Word Order	49
	4.3 Null Pronominals	52
	4.4 Chapter Summary	57

5	English Morphology	60
	5.1 Introduction	60
	5.2 English Articles	61
	5.3 English Verb Morphology	68
	5.4 Chapter Summary	77
6	English Syntax	80
	6.1 Introduction	80
	6.2 Wh-Movement	80
	6.3 Subject Auxiliary Inversion	83
	6.4 Word Order	91
	6.5 Pronominal Use	96
	6.6 Chapter Summary	103
7	Code-Switching	105
	7.1 Introduction	105
	7.2 Code-Mixing: Structure	107
	7.3 Code-Switching: Content	112
	7.4 Code-Mixing: Frequency Over Time	115
	7.5 Chapter Summary	117
8	Ten Years Later	120
	8.1 Introduction	120
	8.2 Theme 1: Korean Language Proficiency and Identity, Belongingness and Family	121
	8.3 Theme 2: Shame	124
	8.4 Theme 3: Finding Themselves	127
	8.5 Analysis	129
	8.6 Chapter Summary	132
9	Conclusions and Implications	133
	9.1 Introduction	133
	9.2 Implications for Linguistic Theory	136
	9.3 Implications for Identity	140
	9.4 Implications for Education	143
	9.5 Next Steps	147
	References	149
	Index	161

Tables and Figures

Tables

1.1	Morphological and syntactic contrasts between Korean and English	14
2.1	Participants' ages and use of Korean and English	20
2.2	Participants' start and end ages	22
2.3	Case markers in Korean	26
2.4	Korean classifiers	27
3.1	Pearson correlations for age and percentage of overt case marking	33
3.2	Logistic regression predicting likelihood of subject marker use based on canonicality	34
3.3	Logistic regression predicting likelihood of object marker use based on canonicality	35
3.4	Chi-square test of homogeneity for subject marker use	36
3.5	Chi-square test of homogeneity for object marker use	36
3.6	Accuracy rates of Korean classifiers	38
3.7	Transitivity marker use by Korean-English bilingual children	42
3.8	Verbs used with transitivity markers by Korean-English bilingual children	42
3.9	Overall accuracy rates for sentence final markers in Korean	44
4.1	Korean word order overall acceptability by child	50
4.2	Word orders used in children's Korean utterances	50
4.3	Rates of accuracy of prodrop	54
5.1	English article use accuracy overall	62
5.2	English article use comparison of Dan and Ben	63
5.3	Proportion of English article errors by child	65
5.4	English verb morphology accuracy	69
5.5	Null copula errors by tense	77
6.1	Stages of auxiliary *do* and supporting evidence	90
6.2	Stages of auxiliary *be* and supporting evidence	90
6.3	Word order used in English declarative utterances	93
6.4	Word order used in English imperative utterances	94

6.5	Types of subjects and objects coded in English prodrop study	97
6.6	Rates of subject and object use accuracy in English overall	97
7.1	Rates of Korean and English word order in code-mixed utterances	108
7.2	Structure of code-mixed utterances	109
7.3	Pearson correlations for age and percentage of language production	117
8.1	Sarah's and Sandy's self-assessment scores	121
9.1	Summary of results from book	134

Figures

2.1	Timeline of children's ages	23
3.1	Range of Korean classifiers used overall	39
4.1	Korean word order types across time: Dan	51
4.2	Korean word order types across time: Ben	51
4.3	Korean word order types across time: Sandy	51
4.4	Korean word order types across time: Sarah	52
4.5	Korean prodrop types: Dan	55
4.6	Korean prodrop types: Ben	55
4.7	Korean prodrop types: Sandy	56
4.8	Korean prodrop types: Sarah	56
5.1	Percent correct for English article use by age: Dan	63
5.2	Percent correct for English article use by age: Ben	64
5.3	Percent correct for English article use by age: Sandy	64
5.4	Percent correct for English article use by age: Sarah	65
5.5	English article errors: Dan	66
5.6	English article errors: Ben	66
5.7	English article errors: Sandy	67
5.8	English article errors: Sarah	67
5.9	English verb morphology accuracy over time: Dan	70
5.10	English verb morphology accuracy over time: Ben	70
5.11	English verb morphology accuracy over time: Sandy	71
5.12	English verb morphology accuracy over time: Sarah	71
5.13	English regular and irregular verb accuracy over time: Dan	72
5.14	English regular and irregular verb accuracy over time: Ben	72
5.15	English regular and irregular verb accuracy over time: Sandy	72
5.16	English regular and irregular verb accuracy over time: Sarah	73
5.17	English past and present tense verb accuracy over time: Dan	73
5.18	English past and present tense verb accuracy over time: Ben	73
5.19	English past and present tense verb accuracy over time: Sandy	74
5.20	English past and present tense verb accuracy over time: Sarah	74
5.21	English verb morphology error types: Dan	75
5.22	English verb morphology error types: Ben	75
5.23	English verb morphology error types: Sandy	76

5.24	English verb morphology error types: Sarah	76
6.1	Rates of English word order over time: Dan	94
6.2	Rates of English word order over time: Ben	95
6.3	Rates of English word order over time: Sandy	95
6.4	Rates of English word order over time: Sarah	95
6.5	Types of English subjects used overall	99
6.6	Types of English objects used overall	100
6.7	Types of English subjects overall: Dan	101
6.8	Types of English subjects overall: Ben	101
6.9	Types of English subjects overall: Sandy	101
6.10	Types of English subjects overall: Sarah	102
6.11	Types of English objects overall: Dan	102
6.12	Types of English objects overall: Ben	102
6.13	Types of English objects overall: Sandy	103
6.14	Types of English objects overall: Sarah	103

Acknowledgements

I want to start by thanking the families that welcomed me into their homes and in their lives, allowing me to spend time with your amazing children, whose languages, thoughts, humor, and creativity continue to astound me to this day. Thank you for letting me be a part of your lives; it means more to me than you will ever know. 감사합니다. And especially to the children – I had so much fun spending time with you, thank you for sharing part of your childhood with me.

I would like to thank the wonderful people at Multilingual Matters, especially my editor Rosie McEwan, series editors Nancy Hornberger and Wayne E. Wright, and the anonymous reviewers who provided insightful feedback and support for this book. I would like to also thank Sarah Shin for the mentorship, collaboration, and empowerment you have provided; it is our conversation over brunch that planted the idea of putting together this book, for which I am immensely grateful. I want to extend my gratitude to Elena Benedicto, who encouraged me to conduct this type of longitudinal research that yielded such riches of language beyond what I could get in an experiment. And to my BBE colleagues Sonia Soltero and Jason Goulah at DePaul: thank you for being my pillars of strength. I could not ask for better, more supportive colleagues and mentors. I also want to acknowledge my amazing research assistants, Alexandra Pflug, Yu Sun Jung, Yeo Jin Yoon, and Marty Buck, for the work they put into these studies: you have my everlasting thanks and admiration.

Finally, 엄마 아빠, thank you for my bilingualism. What an immeasurable, lifelong gift you have given me. Jason, my first unofficial research participant, thank you for your good humor. My deepest appreciation for my loving husband Drew for being the best partner and supporter, and for my incredible children Eunsu and Sungwoo whose sheer presence makes me whole.

1 Introduction

1.1 Introduction

This book is a close-up investigation of the morphological and syntactic development of Korean-English bilingual children in early childhood. The research in this volume comes from a longitudinal study of four Korean-English bilingual children born and living in the United States, growing up in a Korean-speaking household. The data provided in this book are unique in the following three ways. First, while there are numerous studies that have looked at this population in adulthood and adolescence, there is still little known about the earlier stages of development. Perhaps because of the limitations of child research, the specificity of the population, or both, there are not as many studies that look at childhood bilingualism for learners of Korean and English. The data in this book fill that noticeable gap in the research. Second, the data come from a longitudinal study across two and a half years; to have a body of monthly naturalistic production data for four children across several years is a wealth of knowledge that cannot be understated. The data were collected in the children's homes by the same investigator every month during that time. It is perhaps the aforementioned difficulty with researching young children that many studies with Korean-English bilingual children are cross-sectional in nature; the longitudinal data here will allow us to observe moments that are uncaptured in an experimental design, nuanced changes that are missed in a cross-sectional study, and 'messiness' that may not emerge in a lab setting. Finally, much of the research on child bilingualism has focused on the 'ideal' of simultaneous bilingualism. While simultaneous development provides important insight, the nature of this present study allows unique opportunities to witness two vastly different languages developing sequentially while the first is still in development: the children are exposed to Korean from birth and exposed to English just two or three years later while acquisition of the first is still in progress. During this time of life, children also experience a rapid language dominance shift from being Korean-dominant to English-dominant in a matter of a year or two, providing a crucial glimpse into how the brain manages this outward shift internally. The result is a remarkable – but not uncommon – language acquisition scenario that is ripe with consequences for theory and practice.

This first chapter provides an introduction to the topic and a contextualization for the research within a heteroglossic, generative theoretical framework, in which bilingualism is normalized, multilingual and other linguistically diverse individuals are viewed as linguistically complete, and multilingual language systems are complex and rule-governed. The next section familiarizes readers with some critical definitions (e.g. what is sequential bilingualism, who are heritage language [HL] learners) and sets the stage for Korean-English bilingualism, bilingualism in early childhood and the many complexities of learning a new language while the first is still in development. Finally, Chapter 1 discusses the ways in which the study of bilingual children provides theoretical and practical implications in other multilingual contexts throughout the world.

1.2 Theoretical Framework

My work in this volume will draw from two major theoretical views. The first is the heteroglossic framework, which will inform how I view and represent multilingual individuals throughout the book. The second is a generative linguistic framework for examining the structure of language of the individuals discussed in the book. Although these frameworks originate from different disciplines, these two views of thinking about bilingualism are actually complementary and can cohere the complexity and richness of the bilingual experience. Let us consider each in turn, then discuss the way in which the frameworks piece together to help us navigate the linguistic patterns and processes of bilingual children.

The heteroglossic framework stems from the work of Mikhail Bakhtin, philosopher and cultural historian. He (Bakhtin, 1992: 288) defined heteroglossia as 'another's speech in another's language, serving to express authorial intentions but in a refracted way'. In this view, we acknowledge and normalize the coexistence of multiple varieties of language, both in society and within an individual. The heteroglossic stance is that language is never unitary:

> Actual social life and historical becoming create within an abstractly unitary national language a multitude of concrete worlds, a multitude of bounded verbal-ideological and social belief systems; within these various systems...are elements of language filled with various semantic and axiological content and each with its own different sound. (Bakhtin, 1992: 288)

The multiplicity-as-norm core tenet is the crux that informs the work in this book. In other words, the heteroglossic framework views multilingualism as the norm and multilingual and other linguistically diverse individuals as linguistically complete. This is a sharp contrast from the vast majority of literature that historically took a deficit perspective on second language (L2) learners, bilinguals and heritage speakers, focusing on what these individuals cannot do, how they deviate from the monolingual standard and what linguistic inadequacies they must overcome. This deficit perspective has permeated educational and societal ideologies such that they continue to disadvantage these already marginalized groups, shape policy toward monolingualism and prioritize certain languages over others. However, by adopting a heteroglossic framework as we study heritage speakers, we assume their completeness as a speaker, their wholeness as a multifaced multilingual and their unique and valuable contribution to society. Bakhtin also rejects the notion of an official, national language, or the idea that there is 'one reigning language' (1992: 271) in society that prioritizes certain languages and enslaves others. I apply this ideology to heritage speakers and multilinguals, stressing that there are no languages that are inherently superior to others, including those variations spoken by heritage and multilingual communities regardless of how they are viewed in society.

Paired with the heteroglossic framework, I also situate my work in a generative linguistic theory. Chomsky's (1995) theory posits that all human language is equally complex, developed and regulated by an innate internal structure known as Universal Grammar (UG). In this theory, language acquisition is activated by input, with which the human brain can construct language. The crux of this theory that is especially relevant for my work is that this process describes not just monolingual speakers and speakers of socially prestigious languages; this structure is equally available to all. As far as language is concerned, the human brain knows no social hierarchy. All human languages and dialects have regularized rules, regardless of their social status. Some languages have been targeted in society and education fueled by discriminatory ideologies (e.g. African American English), others are wrongfully deemed illegitimate (e.g. Spanglish), while some are ridiculed, belittled and stereotyped (e.g. Korean-accented English). Rather than treating these languages as deviations from the norm, within linguistic generative grammar all languages are analyzed in their own right as complete and legitimate systems. This view also assumes that despite what may appear as errors in heritage grammars, all utterances and structures produced by heritage speakers at all levels are still governed by UG. This entails that utterances produced by heritage speakers, including code-switching and utterances that are not possible for monolingual or homeland speakers of the language, fall under the same principles of grammar that govern socially powerful languages. In adopting this perspective, we flip the narrative: it is not that these languages are wrong, erroneous or underdeveloped, but instead it is that these speakers are far more knowledgeable, creative and remarkable for what they are able to do with two or more languages. By examining the grammatical elements and processes of multilingual speakers and highlighting their abilities, we further shed the arbitrary linguistic hierarchies that society imposes, rejecting language subjugation and language subordination. To examine these languages is to look upon speakers' innovative and brilliant capacities.

Taken together, these theories emphasize additive perspectives of bilingualism to shed light on the extensive linguistic capabilities of multilingual individuals, and in turn expand the collective knowledge of the limitless possibilities of human language. Additionally, we are able to inform not only academia but also educators, policymakers, stakeholders and multilingual communities of the systemic linguistic prejudice that exists for bilinguals in our culture today. By naming the uniqueness that is HL and situating it in a heteroglossic, generative approach, we shed light on the intricate, innovative systems developed by the minds of this unique population. Coursing through both these theories is an undercurrent of inclusivity, acceptance and social justice that animates the research in this book: by seeing the bilingual person as a norm, by focusing on heritage speakers' abilities and by acknowledging the value of minoritized languages, we legitimize the diverse experiences and backgrounds of individuals who are otherwise marginalized in society.

1.3 Definitions

The complex nature of understanding human language and identity result in terms that are used inconsistently or require some examination. In this section I will define some of the terms I will be using throughout the book, but also point out labels that are problematic and potentially misleading. Some identifiers we will discuss include *native speaker*, *bilingual*, *emergent bilingual*, *L2er*, *sequential bilingual* and *simultaneous bilingual*. We will also look at some related terms that refer to the process aspect of bilingualism, such as *second language acquisition* (SLA), *bilingual first language acquisition*, *early L2 acquisition* and *bilingual acquisition*.

1.3.1 Native Speaker

One of the most commonly used identifiers in linguistics and applied linguistics is the notion of the native speaker. It is the native speaker that is assumed to have correct intuition about what is possible and impossible in their language. It is the native speaker that supposedly holds ownership of the language, and learners of that language are secondary to the native speaker. The primacy of the native speaker has been a problem discussed by many scholars (Davies, 1991; Lee, 1995, 2005). One of the issues with the definition is the fact that native speakers are assumed to be monolingual. If we give primacy to the monolingual native speaker, what does that mean for the bilingual individual who happens to be a speaker of the language from birth – natively – but speaks another language as well? Even more controversial is the fact that even if a person is technically a native speaker of a language, that person may be a heritage speaker of that language and has limited proficiency. Heritage speakers never 'make the cut', so to speak, when it comes to their inclusion in the definition of a native speaker even though they have been speaking the language from birth. Another potential issue with the primacy of the native speaker is that regardless of how proficient a person might be in the language, if they did not speak the language from birth, they are excluded from carrying the native speaker banner. An individual who learned English from the age of 3 onward may have indistinguishable characteristics of receptive and productive English from the monolingual native English speaker; yet, that individual cannot by definition claim nativeness and can only be considered 'native-like' in proficiency. The exclusivity of the native speaker club would not be much of an issue if we did not assign such lofty prestige to its members. Nevertheless, native speakers are continually sought after as the control group, the norm by which bilingual, heritage and second language learners are measured. Thus, some caution is warranted as we continue forward to discuss groups of speakers who *are* often compared to the native standard. Linguists consistently reject the notion of the standard language myth; here, we might benefit from rejecting the native speaker myth to avoid overlooking the opportunity to learn from multilingualism.

1.3.2 Bilinguals

As challenging as it is to pinpoint the definition of a native speaker, it is perhaps more confounding to identify criteria for bilingualism. Who is a bilingual? At what level of proficiency does one need to be in order to 'qualify'? Bilingualism entails that a speaker has some level of proficiency in two (or more) languages. Depending on definitions of bilingualism, this requirement of proficiency can vary immensely. At its root, bilingual simply means two languages, but because bilingual is a label that applies not only to a linguistic repertoire but also to an identity, there is a considerable amount of complexity added to the already intricate definition. It is also sometimes difficult to pinpoint who a bilingual is because people use this term inconsistently for themselves. People who have studied a second language for many years will still not admit to others (or themselves) that they are bilingual, despite their high levels of proficiency. Hedging their qualifications, bilingual individuals I encounter will often downplay their abilities:

> 'I studied Spanish for eight years, but I'm not really a bilingual.'

> 'My parents speak Japanese and I try to speak it back but it's hard. I'm not really bilingual…I mix English in a lot.'

This inferiority complex of 'not really bilingual' is, I suspect, in part due to the primacy of the native speaker once again. We are conditioned to not admit to our own abilities because we fall short of the native speaker myth: that one must speak the language from birth in order to claim their identity as a speaker. Too often, my highly proficient bilingual students will downplay their bilingualism because they 'are not really bilingual' or perceive themselves as falling short of some expectation.

In the United States in particular, the term *bilingual* has been so often used synonymously with deficiency and otherness that legislation actually stopped using it by the 1990s. The term *bilingual* (such as in the Bilingual Education Act of 1968) was replaced by terms such as Limited English Proficient (LEP) or English Language Learner (ELL). Of course, these changes then create other problems (namely the primacy of English development over other languages), but the point is that the term *bilingual* was so unfavorable and seemingly inaccurate that the entire US government decided to rename laws and omit it like a taboo.

What is objectionable about the term *bilingual*? What makes it so unattainable? Part of this is due to the mythology surrounding the ideal bilingual person: that they should have perfect proficiency in both languages; that they are able to use both languages equally well in all situations; that they are capable of communicating only in one language or the other without mixing. This myth of the bilingual as two monolinguals in one has been debunked in the literature (see Grosjean, 1989; Zentella, 1997); however, the general public, educators, policymakers and – perhaps most importantly – bilinguals themselves, have internalized the notion. Let us first discuss each myth, then talk about how internalizing such myths can have negative repercussions. First, the myth that bilinguals should have high levels of proficiency in both languages comes from the notion of the United Nations interpreter (Park-Johnson & Shin, 2020; Shin, 2018), a professional who is seemingly able to translate between multiple languages on various topics and be able to do so at any moment's notice. People with this type of ability, however, are limited to highly trained professionals whose job is to bridge communication gaps between speakers of various languages. The typical bilingual person does not have this kind of need nor training, and balanced bilingualism is rather mythological in and of itself. Second, related to the first myth, there seems to be an expectation that bilinguals should be able to use either language equally well in all situations. However, this is rarely the case. Bilinguals might use Language A for work and school, and use Language B for home, religious service and personal relationships. In this scenario, asking this bilingual person to explain, using Language B, what they are learning about at school or explain a work problem might leave them struggling to find the right words; in contrast, they might sound awkward trying to use Language A in an informal, friendly social setting. Lastly, the myth that bilinguals should be able to carry on a conversation without ever needing (or wanting) to switch to the other language is quite limiting and harmful. Most bilinguals, especially if they are using the language that is not the dominant societal language (SL), might find code-mixing a natural part of using that language. For instance, many Spanish speakers who live in the United States might speak Spanish to one another but insert English words or phrases. This is seen with distaste and derision by speakers back in the homeland because the Spanish they speak *is* the dominant SL.

Why are these myths harmful to bilinguals? The unrealistic expectation that bilingual individuals have equal proficiency in both languages excludes most bilingual people from this definition. If the definition does not actually fit most of the people that belong to the category, it behooves us to change that definition. Additionally, for someone to have equal capabilities in either language in any setting would be highly inefficient and a redundancy in the system. It would be generally a better use of resources to have certain ones allocated for one function and others allocated for a different function. But our insistence on this idealized notion of the bilingual is harmful because we can never measure up to it. The two-monolinguals-in-one myth – that to be bilingual one must function as monolingual in both languages but never both at the same time – is harmful because it assumes that the two languages are completely separate. It is as if we acknowledge that we have two hands, but we are only allowed to use one at a time and never together.

In addition to the challenge of defining bilingualism, it is also difficult to know which term to use. In the literature and in society, we see a multitude of terms that sometimes refer to the same group, while at the same time we use a single term to refer to multiple groups. Terms like *emergent bilingualism*, *bilingual first language acquisition* (BFLA), *simultaneous bilingualism*, *sequential bilingualism*, *early L2 acquisition* and *bilingual acquisition* can be defined differently depending on the audience, field and background of the user. Here I will define the terms the way they will be used throughout the book.

Emergent Bilingual Learner (EBL) or Emergent Bilingual is a term used more often in education as an alternative to English Learner (EL) or the more outdated term English Language Learner (ELL). EBL was adopted to shed a more positive light on students whose first language is not English but are learning English in a context where English is spoken as the dominant SL (e.g. United States, Canada, etc.). EBL highlights the direction of the learner's additive bilingualism as they are becoming proficient in more than one language. We rarely hear EBL used in the context of someone who is, for instance, an L1 speaker of English learning Arabic as a second language. The term seems for now to be limited to speakers learning English as a second language.

The terms *bilingual first language acquisition* (BFLA), *simultaneous bilingualism* and *bilingual acquisition* are also used in the literature.

These terms are generally used in linguistics and applied linguistics to refer to children who are learning two languages at an early age. Some scholars further constrain the terms to apply only to children who are exposed to both languages from birth to 2 years of age (De Houwer, 2009). BFLA, simultaneous bilingualism and bilingual acquisition imply that two languages are developing at the same time, but this is not used for, say, an adult who is learning two new languages. Thus, these three terms – BFLA, simultaneous bilingualism and bilingual acquisition – tend to be used exclusively for children.

Sequential bilingualism and early L2 acquisition probably have the most flexibility in use. Technically speaking, sequential bilingualism refers to the development of one language after the first language has already been introduced. This would then mean that sequential bilinguals can be those who were monolingual until adulthood and then developed a language later in life, but the term *sequential bilingual* is generally not used in that way. Rather, sequential bilingualism is usually limited to children, especially those that learned a second language after the first several years (Meisel, 2011). Many would argue that a child who learned a second language at the age of 3 or 4 would probably develop the same level of proficiency and fluency as a simultaneous bilingual child, but the distinction is helpful for discussing the patterns of development. Early L2 acquisition is another term that is used to describe children who learn a second language early in life, but not early enough to be considered 'simultaneous'.

Finally, SLA, which is sometimes seen as the umbrella term for all the aforementioned terms, technically refers to the development of any second language at any time. However, the reality is that SLA is usually reserved for talking about adults or adolescents whose first language is well-established. This is changing somewhat, but still the majority of studies that fall under the SLA umbrella are investigating adult second language development and would see terms like *sequential bilingualism* or *emergent bilingualism* to be an 'offshoot'.

As one can see, it is not just bilingualism that is difficult to define; the process in getting there is also loaded with a multitude of terminology. There is a fair amount of ambiguity around what to call these different types of bilinguals. One has to take into account the age of the learner when exposure began, the spacing between the onset of each language, whether the learner is now an adult or a child and whether the term is being used. It is also crucial to remember that one's own definitions, like identities, are dynamic and always changing. While the intent in this book is not to argue one term versus another, it does help us understand just how complex defining a speaker is. Furthermore, as we delve into the more complex yet set of terms that refer to heritage speakers, it invites us to consider why pinpointing the definition of a heritage speaker is so difficult.

1.4 Heritage Speakers

The first thing to understand about heritage speakers is the great deal of heterogeneity in terms of their experiences, proficiencies, language difficulties and relationship with the language. A population so difficult to define, heritage speakers were not even defined as a category of speakers until the 1990s (Polinsky, 2018). Between heritage speakers, there is a vast amount of heterogeneity in language ability, with variability in the range of receptive versus productive skills and oral versus written skills (Polinsky & Kagan, 2007). However, it is vital that we disaggregate heritage speakers from other types of learners because of the unique context in which they acquire, maintain and use the language. Heritage speakers are 'individuals raised in homes where a language other than English is spoken and who are to some degree bilingual in English and the heritage language' (Valdés, 2000: 1). This makes them different from other bilinguals because most of the time, their L2 is their dominant language and their L1 is the nondominant language.

Heritage speakers typically start out as the children of immigrants whose families have moved to a place where the home language differs from the SL. Children growing up in those homes hear the HL spoken by family members and caregivers and develop whatever variety is spoken by them. It is typical for heritage speakers to be more proficient in the HL as young children and less proficient as they grow older. This is a function of how much of the SL they are increasingly exposed to as children start spending more time with school friends, extracurricular activities and later, work environments. Sometimes the only source of the HL becomes the limited time they spend speaking and hearing the HL at home with their families. Thus, children who started out as monolingual speakers of the home language in the first few years of life quickly become sequential bilinguals of the HL and the SL, then in turn become dominant speakers of the SL.

Heritage speakers do not often have the opportunity to get HL reinforcement in the regular school system. Unless they specifically attend a dual language immersion school where the medium of instruction is both the HL and the SL, most heritage speakers do not get the chance to receive formal education in the HL until adolescence or adulthood, where they can take their own language as – ironically – a foreign language. In the following sections, we will discuss some of the general linguistic characteristics and language external characteristics of heritage speakers. These descriptions are not meant to be an exhaustive summary, but rather a brief primer that will help contextualize the Korean heritage speakers we will discuss in the rest of this book.

1.4.1 Heritage language characteristics

Heritage grammars can be qualitatively and quantitatively different from that of monolingual speakers or even second language learners of a language. Heritage speakers generally have better success with phonetic and phonological patterns of the HL as compared to second language learners. Sometimes, their phonological patterns are almost indistinguishable from L1 learners (Au *et al.*, 2002). However, heritage speakers are known to have more difficulty with morphology and syntax, which are the aspects of grammar we will focus on in this book. Benmamoun *et al.* (2013) provide a comprehensive review of studies that have investigated the various aspects of heritage grammars. Here, they highlight that morphology and syntax are the two areas that are most susceptible to attrition by heritage speakers. For instance, agreement is an area of morphology that diverges between heritage and monolingual grammars. Gender agreement (Polinsky, 2008), verb agreement (Anderson, 2001), possessive agreement (Bolonyai, 2007) and object agreement (Montrul *et al.*, 2012) are examples where we see difficulty for heritage speakers. Additionally, particles and markers that are not reinforced in the dominant SL of the heritage speaker, such as differential object marking (Montrul & Bowles, 2009), case marking (Song *et al.*, 1997) and numeral classifiers (Choi, 2003), often undergo paradigm leveling or deletion. In such a case, heritage speakers may have fewer levels in a paradigm where, for instance, they use the default marker for numeral classifiers when a more specific one is required in the homeland variety (Choi, 2003) or heritage speakers might omit the marker altogether (Montrul & Bowles, 2009).

Furthermore, heritage grammars may take on additional particles or features that are not permissible in the monolingual variety but are allowed in the dominant SL. One such example is preposition stranding, which is allowed in English but not in Spanish (Pascual y Cabo & Gómez Soler, 2015). Another common example is the oversupplying of the overt subject pronoun, which is required in English but is only required in specific uses such as disambiguation or emphasis in Hungarian (de Groot, 2005), Spanish (Montrul, 2004; Silva-Corvalán, 1994) and Arabic (Albirini *et al.*, 2011).

Although these characteristics may reflect some of the same difficulties that L2 learners of the language exhibit, scholars have shown evidence that heritage grammars can be quite different from that of an L2 learner due to the kinds of prior experience and early input that a HL environment provides (Kondo-Brown, 2005; Valdés, 2014). This is the aspect of heritage grammars that has not historically been heavily focused on, but is crucial to investigate if we are to destigmatize HLs and the positive impact that heritage speakers can have in our society and schools. For instance, heritage speakers might have extensive vocabulary that is used in the home and pertain to emotions, food and flavors, caregiver speech, terms of affection, family, profanity, physical feelings, religion and tradition, which many L2 learners struggle with and are not commonly taught or studied. Although they can struggle with vocabulary necessary for technical, academic or professional discourse, this certainly does not mean that they are deficient; rather, they simply have not had the need for developing this kind of vocabulary.

In terms of the four domains of language – listening, speaking, reading, writing – heritage speakers generally have better oral language skills – listening and speaking – than the written language skills because they acquired the language in a home setting. Additionally, because the primary and sometimes sole source of HL input is in the home, learners may only acquire a limited range of registers, usually the informal familiar ones. Finally, the variety they acquire may not be the so-called standard or prestige variety (Valdés, 2014), which adds a layer of social challenges for the heritage speaker.

1.4.2 Language external characteristics of heritage speakers

It is important to discuss some of the language external characteristics of heritage speakers to better understand the population we will discuss in the book. The first and foremost is that many heritage speakers do not realize that they comprise this group and that such a thing as heritage speaker exists. This means that members of this linguistically rich and unique group spend their lives believing they are 'imperfect' bilinguals: from the balanced bilingual myth to the myth-confirming attitudes they encounter when homeland speakers criticize their 'accent', heritage speakers often do not realize their own value. Some may not even admit to others that they are indeed a heritage speaker out of fear that they will be asked to demonstrate or prove their belongingness.

Sometimes referred to as Third Culture Kids (TCK), heritage speakers are generally people who are seemingly nonnative in the area they reside but do not really fit in with the homeland peers either (Useem et al., 1963). A 16-year-old Korean-American who has lived her entire life in the United States might be labeled as 'other' because of her appearance, her bilingualism and her culture. However, when that same teen visits Korea, relatives, peers and the general public might deem her an outsider because of her appearance, her bilingualism and her culture: thus, she is caught between not being American enough but not being Korean enough either. This is a common experience of the TCK and has been well documented in the literature (Fry, 2007; Jeon, 2022; Pollock & Van Reken, 2001), but the discussion of how language plays a role in this balancing act requires further consideration. By speaking a language other than English at home, the aforementioned student might feel embarrassed or otherized by her American peers, while in Korea she may be ridiculed for her American accent and the heritage variety she speaks. Furthermore, this marginalization continues in academic settings, in which language teachers who instruct heritage students will express frustration at their lack of ability to learn the grammar the way L2 students do or because they speak a socially less-prestigious variety of the target language (Valdés, 2005). Through lack of general awareness about linguistic varieties spoken by heritage speakers and bilingualism itself, these ideologies of otherness may be potentially harmful to young people.

Relatedly, many heritage speakers experience linguistic insecurity, a state in which speakers feel self-conscious and anxious due to their language (Labov, 1966; Meyerhoff, 2006; Wolfram & Schilling-Estes, 2005). While linguistic insecurity is generally talked about in the context of people who speak nonstandard marginalized varieties, heritage speakers report linguistic insecurity as well, especially when they use the language with older generations (Goble, 2016). The experience of speaking in a language where one lacks fluency is a difficult enough experience that most people can identify with; the experience of speaking in a language where it is expected – because of your heritage, ethnic or cultural identity – that you have masterful control when in fact you do not is a rather humiliating one.

This brings us back to one of the goals of this book and of HL research. The goal is to bring light to the linguistic innovations of heritage speakers and better understand their linguistic characteristics for the sake of contributing to linguistic theory. Even more importantly, the data can be used to advocate for heritage populations, showing that their language is not a deviation or deficient version of the 'correct' or 'real' language and is a powerful system in its own right. To combat misplaced linguistic insecurity, we must continue to better our understanding of the characteristics of heritage grammars, not just to predict patterns of development but also to show how these speakers innovate with language in unique ways.

1.4.3 Korean heritage speakers

There has been an increasing influx of immigration of South Korean residents to the United States over the past several decades, beginning in the 1960s following the Immigration Act of 1965, which had previously restricted immigration to the United States from Asia. Following steady growth of South Korean immigration to the United States, by 2017 the number of Korean immigrants to the United States surpassed 1 million residents (Batalova, 2022). Given the relatively recent wave of Korean immigration to the United States, there is a large population of second-generation Koreans residing in the country. These second-generation Koreans comprise the majority of Korean heritage speakers in the United States. These speakers tend to grow up hearing Korean in the home spoken by their family members, and some of the children even start out largely monolingual in Korean (Park-Johnson, 2017a). For immigrant families, early childhood is a dynamic time when language is rapidly shifting, as children transition from a monolingual Korean-speaking home environment to an English-speaking world when they begin attending preschool. Like most second-generation children, they quickly learn the SL and become English dominant. In fact, Asian-Americans tend to lose the HL more quickly than other large immigrant populations, e.g. Latinx communities (Rumbaut *et al.*, 2005). Thus, in this book we examine language patterns in Korean and English while dominance shift is happening for HL children.

There are a number of studies that have looked at adult Korean heritage speakers (e.g. Chang & Mandock, 2019; Kim *et al.*, 2009; Lee, 2018; Lee & Zaslanski, 2015; Park-Johnson, 2020a; Shin Kim, 2013). Comparatively, there are fewer studies looking at the development, identity and experiences of Korean heritage speakers during childhood. Sarah Shin's seminal book in 2004 provided a unique, detailed look at the sociolinguistic aspects of Korean-English bilingual children (Shin, 2004). Jin Sook Lee has also conducted important research documenting the many ways in which the cultural identities of Korean heritage speakers impact their lives, with special focus on education (Lee, 2002b; Lee & Oxelson, 2006; Lee & Shin, 2008; Lee & Suarez, 2009). Shin and Lee drew from their experience working with Korean heritage speakers in editing a special edition of the *Heritage Language Journal* in 2008 that explored this previously understudied population of heritage speakers. Hyun-sook Kang's (2002, 2013, 2015a, 2015b, 2016) work has helped us understand the role of parents and families, family language policies and home language practices in language maintenance. Recently, Siwon Lee (2019b, 2023) has looked at the impact of Korean community schools and how the community's language preservation and maintenance efforts intersect with education, specifically in a mainstream educational culture that does not support multilingualism. Jungmin Kwon's (2022a) recent book on the experiences of transnational Korean children has enriched the literature with detailed accounts of children's translanguaging practices.

This present book adds to this growing body of research in two crucial ways. First, it provides a longitudinal view of Korean-English bilingual children during a time in early childhood when they are undergoing the transition from being heavily Korean-dominant (and sometimes monolingual) to becoming English-dominant heritage speakers of English. This is an exciting time of life to capture from a linguistic perspective because children are still in the middle of developing their first language, Korean, when they are quite suddenly confronted with another language, English. Second, this book provides a close documentation of two areas of grammar that are most susceptible to heritage effects, morphology and syntax. In particular, it is especially interesting to examine bilingual children whose languages are typologically distinct: with Korean and English, the languages could not be more opposite in structure. Table 1.1 outlines some of the contrasting morphosyntactic characteristics of Korean and English. As can be seen, Korean and English are typologically distinct,

Table 1.1 Morphological and syntactic contrasts between Korean and English

Korean	English
SOV word order	SVO word order
Extensive classifier system	No classifier system
Case markers and case ellipsis	No case markers
Prodrop	Non-prodrop
Wh-in-situ	Wh-movement
Externally headed relative clauses	Internally headed relative clauses
Highly agglutinative/polysynthetic language	Highly isolating language
Honorific system	No honorific system
Transitivity marking	No transitivity marking

share no genealogical roots and have strikingly different word order, morphology and overall structure. Thus, for the young learner of 3 or 4 years of age, the task of acquiring a new, starkly different language while still developing the first language, is an interesting challenge. The fact that all of these children do acquire English and manage to maintain and continue to develop Korean is quite a marvel. This phenomenon occurs globally for nearly every child growing up in a context where the parents speak a language different from the SL, but there is still much we do not know about the process.

Thus, the aim of this book is to provide a close look at Korean-American children in early childhood as they shift from being nearly Korean monolingual to the heritage Korean speakers they will inevitably become. It is a magnified view of the patterns of morphology and syntax, as well as their code-switching and language usage patterns during this time when their dominance is shifting rapidly. By observing children aged 2–7 who are just entering English-medium preschool and following their development through this time, we are able to see the fine-grained changes that are happening when the two languages collide, interface and intermingle.

1.5 Theoretical and Practical Implications of Studying Bilingual Children

So what? This is a question I would like to pose here and that we will also reflect on at the end of this book. Why study this population of bilingual children, children who learn a second language while the first is still developing, children who soon become heritage speakers, children whose language development is colored with the presence of a SL and language-external pressures to assimilate? Why not focus our studies on the simultaneous bilingual child who receives 50-50 language input and 50-50 language use? The answers to these questions are built directly into the questions themselves: it is this very 'messiness' of the data that makes the population and their language that much more compelling. When one language has just begun to develop and another competing language is introduced, it creates a unique scenario where the child's brain and mind must make sense of this dual input. Much like introducing a new character in a story, a new language allows for different trajectories, more variables and unexpected directions that allow us to learn more about human capabilities.

The complexity of acquiring a new language while the first is still in the midst of rapid development cannot be understated. First, sometimes there are competing parameters that are in direct opposition between the two languages. Bilingual speakers whose one language is prodrop and the other is non-prodrop, for instance, have substantially impacted grammars: oversupplying the pronoun in the prodrop language (e.g. Albirini et al., 2011; Montrul, 2004; Silva-Corvalán, 1994) and undersupplying the pronoun in the non-prodrop language (e.g. Yip & Matthews, 2007) are well-documented patterns in both child and adult language studies. As discussed in Section 1.4.3, Korean and English have structural differences that work in direct opposition to each other, whether it be prodrop, canonical word order, headedness or wh-question formation. Though some might consider the range of differences to be a concern, a problem or a burden to overcome in acquisition, the opportunity to observe and learn about the way a young mind manages these obstacles is a rich and rare opportunity.

Relatedly, we know from bilingual studies that crosslinguistic influence occurs between the two languages of a bilingual individual (Argyri & Sorace, 2007; Genesee & Nicoladis, 2008; Hulk & Müller, 2000; Müller & Hulk, 2001; Yip & Matthews, 2007). Although in adult SLA studies, the direction of transfer is often from the first language to the second language, in child bilingualism there are more opportunities for this directionality to be influenced by factors other than order of acquisition. For instance, there have been many conversations in the literature that are concerned with the directionality of crosslinguistic influence that focus on language dominance, language characteristics and interfaces as possible triggers for the direction of crosslinguistic influence. Here, evidence from early second language learners provides an interesting perspective because these children's language dominance shifts from one to the other in a relatively short span of time. Children of immigrants often begin as monolingual speakers of their home language, but they become speakers of the SL quite quickly and soon become dominant in that language (Berman, 1979; Jisa, 2000; Lanza, 1992; Leopold, 1970; Olsson & Sullivan, 2005; Quay, 2001; Romaine, 1995). Rumbaut (2009) characterizes the United States as a 'linguistic graveyard' because HLs tend to disappear within two to three generations. This relatively rapid language dominance shift provides an interesting opportunity for examining directionality of crosslinguistic influence, especially as a longitudinal study.

Additionally, early second language learners offer a unique insight into studying language acquisition because those very language characteristics, which are assumed to be eventually acquired in monolingual acquisition, are not specifically guaranteed to be acquired or even needed for heritage speakers. If, for instance, honorifics and certain levels of formality are not needed in the daily lives of young heritage speakers who do not interact often with elder members of the community, they simply do not need to develop. This differs from acquisition patterns of monolingual and even older L2 students who learn the language in a classroom setting later in life. What might be considered a benchmark of monolingual acquisition or second language learning is simply unusable or needless for children whose HL is only used in the home in informal settings. This is a unique opportunity to look at just what aspects of language are truly needed in order to *be* a speaker of that language.

Code-switching or code-mixing by young children who are learning two languages in succession is another area that can provide interesting insight. With children who are just beginning to acquire a second language while still developing the first, there is a unique opportunity to see early stages of code-switching. It is also interesting to see what aspects of each language they code mix: is it open class categories like nouns and verbs, or do they also code mix functional elements? For a child of 5 years of age, when switching back and forth from a language that is agglutinative subject-object-verb (SOV) to a language that is isolating subject-verb-object (SVO), how do they fit together the puzzle pieces of these grammars in their minds to construct utterances that are meaningful and also systematic? While adult code-switching is established as rule-based and systematic, for children this is not always assumed, especially by parents and educators, as we will talk about below. Therefore, it is even more crucial to investigate data to provide further evidence that shows code-mixing by young bilingual children is just as grammatically consistent and rule-based as adult code-mixing, and not evidence of confusion or deficiency.

In sum, studying early second language learners contributes an excellent opportunity for unique language data that furthers linguistic theory. Examining the language patterns of this group gives us a glimpse into what is possible in human language development. Historically, the field has spent much time and energy investigating monolingual adult speakers and young children learning one language. However, expanding beyond these populations by including the 'messiness' of children who take different paths of acquisition – learning multiple languages simultaneously, acquiring a language while the first is still developing, learning one language restricted in the home while acquiring a new language only outside of the home – gives us a wider, more robust view of what the human brain is capable of.

The practical implications are more crucial yet. Earlier, we discussed the inherent difficulty of defining the term *bilingual* or *heritage speaker* and the trouble with pinpointing what parameters describe such individuals. For parents, caregivers, teachers, clinicians, social workers and others who interact and support bilingual and heritage speakers every day, this is a crucial gap in our collective knowledge. Understanding the nature of bilingualism is essential for providing the appropriate support for children and adolescents. Often, parents and educators become concerned about the development of their bilingual child because of unfamiliar language patterns, whether it be unexpected errors or behaviors such as code-switching. When their bilingual child does not pattern similarly to monolingual peers, it may raise concerns that they are somehow falling behind or not developing correctly (Jeon, 2008). Although there is overwhelming research to show that is not a concern and bilingualism is an advantage in many facets of the child's life, it places doubt and fear into the minds of parents.

Schools can also benefit from more information about bilingualism, bilingual development and typical language patterns in bilingual children. Unfortunately, there is a history of disproportionately placing bilingual students into special education (Artiles & Ortiz, 2002; Caesar & Kohler, 2007; Gottlieb & Hamayan, 2006; Ortiz et al., 1986); this placement stems from lack of knowledge about typical language patterns of language learners and SLA. Children who code-switch have been labeled as 'non-nons' or 'clinically disfluent', in which educators and clinicians treat the mixing of languages as a sign of deficiency (Cheng & Butler, 1989; Li, 2008; Valadez et al., 2000). Language learners end up receiving services, measures and interventions that are not meant for them and do not actually address their specific needs. The more we are able to uncover and disseminate trends, tendencies and patterns of bilingual speakers' language, the more we can disaggregate students in our schools to provide them the appropriate support for their development.

Thus, in this book I provide a comprehensive picture of the morphological and syntactic development of Korean and English. In Chapter 2, I introduce the participants of this longitudinal study, the children whose grammars we investigate in this book. I also provide a general description of the procedure and the language characteristics of Korean and English. In Chapters 3 and 4, we explore the children's Korean morphology and syntax, respectively, looking specifically at areas that may be particularly difficult to acquire. Chapters 5 and 6 mirror the structure of the previous two chapters, this time isolating English morphology and syntax. In Chapter 7, I examine the languages as they occur together: code-mixing. Chapter 8 is a report of a qualitative study based on interviews of two of the children from the study, a decade after the fact, to see how their languages and identities have taken shape across time. In Chapter 9, I close with theoretical and practical implications to continue the conversation started in this chapter, weaving together the findings presented in this book.

2 Source of Data and Language Overview

2.1 Introduction

In order to better situate our understanding of the findings in later chapters, this chapter will introduce the participants, methods and data that will be used throughout the book. We will first discuss some background information about the participants, such as their ages, home environment, starting language proficiencies and sources of Korean and English input. This chapter also provides information about the children's families, particularly the home language policy, attitudes toward language and bilingualism, socioeconomic status and parents' level of education. Additionally, the chapter covers details of the data collection procedures used to build the Korean-English bilingualism dataset used in this study (e.g. length of data collection sessions, the context and environment in which the children were observed, a typical data collection setup). This chapter allows readers to become familiar with the context of the research participants and methodology. Furthermore, this chapter provides a brief overview of the morphological and syntactic properties of Korean and English as a preview for the topics we will see in the coming chapters.

The Korean-English bilingual children in this study came to be recruited through contact with families in my Korean-American community circles. Although I did not know the children or families directly prior to working with them, their families attended the same church as some of my family members and heard through word-of-mouth about my interest in exploring Korean-English bilingual children's language development. These families reached out to me and we worked together for what ended up being years. It is important to share here, early on, that this type of longitudinal study is not easy to come by without the devotion of families that are willing to take on a long-term study. What is not seen or reported in the data are the relationships that form between the families and researcher. Here, I acknowledge my positionality in this study: because I am a Korean heritage speaker and a member of the Korean-American community myself, the families treated me not like an outsider but a member of the extended family. The children would come running to the door or wait outside for me to arrive, have drawings, cards and art projects they had made for me, and the parents would use my visits as opportunities to ask me questions about their children's schools or translate a note they wanted to send to their child's teacher. Often these kinds of side conversations and relationships do not surface or get reported in academic writing, but I find it important to report the positionality and impact of being an insider, a community member who is also a researcher conducting the study.

The need for longitudinal data, especially for child bilingualism, is two-fold. First, because the vast majority of research on heritage language grammars comes from adults whose languages are relatively more stabilized, there is a need for data from the other side of the spectrum, in which children are just beginning their eventual path to becoming English-dominant heritage speakers. This provides us with the opportunity to link the body of data on adult heritage speakers to their younger counterparts, who are in these initial stages and are typically far better speakers of the heritage language than the adults are. Second, longitudinal data of this nature provide not only a microscopic lens – picking up the nuances and intricacies of the language as they are happening in naturalistic language production – but also allow us to track the paths of development and change of the heritage and societal languages, both in isolation and in conjunction with the other. In this study, the path of acquisition of both the heritage language, Korean, and the societal language, English, is seen across several years, during one of the most robust times of language development and change.

2.2 Participants

2.2.1 Children

The data for this book come from a longitudinal study of four Korean-English bilingual children living in the United States. There are two girls and two boys: Sarah, Sandy, Ben and Dan. Sarah and Ben are siblings where Sarah is the elder, and Sandy and Dan are siblings, where Sandy is the elder.

The children were born in the United States to parents who had immigrated from South Korea during their adulthood and speak Korean in the home. Thus, the children acquired Korean first, and then were exposed to English when they entered preschool. The two elder children, Sarah and Sandy, did not receive English input until they began preschool at age 2;6 and 2;7, consecutively. The younger children, Ben and Dan, heard some English from the older sibling, but still were heavily Korean-dominant and not producing any English utterances until they entered preschool themselves. At the onset of the study, the two younger children were not yet able to produce much English. Table 2.1 shows the children's demographic information and use of each language at the onset of

Table 2.1 Participants' ages and use of Korean and English

Code name	Age	Sex	% use Korean	% use English
Dan	2;4.20	M	90	10
Ben	3;4.16	M	90	10
Sandy	4;8.29	F	50	50
Sarah	5;3.27	F	60	40

the study as reported by the parents. All of the children were exposed to Korean from birth as their primary language and were quite comfortable and proficient in its use. Below I provide further information about each child with respect to their language ability at the start and end of the study, as well as some personality and tendencies that may contribute to their language development.

Dan

Dan, at age 2;4, had not begun attending preschool and was using Korean exclusively, although he did seem to understand some English, most likely due to his older sister's influence. By the end of the study, however, he was using full English sentences and seemed to favor using English even with his mother, despite her attempts to steer him toward the home language. Dan has a rambunctious personality and his parents characterized him as a 'trouble-maker' in a fond sort of way.

Ben

At the onset of the study, Ben had had only one month of English input, and like Dan, he used Korean almost exclusively as well. He did display that he was able to understand English, though at the beginning he only used one-word English utterances. Ben was often more reserved and quiet compared to the other children in the study. I do suspect that given his highly vocal older sister, he was somewhat used to taking on a quieter role in the home dynamic.

Sandy

Sandy had already been attending preschool for a year and receiving English input regularly by the start of the study. Sandy was highly proficient and conversational in English at that point. Her Korean was also the strongest compared to the other children throughout the study. By the end of the study, Sandy was a strong Korean and English speaker. Sandy also has a very patient, caring personality.

Sarah

Sarah is the oldest child in the study. Like Sandy, Sarah had been exposed to English through preschool. Her parents reported that she had not spoken any English prior to starting school at 2;6, but by the time we began the study, Sarah was 5;3 and was very fluent and proficient in the language. At the onset of the study Sarah was also very fluent in Korean and used it productively with her mother and brother, Ben. Sarah was outspoken and outgoing from the very start of the study.

2.2.2 Language environment

Korean was the primary home language in each of the families. Although the children spoke some English through code-mixing (see Chapter 7), the home language was consistently Korean throughout the duration of the study. The parents always spoke to the children in Korean, and their social circles were almost exclusively Korean-speaking communities. The parents noted that while the working members of the family had frequent interactions in English at work, their social interactions – and what the children would hear – were always in Korean.

A large part of the family's social center is the church community. Both families attend a Korean church that consists mainly of first-generation immigrants from South Korea, with services conducted in Korean. There are social events, interest groups and committees that stem from the church as well, where Korean is spoken. There is also a large population of second-generation children and adolescents who also attend the church with their families. These children tend to speak English among themselves, and there are religious services, events and activities conducted in English specifically for the younger population at the church.

The parents were strongly aware of the importance of maintaining Korean. The families spoke of friends whose children were no longer speaking Korean at home, and they expressed that this was unacceptable and wished to avoid this. Both families had relatives back in Korea that they visited with the children every several years, and one of those trips actually coincided with the study during one of the summers, which impacted the children's Korean development positively. The parents filled the house with books, music, TV shows and other materials written or spoken in Korean in order to provide as much of the home language as possible.

Lastly, almost all the children attended Korean language and culture school on the weekend, programs that were run by the aforementioned church or local Korean community. The medium of instruction was entirely in Korean, and there the children learned songs, heard stories and played games that taught them about the Korean language and culture.

One would expect that with all the Korean influence in the home, church and Korean school, that English would not be so quickly adopted by the children once they start receiving English input in school. However, it seems that the hegemonic power of English in the United States is not to be underestimated; the children still became fluent in English in a short amount of time, as we will see in later chapters.

2.2.3 Parents

The four children in this study live with their mother and father, both of whom were born and raised in Korea. The parents of the children lived in Korea until their 20s and 30s, then voluntarily immigrated to the United States for work or to pursue further education. The parents spoke almost exclusively in Korean, both to each other and to their children. The fathers of each family, however, did work in English-speaking environments, and the mothers also had conversational abilities in English. All parents had a four-year university degree, and Sandy's mother had a master's degree as well.

The families live in middle-class, suburban areas of the US Midwest in single family homes. The families themselves were middle-class, and the fathers worked in professional jobs. Their neighborhoods were predominantly white, and the children attended schools that were enrolled by predominantly white, monolingual English-speaking children. Thus, the only place where the children would interact regularly with other Korean peers was at their church and Korean school.

2.3 Data Collection

2.3.1 Overall design

The design of this study is longitudinal observations. The children in this study were audio- and video-recorded during naturalistic play interactions across two and a half years in monthly sessions. The ages of the children throughout the data collection sessions can be found in Table 2.2 and in Figure 2.1. Although I attempted to keep the recordings almost exactly one month apart, there were a few instances where the sessions were closer together in time, and other instances when the recordings took place farther apart due to the families' availability.

The recordings took place in the children's homes in order to maintain a comfortable, relaxed language environment. Part of this decision was to make the sessions as easy for the families as possible. The other part was that the home environment is one that encouraged the use of Korean in a more organic environment where Korean was typically used, as opposed to conducting the sessions in a school or lab setting where

Table 2.2 Participants' start and end ages

Child	Start age	End age
Dan	2;4	4;3
Ben	3;4	5;11
Sandy	4;8	7;3
Sarah	5;3	7;11

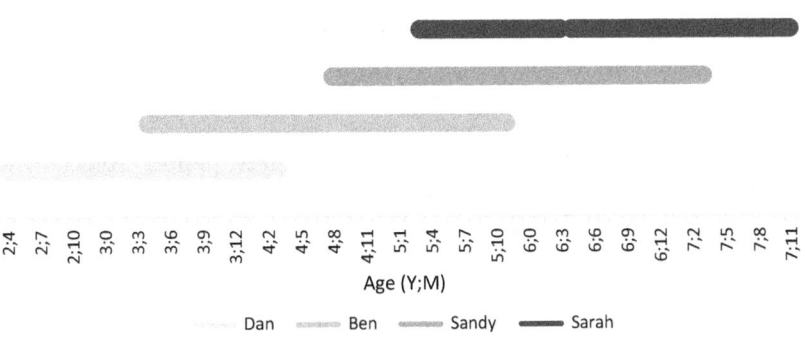

Figure 2.1 Timeline of children's ages

children might feel as though they need to use English more. Each month of observation consisted of two language segments: one language segment involved the children interacting and playing with their parent in Korean, and the other language segment involved the children interacting and playing with me in English. The order in which we conducted these language segments was counterbalanced each time to offset any ordering biases or priming that may occur. For instance, in Month 1 we conducted the Korean language session first then English language session second, in Month 2 we reversed the order to English then Korean, and then continued this pattern going forward.

The Korean and English language sessions were generally similar in nature: both occurred on the same day, both were naturalistic play interactions with an adult and both were child-led in terms of what we did and talked about. Each language session was about 45–60 minutes long. In the Korean sessions, parents were encouraged to speak Korean the way they always do with their children. In the English sessions, the children would quickly change to English with me, and although they knew I was a Korean speaker (I interacted with the parents in Korean), they almost never spoke Korean to me. In both language sessions, we tried to stay in one place in the room so that the camera and microphone would not have to be moved and could capture the video and audio.

2.3.2 Procedure

Ahead is a description of a typical data collection session.

The families would welcome me into their homes for each monthly session. After initial greetings and chatting, I would mount the digital camera (micro SD) on a tripod and connect the microphone, setting it up so that it would clearly capture the part of the room the adult and children were in, but not be distracting. If the first segment was the Korean language segment, I would turn on the record button and sit in a different room within earshot so that I could troubleshoot if needed but would not affect the data. For the English language segment in which I interacted with the children, the parent would leave the area as well.

In each language segment, the children would interact with the adult through looking at a book, constructing Lego, doing an art project, coloring, playing make-believe with dolls and figures, puppets, blocks and role play (e.g. from the more typical like house and school, to the more inventive like pet store and aliens on a spaceship). Although there was not much procedural difference between the English and Korean language segments other than the target language used, the children's attitudes during each session differed somewhat; the children were generally much more enthusiastic about the English language segment (the presence of a fun novel person coming over to play was more exciting than playing with the parent). Therefore, the English sessions typically were slightly longer.

Because each household had a sibling pair, both the parent and I worked to make sure the younger sibling had ample opportunities to talk. Because there were only three people, this was generally not an issue, but in the first few months for both Ben and Dan – the younger brothers of Sarah and Sandy, respectively – the parent and I both had to gently remind the older sisters to allow the young brothers to speak for themselves.

At the end of the first language segment, I would turn off the camera and reposition (if necessary), take a quick break, then move on to the second language segment.

At the end of both language segments, the camera would be turned off, the equipment put away and the children were invited to select an item from the prize bag. The prizes included books, art supplies, school supplies and toys valued at approximately $5.

Video recordings were then taken back to the lab setting and were transcribed by Korean-speaking research assistants. All transcriptions were reviewed and revised by myself or a Korean-speaking senior research assistant. Coding for the studies in this book were conducted by me and a Korean doctoral student.

2.4 Language Overview: Korean

In this section, I will provide a brief overview of the Korean language with respect to morphology and syntax. This is not meant as a comprehensive grammar of the language (see Choo, 2008, for instance, for a fuller description of the Korean language), but rather a background primer on the aspects of Korean morphology and syntax that will be specifically pertinent to the topics in this book. In Chapters 3 through 6, I will discuss each aspect of Korean and English morphology and syntax as I present the research and data. For the Korean used in this book, I adopt the Yale romanization convention, which is the standard romanization that is used in Korean linguistics and linguistics research due to its emphasis on morphological and phonological structure.

2.4.1 Morphology

Korean is an agglutinative language, whose nouns and verbs can be affixed with multiple morphemes in a particular, fixed order. For instance, Korean verbs can take on multiple morphemes that encode for tense, aspect, mood, voice, transitivity, modality, honorific and sentence type. The utterance in (1) is a full sentence containing just a verb; however, the verb contains a complex series of morphemes that supply semantic, syntactic and pragmatic information.

(1) *Mek-ul-su-issul-kka-yo*
Eat-future-can-be-past-inquisitive-honorific
[do you think] [this] can be eaten?

Korean verb morphology can express tenses, including present, past and future, and it can also add aspectual information (perfective, imperfective). Mood and modality are also expressed through agglutinative verb morphology, as is sentence type (e.g. imperative, interrogative, propositional, declarative, vocative, quotative). Korean also has a complex system of honorifics that are obligatory for every verb when addressing a formal, older or socially higher-status interlocutor. Korean is generally said to have six levels of formality (Sohn, 1994).

Korean noun morphology is complex as well, and it exhibits more variability and optionality. Korean nouns can bear plural endings (*-dul*), but this can be omitted in informal contexts. Like English, Korean is a nominative-accusative language, where the subject of both transitive and intransitive verbs behaves alike and the object of both transitive and intransitive verbs behaves alike. In Korean, subjects appear with the nominative marker *-ka/-i*, where the suffix *-ka* is attached to nouns ending with a vowel, and *-i* is attached to nouns ending with a consonant. Korean objects are marked with the accusative marker *-lul/-ul*: nouns ending with a vowel take the *-lul* suffix and nouns ending with a consonant take the *-ul* suffix. Korean also allows the topic marker *-nun/-un* frequently in place of the nominative or accusative marker: *-nun* is used for nouns ending with a vowel, and *-un* is used for those ending with a consonant. See Table 2.3 for examples of each marker.

However, case markers are not required in all contexts and can be omitted in certain situations. This omission of case markers, or case ellipsis, is more common for objects than subjects, in informal situations, object-verb adjacent word orders, familiar topics or determiner phrases (DP) and with familiar interlocutors.

Classifiers, on the other hand, are obligatory in Korean when using numerals with nouns for counting purposes. The noun is followed by a numeral and a semantically appropriate classifier:

Table 2.3 Case markers in Korean

	Root noun	Nominative	Accusative	Topic
Nouns ending with vowel	*chinku* 'friend'	*chinku-ka*	*chinku-lul*	*chinku-nun*
	emma 'mom'	*emma-ka*	*emma-lul*	*emma-nun*
	nuna 'older sister'	*nuna-ka*	*nuna-lul*	*nuna-nun*
Nouns ending with consonant	*sensayngnim* 'teacher'	*sensayngnim-i*	*sensayngnim-ul*	*sensayngnim-un*
	hyeng 'older brother'	*hyeng-i*	*hyeng-ul*	*hyeng-un*
	haksayng 'student'	*haksayng-i*	*haksayng-ul*	*haksayng-un*

N+NUM+CLASSIFIER. For instance, to express 'three books', the language requires a classifier for books (*kweun*), thereby resulting in *chaek se kweun*, or 'book-three-CLASSIFIER'. A list of common classifiers can be found in Table 2.4.

2.4.2 Syntax

Korean has a canonical subject-object-verb (SOV) word order. However, Korean allows for relatively flexible word order, as compared to English, likely due to its rich morphology. SOV word order comprises about 97% of Korean utterances (Lee, 2016), but Korean sentences can present as SVO, OVS, OSV or even VSO depending on context and prosody.

Korean is a prodrop language, allowing for both the subject and object to be dropped if understood from context. Thus, it is not uncommon to find a sentence that is simply a verb (as we saw in (1)).

Korean is also a wh-in-situ language, which means that wh-words appear in the exact location within the sentence where the gap would be. For example, to form a wh-question based on the sentence in (2) (where the constituent in question is 'the apple'), one simply has to replace the 'the apple' *sagwa* with 'what' *mwe*, then replace the declarative marker *-ta* with the question marker *-ni* (3).

(2) *Sungwoo-ka   sagwa-lul   muk-ess-ta.*
    Sungwoo-NOM   apple-ACC   eat-PAST-DECL
    "Sungwoo ate an apple"

(3) *Sungwoo-ka   mwe-lul   muk-ess-ni?*
    Sungwoo-NOM   what-ACC   eat-PAST-Q
    "What did Sungwoo eat?"

Table 2.4 Korean classifiers

Classifier	Romanization	Semantic category
개	kay	generic/default
명	myeng	people
분	pun	serving; minute; people (formal)
마리	mali	animals
권	kwen	books
그루	kuru	trees
대	tay	cars and vehicles; injections
매	may	sheets of paper (formal)
벌	pel	clothes and silverware
부	pu	periodicals
송이	songi	stem; bunch
다발	tapal	bouquet
자루	caru	long slender object; bag
장	cang	thin, flat objects
점	cem	pieces of art
채	chay	buildings
척	chek	ships
켤레	khyelley	pair of socks, shoes, gloves
통	thong	letters in an envelope; round-shaped fruit; phone calls
단	tan	bunch of vegetables
모	mo	block-shaped food like tofu or jelly
알	al	small round-shaped things
잔	can	liquid in glass/cup
페이지	peiji	page
번	pen	times (as in, number of times)
살	sal	age (years)
가지	kaci	sort or type

Another notable syntactic feature in Korean that will be relevant in this book is the fact that Korean does not have an article system.

2.4.3 Lexicon

One of the areas that causes difficulty for learners of Korean and heritage speakers of Korean are lexical items with semantic specificity as discussed below. One is that in formal contexts where one would be expected to use the honorific, it is also common that entire lexical items are replaced by formal versions of those roots. For instance, the verb 'to eat' *mekta* is the generic term; however, in polite company the word more commonly used is *telta* or *chapseta*.

Second, another common area of lexical difficulty arises from the multiple versions of a single English word. For instance, the verb 'to wear' can appear in multiple forms depending on the type of worn item. In English, 'to wear' can apply to anything worn on the body; in Korean, there are specific individual lexical verbs for wearing items on different body parts: *kkita* 'to wear fitted, as a glove or ring', *sseta* 'to wear on head, such as a hat or face mask', *ipta* 'to wear on the body (generic)', *sinta* 'to wear on feet', *meta* 'to tie or hoist, such as a tie or belt or backpack', and *chata* 'to clasp, as in a watch'. In heritage Korean grammars, it is common for the speaker to default to the generic *ipta* for some of the more specific terms. Korean lexicon contains many of these types of examples (e.g. family terms, flavor descriptors, classifiers) where there is a one-to-multiple ratio between the English term and Korean terms.

2.5 Language Overview: English

In this section, I will provide a brief overview of English morphology and syntax as it relates to or contrasts with what was discussed with Korean. Though some of these tendencies extend to most varieties about English, the variety I will specifically focus on is the American Midwestern variety of English, which is the variety spoken by the children and in their geographical area.

Morphology in English differs substantially from Korean. English has an isolating verb morphology, in which words expressing features such as aspect, transitivity, modality and mood are expressed through free morphemes, often in combination with auxiliaries *have* and *be*, and modals such as *will*, *would*, *should*, *can* and *might*. Only regular past tense (e.g. *played, laughed*) and third person singular present (e.g. *plays, laughs*) are expressed as bound morphemes attached to the root lexical verb. For instance, if expressing passive voice, past tense, progressive aspect, as in (4) below, the lexical verb *count* simply takes on the past participle form *prepared*, and the auxiliaries preceding the lexical verb – *was* and *being* – along with the syntax (be + past participle + by-phrase construction) accomplish the expression. In contrast, Korean would employ bound verb morphology attached to the verb to accomplish the same expression, as in (5).

(4) The food was being prepared by the chef.
(5) *yolisa-ka   umsik-ul   cunpi-hako-iss-ess-supni-ta*
   Chef-NOM food-ACC prepare-prog-be-past-honorific-declarative

The challenge with English verb morphology is that multiple conjugations, voice and tense can appear with the same surface form. *Played* can be a nonfinite past participle in active voice (*I have played the game*), a nonfinite past participle in passive voice (*The game was played last week*) or a finite first person main verb (*I played yesterday*).

English nouns take plural morphology like Korean, and also take on possessive ('s) morphologically, but do not have a system of case marking nor classifiers. However, English nouns can be preceded by a complex system of articles, *the*, *a/an* and *ø*, which demarcate the noun phrase for semantic categories such as definiteness and specificity. The English article system is notoriously difficult for learners of English (Ionin *et al.*, 2004, 2021; Ko *et al.*, 2009) and is a stark contrast from the article-less Korean language.

As for syntax, English has a stricter word order than Korean, most often appearing as SVO, and rarely allows for other word orders save for some exceptional cases. The language is also non-prodrop, in which the overt presence of a subject and object pronoun is required, even when the nominal's reference is understood through context. English also employs wh-movement and subject auxiliary inversion in questions, in which the wh-interrogative (e.g. who, what, why) must move to the front of the sentence and the tensed auxiliary must move to a position immediately following the wh-word. Thus, the question form of *Mary is painting a picture*, where the noun phrase *a picture* is the object of the question, the substituting word *what* and the auxiliary *is* must move to the front of the sentence, resulting in *What is Mary __ painting __?*, leaving behind gaps where the wh-word and auxiliary used to be. Again, this is different from Korean in which the only step would be to insert the wh-word in place of the object of the declarative sentence.

2.6 Chapter Summary

This chapter provided detailed information about the source of data for the research presented in this book. Background information about the children and their families, languages, home environment and other background factors were provided to set the stage for the longitudinal study from which the data arise. This chapter also gave a detailed account of the data collection procedure. I also introduced some of the aspects of the syntax and morphology of each of the two languages, Korean and English, that will become relevant for this book.

While there are many notable studies where children's language development has been tracked across time by language acquisition researchers, there are far fewer such studies for bilingual children, and especially ones that have dedicated language sessions. Kenji Hakuta set the stage for longitudinal case studies for bilingual children in his seminal work (Hakuta, 1976), and I aim to replicate his work for this population of Korean-English bilingual children. Rather than focusing on a few cross-sections of the child's development, where we are much more likely to miss important developmental stages or patterns, this type of study provides more opportunities to see features, characteristics and 'language moments' than we might in a traditional experimental study. Although longitudinal studies of this nature are arduous in the data collection and analysis portion, it allows us to gain a much more holistic and complete picture of the child's development, as we will see in the coming chapters.

3 Korean Morphology

3.1 Introduction

This chapter describes some of the main trends in Korean morphological development for Korean-English bilingual children. Specifically, the chapter focuses on trends that may differ from monolingual Korean-speaking children, highlighting the ways in which Korean-English bilinguals acquire, maintain and use some of the more challenging features of Korean morphology. I start here with Korean morphology for a couple of reasons. The first is that morphology tends to be one of the areas that heritage speakers generally struggle with; this is certainly seen in the body of literature we have on Korean morphology by heritage speakers (Benmamoun *et al.*, 2013; Hakansson, 1995; Laleko & Polinsky, 2016; Montrul & Sanchez-Walker, 2013; Montrul *et al.*, 2015; Polinsky, 2008, 2018). Second, we know that Korean has a rich system of inflectional morphology whose complexity makes for subtle nuance and implication: a single monosyllabic marker on the final verb can turn an entire sentence into a polite accusation with playful undertones or a last-minute end-of-sentence shift of blame and agency on the part of the speaker. Korean nominal and verbal morphology plays a monumental role in conversation, meaning, nuance and pragmatic play, and it is perhaps this layered complexity that makes it difficult for adult heritage speakers (Choi, 1997; Kim, 2014; Lee, 2018). However, although there is evidence for Korean heritage speakers struggling with Korean morphology, the data come predominantly from adult speakers who have lived their lives with the SL English influencing their Korean. What of children, who have yet to experience years of language use, paired with language-external messaging from schools, society, peers and even families that Korean is allegedly less important than English? At the age of 3–7, how are children able to handle the complex nuanced set of Korean morphemes?

The chapter is organized as follows: in Section 3.2 we will look at the children's use and acquisition of Korean case markers and case ellipsis. Section 3.3 explores their acquisition of Korean classifiers, 3.4 their acquisition of transitivity marking in Korean and 3.5 their development of sentence final markers. Finally, in Section 3.6 we discuss the impact of these results on theory and its implications and insight for other bilingual language pairings.

3.2 Case Markers and Case Ellipsis

As discussed in Chapter 2, Korean nominals can appear with case markers, a functional morpheme that denotes the relationship of the noun to the verb and how that noun functions within the clause. For acquisition, however, the challenge with Korean case markers is that they are not always present or necessary. In Korean, case markers can be optionally omitted, and the original utterance can still maintain the same meaning. Compare (1) and (2) below, where both are perfectly grammatical. This phenomenon where the case marker is dropped is referred to as case ellipsis (CE).

(1) *Sungwoo-ka*   *cemshim-ul*   *mekesse*
    Sungwoo-NOM lunch-ACC   eat-PST-DECL

(2) *Sungwoo*   *cemshim*   *mekesse*
    Sungwoo   lunch   eat-PST-DECL

While CE appears simple on the surface, the grammatical, semantic and pragmatic contexts that allow for CE are nuanced and complex. For instance, researchers have shown that CE in Korean is triggered by animacy, definiteness and the person feature of argument noun phrases (NP) (Fry, 2001; Kim, 2008; Lee, 2006a; Lee, 2006b, 2007). CE can also be predicted based on specificity of the object (Kim, 1993), syntactic position of the argument (Ahn & Cho, 2006, 2007), utterance length and proximity of the NP to the predicate (Fry, 2001; Kim, 2008) or contrastiveness (Kim, 2008; Ko, 2000; Lee, 2002a). In addition to the syntactic and semantic factors listed above, CE in Korean can also be affected by pragmatic features such as formality and familiarity with interlocutors (Ko, 2000; Lee & Thompson, 1985). Case markers are less likely to appear in informal contexts and between familiar interlocutors. Lee and Thompson also found that the more information is shared between speakers, the more it is permissible to drop the case marker. In fact, even among native adult speakers of Korean, acceptability studies have shown that most Korean speakers have gradient preferences for the provision or omission of case markers and cannot necessarily pinpoint why they feel the case marker is needed or not (Lee, 2006b, 2008).

Why are we interested in case marking and CE for Korean-English bilingual children? First, while case marking is not obligatory, it plays an essential role in clarifying the function of each nominal in a clause; Korean's relatively flexible word order is certainly associated with case marking. It also establishes focus, clarifies ambiguity and it even signals formality and respect in some cases, as provision of case markers is more common in formal pragmatic contexts. As for CE, it is interesting to investigate Korean heritage speakers' proficiency with such a nuanced optional element. CE is, as discussed, quite grammatically and pragmatically complex. Chung (2013: 2) asserts that CE is particularly difficult for acquisition given that 'it involves the interaction of syntactic, semantic, and discourse principles and requires integration of contextual information with structural information (Kwon & Zribi-Hertz, 2008; Lee, 2006a)'. Even monolingual Korean children, who acquire the use of case markers by 2;6–3;0 (Chung, 1994), do not acquire adult-like use of CE until ages 5–6 (Chung, 2015). Thus, it stands to reason that heritage speakers of Korean would also have difficulty acquiring the case marker and CE system.

Furthermore, heritage speakers typically have reduced input due to the fact that their exposure to the heritage language is limited to the home and typically only spoken by a small percentage of their interlocutors. Frequency of occurrence is further decreased for variable aspects of grammar such as CE. In particular, for bilingual and heritage speakers whose other language – English, in our case – does not reinforce case markers, it poses even more of a challenge to acquire an element that is usually overt but not always present. Although there are only a few studies that have examined child Korean heritage speakers with respect to case markers, these studies have shown what we might expect. Choi (1997) examined Korean heritage children and their use of case markers. The findings indicated that the children had difficulty with the accusative marker -*lul*. Song *et al.* (1997) also looked at Korean heritage speakers' interpretation of case markers in children ages 3–8. They found that the children had difficulty interpreting Korean case markers if the word order of the sentences was atypical, such as object-subject-verb (OSV) order. These studies already start to suggest that case marker acquisition alone may provide some difficulty for heritage children.

When it comes to CE for heritage language acquisition, the plot thickens. Because case markers are only occasionally elided and this is often contingent upon subtle syntactic, semantic and/or pragmatic factors, the amount of input learners receive is reduced further still. Additionally, because case markers are more likely to be dropped among familiar interlocutors in informal contexts – precisely the context in which heritage speakers use and hear the heritage language – there are fewer examples of case markers in the input. Thus, here we not only look at case marker use, but also the heritage children's ability to elide the case marker as well.

Below I report on my study of Korean heritage children's use of case markers and ellipsis (Park-Johnson, 2019b). While there are a few studies on child heritage speakers of Korean and their knowledge of case markers (e.g. Choi, 1997; Song *et al.*, 1997), in my study I focused on children's production of case markers and their ability to employ CE when appropriate (Park-Johnson, 2019b). Here I investigated these questions by analyzing the Korean productions by Sarah, Sandy and Ben, spanning ages 3;7 to 7;11. Each utterance that contained either a subject or object was coded for the presence or absence of subject, object or topic markers. Only utterances that were entirely in Korean were part of this analysis; utterances that had any code-mixing with English were not included.

Overall, the findings indicated that all three children used overt subject marking 51% to 70% of the time and overt object marking 10% to 18% of the time. All three children also used the overt subject case marker (-ka/-i) significantly more frequently than the object case marker (-lul/-ul). This pattern of subject-object asymmetry is a prominent feature of adult Korean speakers in Korean CE literature (Ahn & Cho, 2006, 2007; Chung, 2013, 2015; Hong, 1994; Kim, 1998; Lee, 2016). In other words, Korean heritage speakers in early childhood appear to use Korean case markers in a discernable pattern that mirrors that of monolingual adult speakers of Korean (Park-Johnson, 2019b).

Next I examined how children's case marker use changed over time. Pearson's product-moment correlations were used to identify the relationship between time (each child's age in months) and the percent use of overt case markers. Here, correlation was used to determine whether there is a significant increase or decrease of case marker use with respect to time, or children's ages; if time is significantly correlated with change in case marker use, it would show that age makes a meaningful difference. Analyses indicated no significant correlations for the use of subject overt case marking across time for all three children, which suggests that the use of subject case did not change over time. For objects, the findings are similar for Ben and Sarah: no significant correlation was found between age and use of object case markers. However, for Sandy, a significant correlation was found for object case markers. Table 3.1 shows correlation values and significance between children's age and use of overt subject and object case markers.

With the exception of Sandy's object marker use, there was no significant change over time in children's usage of overt case markers.

Having established that the young heritage speakers do use case markers, the next question is whether the children use CE. Ellipsis is a

Table 3.1 Pearson correlations for age and percentage of overt case marking

	Subject		Object	
	r	p	r	p
Ben	0.215	0.377	−0.228	0.349
Sandy	−0.141	0.588	0.544*	0.024
Sarah	0.030	0.902	−0.041	0.869

Source: Park-Johnson, 2019b.

Note: * = statistically significant at $p < 0.05$ level.

tricky element to measure: absence of the case marker can mean either that the children know how to elide it or they have simply forgotten it. In other words, one ascribes nuanced knowledge, and the other is the lack thereof. Thus, to shed light on this question, we have to identify whether the use of the children's case markers follow a particular pattern. I have already shown that there is significant subject-object asymmetry. The question is, are there other factors that trigger the use of overt case markers? The idea is that if the children truly do not understand how to use case markers, there would be no discernable patterns: it would indicate the children are dropping case markers randomly and haphazardly.

We have previously discussed that case marking and CE is triggered by syntactic factors. One well-documented pattern is that CE is more likely to occur when the word order is canonical (Ahn & Cho, 2006, 2007; Fry, 2001; Kim, 2008). In other words, when the word order follows the expected SOV pattern, speakers are more likely to drop case markers than when the word order is a less common configuration. To investigate this factor for the children in this study, the data were coded for word order. Word orders that were considered canonical were SOV, OV and SV. Noncanonical word orders included OSV, SVO and OVS. The prediction is that children will be more likely to supply the overt case marker when they use a noncanonical word order and more likely to drop the case marker for utterances that follow canonical word order. A binomial logistic regression was conducted to predict the probability of the dichotomous dependent variable – presence or absence of the case marker – based on word order, a categorical variable.

The analysis revealed that for subject case markers, canonicality of word order did not significantly predict the presence or absence of subject case marker -ka/-i for any of the children (see Table 3.2).

For the object case marker, however, canonicality of word order was a significant predictor for the use of object case marker -un/-nun for Ben and Sandy. The findings revealed that these two children are significantly more likely to use the object marker when the word order is noncanonical (Table 3.3). The implication of this result is that at least for object marking, the use of the case marker is predictable by word order, a well-documented factor in Korean CE literature. Here we also see yet another

Table 3.2 Logistic regression predicting likelihood of subject marker use based on canonicality

Child	B	SE	Wald	df	p	Odds ratio	95% CI for odds ratio	
							Lower	Upper
Ben	−1.709	1.091	2.453	1	0.117	0.181	0.021	1.537
Sandy	0.811	0.588	1.902	1	0.168	2.250	0.711	7.124
Sarah	1.879	1.233	2.322	1	0.128	6.548	0.584	73.440

Source: Park-Johnson, 2019b

Table 3.3 Logistic regression predicting likelihood of object marker use based on canonicality

Child	B	SE	Wald	df	p	Odds ratio	95% CI for odds ratio	
							Lower	Upper
Ben	−4.394	1.419	9.596	1	0.002	0.012	0.001	0.199
Sandy	−1.907	0.659	8.387	1	0.004	0.148	0.041	0.540
Sarah	−1.863	1.244	2.242	1	0.134	0.155	0.014	1.778

Source: Park-Johnson, 2019b

example of subject-object asymmetry that mirrors what we find for adult Korean speakers (Lee, 2016).

To further investigate predictability of case marking, we look now at a pragmatic factor that triggers CE. We have evidence that CE is more likely to occur between interlocutors who are familiar with one another, which is certainly true for the parent-child context in our study. Furthermore, CE is more likely to occur when there is shared information between speakers (Lee & Thompson, 1985). In other words, when there is more shared knowledge between the interlocutors and when there is an immediate referent, CE is more likely to occur. For parent-child interactions, especially with younger children, the topics of conversation typically consist of those in the immediate environment: for example, a toy or book they are looking at together, commenting on something in the room they can point to or commentary about the people present in the room. Demonstrative pronouns such as *this* and *that* are among the most referential nouns used in face-to-face conversations: the child or parent often points to an object to ask 'what is that?' or say 'this is mine', where the demonstrative is used to identify and refer to that which is immediately visible and shared. Thus, if CE is more likely to occur with shared information, we could predict that these highly referential deixis terms would be less likely to take case marking than other NPs that are less referential. In our dataset, we have the unique opportunity to observe young heritage Korean children interacting with parents to explore this particular potential trigger for CE. To do so, all utterances across all data containing a subject or object were coded for what type of subject or object was used, namely, words meaning 'this' or 'that'.

Demonstrative Pronouns
(a) *ike(t), iken, ikey* 'this'
(b) *kuke(t), kuken, kukey* 'that'

Analysis consisted of a test of two proportions, or the chi-square test of homogeneity, to determine whether there is a difference between the binomial proportions of two independent groups (case marker use, deixis). It was predicted that because demonstrative pronouns are highly referential, they would be less likely to appear with case markers.

The analysis revealed that this was indeed the case for subject markers (Table 3.4). However, the prediction was not borne out for object markers; no significant association was found between the use of demonstratives and the appearance of overt accusative case marking (Table 3.5).

To summarize the findings from this study on case markers and CE, the following trends can be reported:

(1) Ben, Sandy and Sarah used subject and object case markers, and they displayed subject-object asymmetry, a normal pattern among monolingual adult Korean speakers.
(2) No correlation was found between age and use of subject markers. No correlation was found for object markers as well except in one child.
(3) Canonicality of word order was found to be a significant factor for the use of the object marker for Ben and Sandy. No significance was found for subject markers.
(4) There was a significant association between the use of demonstrative pronouns and the appearance of overt subject case markers. No significance was found for object markers.

We will return at the end of this chapter to discuss what these results might indicate with respect to Korean heritage speakers' development of Korean morphology.

Table 3.4 Chi-square test of homogeneity for subject marker use

Child	Pearson's Chi-square	df	p
Ben	3.723	1	0.054*
Sandy	25.216	1	0.000
Sarah	16.092	1	0.000

Source: Park-Johnson, 2019b.

*Although Ben's subject use did not technically reach the $p < 0.05$ threshold for significance, there is undeniably a trend for subjects that are not found for objects, as we will see.

Table 3.5 Chi-square test of homogeneity for object marker use

Child	Pearson's Chi-square	df	p
Ben	0.146	1	0.703
Sandy	0.386	1	0.535
Sarah	3.723	1	0.087

Source: Park-Johnson, 2019b.

3.3 Classifiers

Nominal morphology in Korean does not end with case markers. Like many other Asian languages, Korean employs classifiers when using count nouns with numerals. The classifier, a particle that in Korean follows the noun and numeral, agrees semantically with the type of the noun, as seen in (3). Unlike case markers, Korean classifiers are obligatory when using a numeral.

(3) Classifiers in Korean
  noun + numeral + classifier
  koyangi han-mali
  cat   one-CL
  'one cat'

The complexity of classifiers is not necessarily in its structural usage, but rather in choosing the appropriate one. There is a wide range of classifiers in Korean, as we saw in Chapter 2, and although there is a generic default classifier (*-kay*) that is used for objects, there are a great many others that speakers have to know. Certainly there are high-frequency classifiers that heritage speakers may often hear in the home or in social settings, such as the classifier for people (*-myeng*), animals (*-mali*), flat thin sheets (*-cang*) and glass/cup of liquid (*-can*). However, there are also infrequent noun types that young heritage speakers are not likely to hear, such as buildings (*-chay*), pieces of art (*-cem*) and agenda items (*-ken*).

Classifiers are important in Korean not only because they are obligatory particles, but also because using the wrong classifier can range from sounding non-native to being rather insulting (e.g. using the generic classifier for 'thing' instead of the classifier for a human). Studies that have investigated heritage speakers' use of classifiers show that speakers tend to favor the default markers (Jia & Paradis, 2015; Kan, 2019; Ming & Tao, 2008). For the Korean heritage children in this book, we examine their use of classifiers in naturalistic settings, namely to identify (1) whether they use them at all, (2) whether they use the correct ones when supplied and (3) what range of classifiers they use over time. Because classifiers only appear when indicating quantity, it is expected that the children do not hear examples often in the input. Therefore, if they do acquire it and use it, that alone would be a notable result.

To investigate, every utterance produced by each child across the entire data range that contained a numeral was coded for presence or absence of a classifier, which classifier they used (if any) and whether or not that classifier was target-like.

Table 3.6 Accuracy rates of Korean classifiers

Child	Total CL	Correct CL (%)	Default CL (% of total)
Ben	23	20 (87.0)	5 (21.7)
Sandy	59	54 (91.5)	36 (61.0)
Sarah	73	73 (100)	33 (43.4)

Findings indicated that classifiers, while not a frequent occurrence, did appear in the data for three of the children: Sandy, Ben and Sarah. The earliest age that classifiers appeared was at 3;10 by Ben. Dan, whose oldest data point was 3;11, did not exhibit any classifiers in any of his data. Given that classifiers did not appear in Ben's productions until 3;10 and we did not see any in the youngest child, we can tentatively say for the moment that classifiers may not be acquired until at least 3;10. Going forward in this section, we will focus on the three children that did produce classifiers.

Impressively, Sandy, Ben and Sarah had relatively high success rates with target-like use of Korean classifiers (Table 3.6). Ben produced a target-like rate of 87%, Sandy 91.5% and Sarah 100% of the time. Considering the limited appearance of classifiers in the input, this was an unexpected result. This indicated that when the children used classifiers, they were able to use them in a target-like manner. For the majority of the classifiers, the children used the default classifier, *-kay*. Sarah used *-kay* 46.5% of the time, Ben used them 25% of the time and Sandy used them 36% of the time. Other classifiers that appeared include *-pun* (minutes), *-to* (degrees), *-peiji* (pages) and units of time such as *-il* (day), *-wel* (month) and *-nyen* (year). A graphic representation of the range of classifiers used can be found in Figure 3.1.

Because of the relatively low occurrence of classifier errors (only three across all of Ben's utterances and only five across Sandy's), it was not possible to make any predictions about change over time. When errors did occur in the children's use of classifiers – eight total instances across years' worth of data – the errors were primarily those involving non-target-like classifier choice, with the children often using the default classifier *-kay* in place of one more specific. This is consistent with previous studies with other learners defaulting to the generic marker (Jia & Paradis, 2015; Kan, 2019; Ming & Tao, 2008). Some examples from the data can be seen in (4) below.

(4) Non-target-like classifier use

    (a) Killer whale *tu-*kay*   (Ben 5;4)
         two-CL$_{default}$
        'two killer whales'
        expected classifier: *-mali*, animal classifier

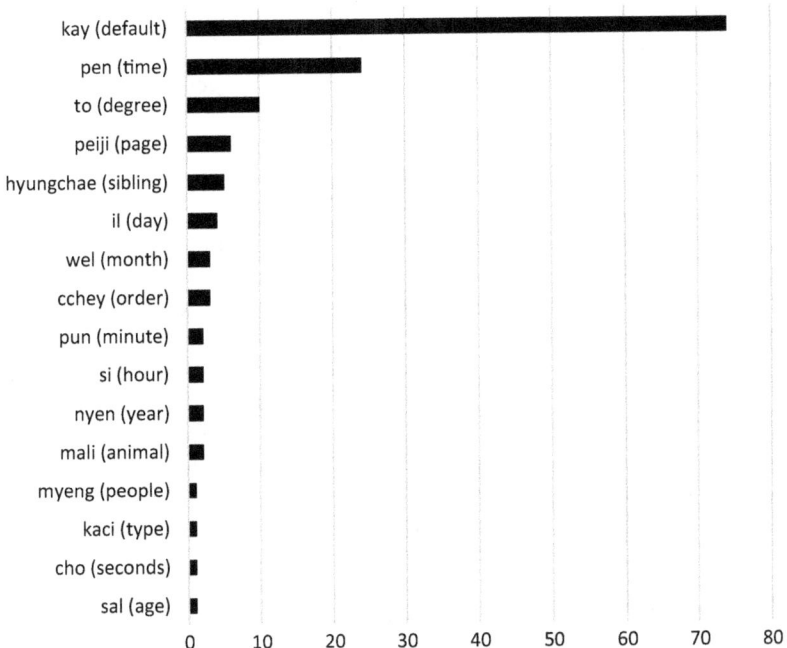

Figure 3.1 Range of Korean classifiers used overall

(b) *pihayngi ney-*kay* (Sandy 6;5)
    airplane four-CL$_{default}$
    'four airplanes'
    Expected classifier: *-tay*, vehicle classifier

In some cases, the children omitted the classifier altogether, as seen in example (5).

(5) Omitted classifier
    (a) *say twayci-*ø* (Sandy 4;10)
        three pig
        'three pigs'

    Expected: *twayci say-mali*
              Pig   three-CL$_{animal}$

Again, although we bring up these examples, the crucial point is there are only eight of these instances across the entirety of the data of 161 occurrences of Korean classifiers, and these errors account for just 5% of the data. The remaining 95% were used correctly.

The findings from this study of classifiers revealed the following trends:

(1) The earliest age that classifiers appeared among these Korean-English bilingual children was at 3;10.
(2) The children produced classifiers at a high target-like rate: 87% to 100% accuracy.
(3) The children used 17 different types of Korean classifiers.
(4) They used the default classifier -*kay* 74 times of the 161 total instances of classifiers across the data.
(5) Errors occurred eight times out of 161 total instances of classifiers.

These results show that while classifiers are not common, the Korean-English bilingual children in this study do know how to use them, when to use them and seem to use them quite productively. Furthermore, they seem to have a working knowledge of classifiers other than the default marker -*kay*, although they clearly use -*kay* more frequently than the other markers. Finally, the results show that the children have relative success with using classifiers in a target-like manner, with only eight errors across the entirety of the dataset.

3.4 Transitivity Markers

In the next two sections, we explore verbal morphology, which is quite complex given Korean's agglutinative nature. One area of potential difficulty for Korean heritage speakers is transitivity alternation, or the process by which derivationally or morphologically related verbs change from transitive to intransitive, or vice versa (Shin, 2010a; Yeon, 2001). In a transitive clause, the verb enacts an action or change of state on a direct object, such as in (6). In (6), the agent *Vincent* enacted the verb *melted* onto the direct object, *the ice*. In this transitive reading, the agent might be using a source of heat to melt the ice.

(6) Vincent   melted   the ice
    subject   transitive-verb   direct-object

In an intransitive clause, however, there is no requirement for a direct object, as in (7).

(7) The ice   melted
    subject   intransitive-verb

The intransitive reading of the sentence in (7) might call to mind a piece of ice that is melting on its own, not because someone is forcing it to, but simply because the weather is hot. In English, both the transitive and intransitive versions of the verb *to melt* appears identical.

However, in Korean, transitivity is specifically marked. Transitive verbs are marked with an inflectional morpheme that is attached to the verb root. For example, the attachment of the derivational affix –*i* will change the verb *nok-ta* 'to melt (intransitive)' to transitive verb *nok-i-ta* 'to melt (transitive)'. The transitive reading requires the presence of the –*i* particle immediately following the verb root, as in (8). Other transitivity particles include *-hi, -ki, -li, -wu, -ku* and *-chu*. In Korean, intransitive readings of the verb do not – and cannot – take the transitivity particle, as shown in (9).

(8) *Mul-ul   kkel-i-ess-ta*
    water-ACC boil-TRANS-PST-DECL
    '(pro) boiled the water'

(9) **Mul-i   kkel-i-ess-ta*
    water-NOM boil-TRANS-PST-DECL
    'the water boiled'

(10) **Mul-ul   kkel-ess-ta*
     water-ACC boil-PST-DECL
     'the water boiled'

For heritage speakers of Korean, transitivity alternation is of particular interest because this is yet another area of morphology where Korean contains an overt morphological distinction where English does not. In Park-Johnson (2020a), I conducted a study with adult Korean heritage speakers that showed that they had overall control over the particle, a finding that was surprising given that transitivity markers are not supported by their dominant language of English. For children, this might still be the case because the transitivity particle is also not phonologically salient and quite easy to miss in natural speech. In the present study, we are interested in seeing if young Korean heritage speakers develop and use this marker. To investigate, all instances of overt transitivity marking were identified in the children's production data. Of the ones that were found, each instance was coded for target-like usage and type of transitivity marker.

Results showed that much like classifiers, transitivity marking did not appear very frequently in the spontaneous productions by the Korean-English bilingual children. There was a total of 120 occurrences in the dataset across all four children. The earliest appearance of a transitivity marker was at 3;0 for Dan. Table 3.7 shows the number of transitivity marker occurrences per child.

Across the children, Ben and Sandy produced the most transitivity markers among the children. Accuracy ranged from 71% (Ben) to 100% (Dan). The list of verbs used by each child with a transitivity marker can be found in Table 3.8.

The verb list shows that not only was there a wide range of verbs used with the transitivity marker by the children, but they also used

Table 3.7 Transitivity marker use by Korean-English bilingual children

Child	Total transitivity markers	Total correct (%)
Dan	3	3 (100)
Ben	28	20 (71.4)
Sandy	42	38 (90.5)
Sarah	24	22 (91.7)

Table 3.8 Verbs used with transitivity markers by Korean-English bilingual children

Sarah	Sandy	Ben	Dan
English word + do (1)	Feed (2)	Erase (1)	Show (3)
English word + make do (1)	Raise (1)	Show (2)	
Stop (1)	Show (20)	Become (4)	
Hit (1)	Laugh (5)	Leave (1)	
Take off (as in clothes) (1)	Cut (1)	Match (2)	
Show (9)	Put on (clothes) (1)	Attach (6)	
Attach (9)	Attach (7)	Become red (2)	
Put on (clothes) (1)	Contain (1)	Puff out (1)	
Disappear (1)	Combine (1)	Wither (2)	
Cry (1)	Press (1)	Disappear (1)	
Laugh (2)		Make + come (1)	
Spread out (1)		Fall (1)	
		Splash (1)	
		Drop (1)	
		Detach (2)	
		Rip (1)	
		English word + become (3)	

them in ways that are typical among adult Korean speech. For instance, the verb meaning 'attach' (*puth-ta*) can be used intransitively to express the meaning that something has stuck itself to another object, for example, a piece of tape got stuck to a sock. However, with the transitive marker -*i* (transcribed as -*y*), the usage becomes transitive to mean that a person has attached one thing to another object, for example, stick a note on a wall. The alternation between those two uses by a single child in a single session, deftly oscillating from one usage to another, shows that she has the ability to discern the meaning of the particle and use it appropriately for intransitive (11) and transitive (12) purposes.

(11) *Mwe-ka   kuke   kunyang puth-enunke   ya*
     What-NOM   that   just   attach-that-thing Q
     'what's that thing that's attached?'

(12) *Neykke-nun   yeki-ta   puth-ye*
     Your-ACC   here-LOC   attach-TRANS
     'you attach yours here'

The results of this study of Korean transitivity marking are summarized as follows:

(1) All four of the children use transitivity markers in Korean, with 120 occurrences across the dataset.
(2) The earliest appearance of the transitivity marker is 3;0 (Dan).
(3) The children tend to use the transitivity marker appropriately. Other than Ben, who used transitivity marking at 71% accuracy, the other three children used them at an accuracy rate of 90% (Sarah), 92% (Sandy) and 100% (Dan).
(4) The correct uses of the transitivity marker showed a wide range of lexical verbs, all of which are used in adult-like Korean for causative and/or agentive meanings.

3.5 Sentence Final Markers

Korean has a rich system of verbal inflectional morphology as we discussed in Chapter 2. In Korean, information that is pertinent to the tense, aspect, modality, evidentiality and formality of a clause is attached to the root verb. Together, these are often grouped together as sentence final markers, and we will examine them together for the purposes of this section. Some examples are as follows: clausal markers *-ca* (proposal) or *-la* (command); honorifics such as *-yo* and *-si*; tense markers such as *-ess* (past) and *-koissta* (present); aspect markers that denote continuation, completion or repetition such as *-keytoyta* (to become), *-komalta* (to manage to complete) and *-epelita* (to do completely to one's regret or relief); modality markers that denote speaker attitudes and intentions such as *-cikulay* (why don't you), *-mot* (not able to) and *-cikulaysse* (wish you had); and evidentiality markers, or markers that indicate how speakers have come to know or report on a fact, such as *-kekatta* (seems like), *-epointa* (looks like, based on immediate sensory experience) and *-kuna* (first realization). These markers can also be combined with others to create various meanings and functions.

There are very few known studies that look at Korean heritage speakers in early childhood and their acquisition of sentence final markers in Korean. Some evidence from adult heritage speakers exists in the literature. For instance, Choi (2003) found that adult heritage speakers of Korean do show difficulty with irregular verb endings. Lee (2018) also showed that adult Korean heritage speakers and L2 learners of Korean tend to struggle with tense-aspect morphology in Korean, which is expressed in sentence final markers as well. The present study aims to establish a baseline for what Korean heritage children do with the complex sentence final morphology of Korean. Sentence final markers are also completely unavoidable; Korean verbs cannot exist in root form without a morpheme attached, and thus every utterance that contains a verb should contain a sentence final marker. Given their vastness in meaning and usage, it is important that while we give a single name to the marker, we do tease apart the different categories of markers to showcase the variety that the children are using to avoid oversimplifying their abilities. The research questions are as follows:

(1) Do Korean-English bilingual children use sentence final markers?
(2) What is the rate of accuracy for each child overall?
(3) What is the earliest occurrence (age) of sentence final markers?
(4) What is the range of sentence final markers used?

To investigate, all utterances containing a verb were coded for which marker was used and whether or not the child used it in a target-like manner as assessed by a native speaker of Korean. I also noted the range of markers used across time and by each child.

Results indicate that sentence final markers are robustly used in the Korean productions by the Korean-English bilingual children in this book. All four children used sentence final markers in every single session. Sentence final markers appeared at the youngest age data point available, Dan at age 3;0. The overall accuracy rates for each child can be seen in Table 3.9.

The rates of accuracy are especially notable given the range of final markers available and required in Korean. Across all the utterances, Dan and Ben – despite producing fewer utterances overall – only made one error each. For Sandy and Sarah, who produced over a thousand utterances that required sentence final markers, they each only made 15 and three errors, respectively. These errors – which again only make up 0.1% of total utterances – were typically due to use of the wrong verb form or missing inflection, as in (13).

(13) *emma   kuntey   kurekey   mantule   tway   (Sandy 4;8)
      Mom   by-the-way   that-way   make   can
      'By the way, Mom, can I make it that way?'

Table 3.9 Overall accuracy rates for sentence final markers in Korean

Child	Number correct over total	Accuracy rate (%)
Dan	51/52	98.1
Ben	392/393	99.7
Sandy	1687/1702	99.1
Sarah	1220/1223	99.8

In (13), there is a marker expected after the verb form *mantule* to connect to the marker *tway*, which could be either *-ya* or *-to*. These exceptional cases were highly uncommon and usually involved more complex syntactic structures such as the example given here.

To answer Research Question 3, we looked at the earliest occurrence of sentence final markers in the data. Sentence final markers appeared in the earliest session with the youngest child, Dan, at age 3;0. The other children also showed examples of sentence final markers from their first session, which leads us to hypothesize that they begin to occur quite early (prior to 3;0) in Korean-English bilingual children.

Finally, Research Question 4 explored the range of sentence final markers used by the children. Unlike what we saw above for classifiers, the children used an extensive range of sentence final markers throughout the study. Dan used 25 different types of markers, Ben used 91, Sandy used 447 and Sarah used 240 different types of sentence final markers. The children did favor certain markers over others: all four children used the *-e* marker extensively, comprising 9.6% of Dan's final markers, 10.7% of Ben's, 9.7% of Sandy's and 8.8% of Sarah's. The *-e* marker is a default declarative sentence final marker that is often used in an informal setting, as with close family members. Some examples can be found below:

(14) *pinu   yeki-ss-e*   (Dan 3;0)
     Soap here-is-SFM
     'Here is the soap'

(15) *ike him-tel-e*   (Ben 4;11)
     This strength-take-SFM
     'This is hard'

(16) *mini-to kati mek-e*   (Sandy 5;8)
     Minnie-also together eat-SFM
     'Minnie also eats together'

(17) *acu   yeyppess-e*   (Sarah 7;5)
     Very pretty was-SFM
     'It was very pretty'

The three older children also used the *-iya* marker, which denotes declarative presentation, used in utterances when the speaker is presenting a fact to the listener. This is used quite frequently in familiar, informal contexts as well. The *-iya* marker comprised 9.2% of Ben's sentence final markers, 6.3% of Sandy's and 5.1% of Sarah's.

The results of this study of Korean sentence final markers are summarized as follows:

(1) All four of the children used sentence final markers in Korean, with 3370 occurrences across the dataset.

(2) The overall accuracy rate for sentence final markers was very high, ranging from 98.1% to 99.8%.
(3) The earliest appearance of a sentence final marker was 3;0 (Dan).
(4) The children used a vast range of sentence final markers, with Dan using 25 different types and Sandy using 447. The children did favor certain markers over others, such as the *-e* marker (default declarative informal) and *-iya* marker (presentation declarative informal).

3.6 Chapter Summary

In this chapter we have looked at Korean-English bilingual children's development of Korean morphology. Specifically, we have examined four areas of grammar that have the potential to pose difficulty for learners of Korean: case marking and ellipsis, nominal classifiers, transitivity marking and sentence final markers. Each study described above shows aspects of Korean morphology that play a crucial role in Korean language use and are unsupported by the children's other language, English. Certainly, children did show difficulty with each of these areas. For instance, in the classifier study, we discovered that the youngest child Dan did not display any use of classifiers, and Ben produced errors with them 13% of the time. The transitivity marker also posed difficulty for some of the children: Ben produced errors 29% of the time and Sandy 10% of the time overall.

However, the overwhelming result across all four studies showed a remarkable pattern: not only did they acquire these difficult Korean morphological forms and processes, but they also excelled at the use of them much of the time. For instance, case markers, which are required in some contexts and are permitted to elide in other contexts, pose difficulty due to their variable nature. Other morphemes like transitivity markers and classifiers are challenging because the contexts in which they are used are infrequent in the input. Sentence final markers are vastly diverse: the fact that the two older children were using hundreds of different types of sentence final markers shows that they are not the restricted users of the language we might believe heritage speakers to be. The longitudinal study also reveals that the trend of development over time is always positive; there is ongoing growth and increasing accuracy of the children's Korean as they progress. This is particularly notable given that as the children get older, they are increasingly exposed to English during their waking hours, and the two languages may be in 'competition' with one another, at least in the input. However, even with partial Korean input, it is rich enough input for children to acquire these challenging areas of Korean morphology. This provides counterevidence for the fallacy that the more English they are learning, the less Korean is able to develop. So far, even with the increasing English they are exposed to, the children are still in the upward development of Korean. We will return to this point as we explore the children's Korean syntax development in the next chapter.

The theoretical implications of these results are important as well. First, it shows us that frequency in the input does not necessarily translate to facility of acquisition. If we look at the examples with case marking and ellipsis, we found that children can acquire all forms in both subject and object NPs, despite the variable nature of case marking in Korean, especially in informal contexts. For transitivity marking, which only appears with verbs that allow for transitivity alternation, children are still able to acquire it and use it productively. Although frequency has often been attributed as an explanation for facility of acquisition in language acquisition, here the inverse case is not necessarily borne out. This is a profound result that supports the generative perspective of language acquisition: grammatical features that are low frequency are still robustly acquired in early childhood bilingualism and in heritage contexts.

Second, this investigation of Korean-English bilingual children also has implications and insight for other bilingual language pairings. What we see here is that typological difference between languages does not necessarily mean that the languages will be more difficult to acquire than between two languages that are typologically similar. Studies have indeed shown that typological closeness does not necessarily equate to facility of acquisition; in fact, there are times when that similarity of structure can contribute to difficulty (Kolb *et al.*, 2022). In the examples of sentence final markers or classifiers – features of Korean morphology that do not have a counterpart in English – the children are able to acquire it, use it and continue to develop it with relatively high levels of accuracy. Their capacity for learning both languages does not seem to be strongly affected by their reduced input in both languages.

Overall, the message is this: despite their heritage status, these Korean-English bilingual children are successfully and productively using Korean morphology at this stage of language development. Furthermore, this has consequences for the attrition versus lack of attainment debate: considering that adult heritage speakers have difficulty with these areas, it may mean that those same adults once had those features in early childhood and then lost them over time, rather than never having acquired them in the first place. The consequence of this is positive: it means that the grammatical features can be maintained as opposed to having to acquire them anew later in life. As we look closely at the children's Korean syntax in the next chapter, we will return to this debate.

4 Korean Syntax

4.1 Introduction

In this chapter, we explore the development of Korean-English bilingual children's Korean syntax, an area of particular interest due to its distinct structural difference from English. This chapter investigates areas of Korean syntax that are predicted to be difficult for Korean-English bilingual individuals: Korean word order and null pronominals. Recall from Chapter 2 that Korean has canonical subject-object-verb (SOV) word order while English has SVO order. Korean also allows for both subject and object drop, a feature that is not supported in their English. Although there is a fair amount of coverage of Korean heritage syntax for adults, there are fewer studies that report on children's development of heritage Korean syntax. For adults, there has been comprehensive work done on Korean binding interpretations (Kim *et al.*, 2009, 2010), relative clauses (Lee-Ellis, 2009; O'Grady *et al.*, 2003) and negative polarity items (Kim, 2013). However, word order or prodrop studies for Korean heritage speakers, particularly for children, are few and far between. The results presented in this chapter are offered to help fill this gap. We also focus on word order and prodrop in this chapter because these are features that are likely to be part of child syntax. Though Korean does have syntactic features that differ from Korean (e.g. internally headed relative clauses), these generally do not arise in child grammars, especially when looking at naturalistic data.

Furthermore, at the end of Chapter 3, I raised the question that has been posed in heritage language literature many a time: do adult heritage speakers lose features in their heritage language over time, or do the learners never acquire them in the first place as children? Evidence from Chapter 3 suggested that the children do have features that later adult heritage speakers of Korean struggle with. After examining the data from this chapter on Korean syntax, I will return to this question at the end of this chapter with respect to Korean development overall.

This chapter will begin with an investigation of children's development of Korean word order. In the subsequent section, we will look at their use and development of null pronominals. To conclude, Section 4.4 provides an analysis of how these results impact theory and practice.

4.2 Word Order

Word order is one of the primary areas of interest for Korean-English bilingual development, as it is one of the most salient ways in which the two languages differ syntactically. Because of its large syntactic scope, word order errors tend to have more significant and noticeable consequences. Korean follows SOV word order as its canonical pattern. However, the added complexity for Korean is that partly due to its rich morphology (case marking in particular), Korean has relatively flexible word order, allowing objects or even verbs to be fronted in pragmatically licensed contexts. English, on the other hand, has a strict word order of SVO, and changing of the subject and object arguments can completely change the meaning: *Sunny kicked a chair* and *A chair kicked Sunny* yield two very different mental pictures. Although word order does not seem as though it would be a challenge to learners because of its overall salience, research in second language acquisition of Korean by L1 English speakers shows that Korean word order does pose difficulties for learners (Ha & Choi, 2012). Other studies investigating younger children acquiring two languages with different word orders show similar difficulties: for instance, Cantonese-English bilingual children have shown crosslinguistic influence of word order from English to Cantonese (Yip & Matthews, 2007). Norwegian-English bilingual children have also shown considerable word order language transfer from Norwegian into English (Westergaard, 2003). It is predicted that the children in the present study who are learning Korean at home as a heritage language would also have similar difficulties given that their societal language of English has differing – and rather inflexible – canonical word order.

In our dataset, we investigate the production of Korean by the four children – Dan, Ben, Sandy and Sarah – and specifically ask the questions:

(1) Do Korean-English bilingual children produce target-like word order in their Korean utterances?
(2) What word orders do Korean-English bilingual children use when producing spoken Korean?
(3) Does the children's Korean word order change over time?

To answer these research questions, all Korean productions throughout the entire body of data were coded for word order. Utterances that contained any English were eliminated from this analysis because of the possible competing trigger that could occur when English grammar is activated. Single word utterances or utterances not containing a verb were eliminated from this analysis as well, as word order is either irrelevant or cannot be discerned from these types of utterances. A Korean-speaking graduate student coded the utterances for word order and also judged the acceptability of those utterances. Acceptability was necessary because while Korean has canonical word order of SOV, other orders are permissible in context (e.g. OSV, when focus is on the object).

Research Question 1 inquired about the overall acceptability of the word order used by the children in their Korean utterances. Table 4.1 displayed the accuracy overall for each child. The findings indicate that the children scored at ceiling overall for their use of Korean word order. In fact, only one utterance across all four children was deemed unacceptable.

In examining types of word orders the children use for the second research question, we looked at the most frequent word orders as well as the range of word orders the children employed in their Korean utterances. Table 4.2 provides an overall picture of the range of word orders used by each child. The results show that all four of the children used V or SV word orders, with those two categories making up 67% to 80% of all the children's word orders.

While noncanonical word orders are permissible and certainly used among the older children, the overwhelming majority of the utterances still fell under the canonical (S)(O)V category: Dan 100%, Ben 98%, Sandy 98% and Sarah 99%. This is consistent with findings for native speakers of Korean, whose Korean utterances follow SOV word order 97% of the time (Lee, 2016).

We also have the advantage here of looking at the children's word orders across time for each child for the four canonical word orders (Figures 4.1 to 4.4). Because tokens vary from session to session, it is more useful to compare proportions than number of occurrences.

Table 4.1 Korean word order overall acceptability by child

Child	Overall acceptability % (tokens correct/total)
Dan	100 (35/35)
Ben	100 (334/334)
Sandy	100 (969/969)
Sarah	99.9 (867/868)

Table 4.2 Word orders used in children's Korean utterances

Child	SV	V	OV	SOV	SVO	VO	VS	OVS
Dan	7	22	4	2	–	–	–	–
Ben	120	115	43	47	1	2	3	3
Sandy	228	442	195	91	–	13	7	13
Sarah	278	394	119	64	2	3	7	–

Korean Syntax 51

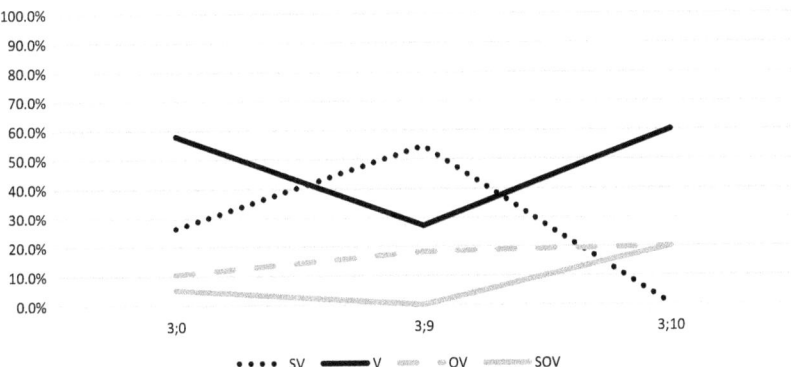

Figure 4.1 Korean word order types across time: Dan

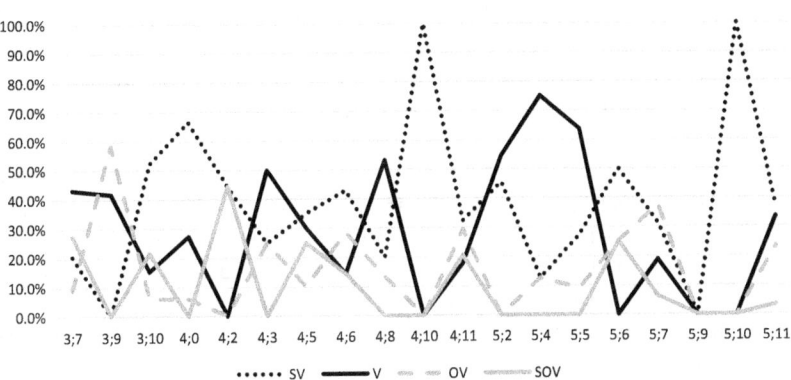

Figure 4.2 Korean word order types across time: Ben

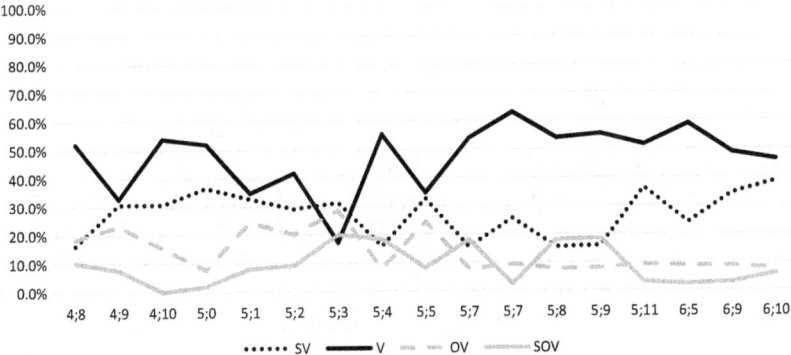

Figure 4.3 Korean word order types across time: Sandy

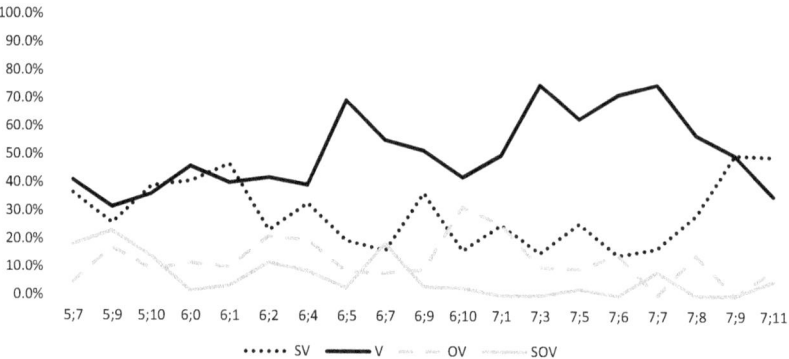

Figure 4.4 Korean word order types across time: Sarah

Longitudinal analyses show that the rate of each type of word order stays relatively constant across the data. Sarah and Sandy do show a slight increase over time with respect to the V-only construction (around late age 5 and throughout 6s), but the change is only slight over time.

The results of the word order study can be summarized as follows:

(1) The Korean-English bilingual children produced highly accurate word orders that were near or at ceiling (99.9%–100% accuracy).
(2) The children had a strong preference for the (S)(O)V word orders, indicating that despite their ability to use noncanonical word orders they tend to use canonical structures.
(3) There were not many changes over time in the types of structures children preferred to use.
(4) Sandy and Sarah showed a slight increase of V type word order as they got older.

4.3 Null Pronominals

Closely related to Korean word order – and what makes Korean word order more complex – is the prodrop parameter. However, unlike many Romance languages that allow just the subject to be dropped, Korean allows for both the subject and the object to be omitted in contexts where the arguments are presumably known and understood by the speaker and listener (Nam & Ko, 2013). Therefore, Speaker A in (1) may produce a sentence without the subject, as it is understood that they are asking a direct question of 'have you eaten rice/meal' to Speaker B, and in turn, Speaker B can answer with just the verb with the understanding that the subject is 'I' and the object is 'rice/meal'.

(1) A: *pap   mek-ess-e*
        Rice/meal eat-PST-Q
        Did you eat rice/meal, or 'have you eaten'

B: *Ung, mek-ess-e*
     Yeah, eat-PST-DECL
     Yeah, I ate rice/meal, or 'yeah, I've eaten already'

What is notable here is that inserting the subject 'you' or 'I' in A and B's utterances respectively, would sound either awkward, slightly accusatory or at best making it a point to ask just about B and excluding other participants. In other words, like many prodrop languages, inserting the pronoun when it is not necessary makes for redundancy and possible awkwardness. It may present as being a little too focused on oneself.

For language acquisition, this is a challenge because learners must acquire the exact nuanced pragmatic contexts and situations where it is not allowed and where it would be natural to drop the pronoun(s). Many studies have explored this for adult second language learners of prodrop languages (Al-Kasey & Perez-Leroux, 1998; Chen, 2003; Forsythe *et al.*, 2019; Glass & Perez-Leroux, 1998; Isabelli, 2004), for first language acquisition (Rizzi, 1994; Serratrice, 2008; Wang *et al.*, 1992) and for child bilingualism (Haznedar, 2003; Paradis & Navarro, 2003; Serratrice & Sorace, 2003; Sopata *et al.*, 2021). The resounding consensus across these studies is that learners have difficulty acquiring prodrop, particularly when the other language of the speaker is non-prodrop, like English. Because English does not allow for subject or object drop, this causes more difficulty for learners who are learning both English and another language at the same time. Further challenges are posed when there are opposing parameters with a small overlap: English allows only overt pronouns, but Korean allows both overt and dropped pronouns. Thus, the goal of the present research is to inquire whether Korean-English bilingual children have this difficulty as well. Below is a formalization of the research questions:

(1) Do Korean-English bilingual children drop and supply pronouns appropriately?
(2) How often do they supply pronouns when it is not necessary?
(3) What are the most frequent types of prodrop?

The prediction was that because they are also learning English, the children may use more overt Korean pronouns than expected, and that this rate of overt pronoun use will increase over time as English becomes more dominant for each child. However, the bilingual children in this book were exposed to English several years after Korean; having been exposed to Korean from birth may supply better chances of target-like prodrop rates in in Korean.

All Korean utterances that contained a verb were coded for the presence or absence of an overt pronoun in both subject and object position. Only utterances that followed canonical word order were examined.

Table 4.3 Rates of accuracy of prodrop

Child	Overall	Prodrop	Non-prodrop
Dan	96.3% (26/27)	96.2% (24/25)	100% (2/2)
Ben	98.6% (278/282)	100% (158/158)	97.8% (120/124)
Sandy	97.9% (943/963)	100% (651/651)	93.6% (292/312)
Sarah	98.7% (747/757)	100% (434/434)	96.9% (313/323)

Utterances that contained any English words were omitted from this analysis, as were utterances not containing a verb. Acceptability judgment of the utterances was conducted by a native Korean-speaking graduate research assistant.

The first research question prompted an inquiry about children's accuracy overall with Korean prodrop. The rates of acceptability are reported in Table 4.3. Overall, the children exhibited near-ceiling levels of proficiency with prodrop in their Korean utterances, all scoring between 96.3% and 98.7%. Table 4.3 also displays the rates of accuracy for utterances with prodrop (i.e. the child dropped the pronoun appropriately) and for utterances with non-prodrop (i.e. the child supplied the pronoun appropriately). To address Research Question 2, we see that although both categories showed high levels of accuracy, children tended to have slightly less accuracy with non-prodrop categories. These errors with non-prodrop were ones in which children dropped a pronoun when it was more acceptable to supply the pronoun, indicating an error of omission.

Of particular note is the direction of the pattern we see in Table 4.3 between the prodrop and non-prodrop categories. Given that the children are increasingly being exposed to English, we would expect that children would be more likely to oversupply the pronoun than undersupply. Indeed, that is what we see in other studies among children who are exposed to a non-prodrop and prodrop language (Yip & Matthews, 2007). However, here, the children are more likely to drop the pronoun in a non-prodrop context – that is, undersupply the pronoun – in an error of omission, the opposite of what we might expect. It is possible the children are at some level aware that Korean permits the dropping of pronouns, and thus children omit the pronoun more readily. We will study children's English pronoun use in Chapter 6, then compare these results in Chapter 9.

Finally, Research Question 3 inquired as to which types of prodrop are most likely. To that end, every utterance in this analysis was coded for the type of (non)prodrop the children employed. The nine different types are defined below:

(1) Sdrop – subject pronoun is dropped, object pronoun is unnecessary because predicate is intransitive or object is a full determiner phrase (DP).
(2) SdropO – subject pronoun is dropped, object pronoun is supplied.

(3) Odrop – object pronoun is dropped, subject is full DP.
(4) SOdrop – object pronoun is dropped, subject pronoun is supplied.
(5) S – subject pronoun is supplied, object pronoun is unnecessary because predicate is intransitive or object is a full DP.
(6) SO – subject pronoun is supplied, object pronoun is supplied.
(7) SdropOdrop – subject pronoun and object pronoun are dropped.
(8) None – for utterances with unnecessary subject and object, such as when both the subject and object are full DPs.
(9) NoneIntrans – when verb is intransitive and has full DP subject with verb (often for verb *issta* 'to be').

For each child, the proportions of each type of prodrop context are reported in Figures 4.5 through 4.8. The comparisons across the four

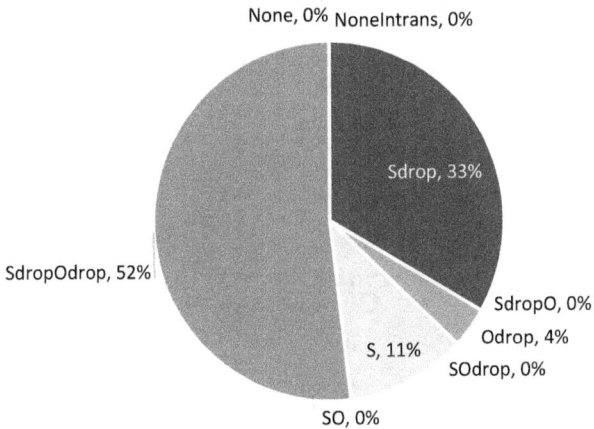

Figure 4.5 Korean prodrop types: Dan

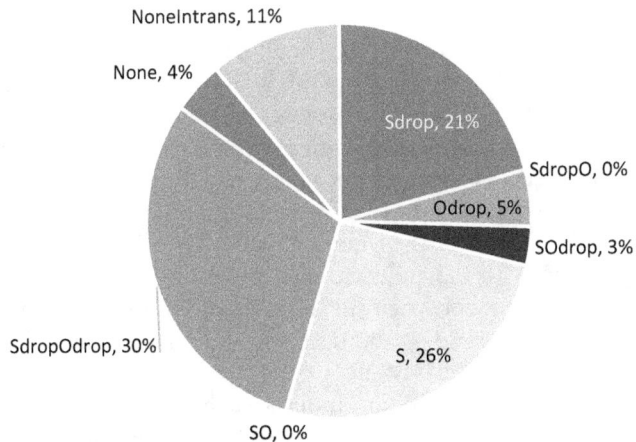

Figure 4.6 Korean prodrop types: Ben

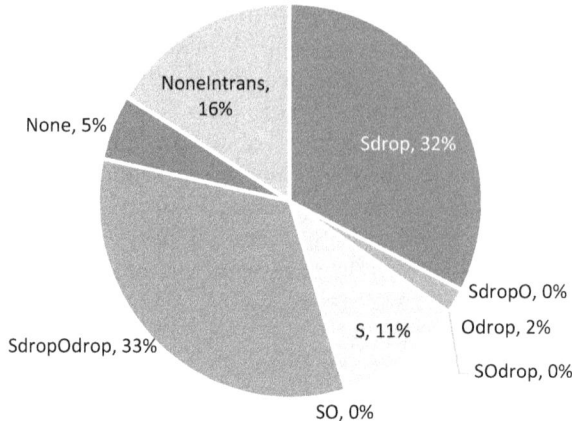

Figure 4.7 Korean prodrop types: Sandy

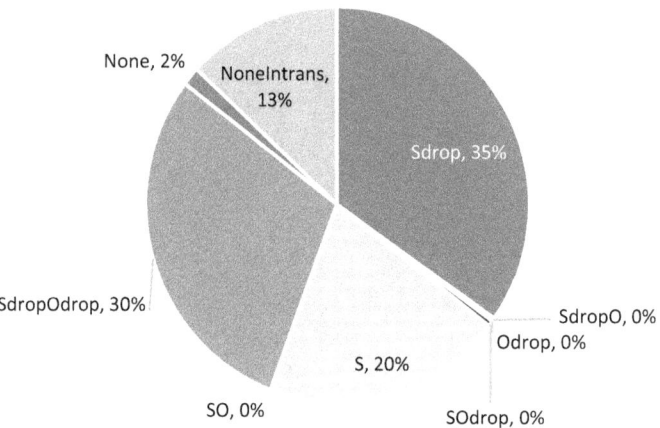

Figure 4.8 Korean prodrop types: Sarah

children indicate that SdropOdrop – in which both the subject and object pronoun is dropped and the verb stands alone – is the most common type of prodrop found in the children's utterances. Sdrop, or dropping just the subject pronoun, is the second most common type, followed by S, where the subject is supplied but object pronoun is unnecessary. This actually patterns quite similarly to monolingual-like Koreans, who drop pronouns 68% to 79% of the time (Lee, 2019a; Park, 2012). The higher rates of prodrop with the children here are also to be expected because prodrop is more frequent when speaking to an interlocutor who is older (Lee, 2019a), as in a child speaking to their parent. It is also interesting to note that there are no instances of SO, or utterances with both an overt subject and overt pronoun. Indeed, such cases are rare, because it would entail that neither the subject nor object are previous mentions and neither are understood by the speaker or interlocutor. Since the likelihood of such utterances is rare in parent–child interactions, it makes sense that utterances with an overt subject and object are not seen here. Again, if English had imposed more influence on their Korean structure, we would expect to see more of them.

To summarize the results from the prodrop study, below are some of the most salient trends:

(1) Korean-English bilingual children had high rates of accuracy with prodrop and non-prodrop in Korean production (>96.3% overall).
(2) The children generally had higher success rates with prodrop over non-prodrop, favoring errors of omission rather than errors of commission.
(3) The most common type of prodrop was SdropOdrop (omit both subject and object pronouns) and Sdrop (omit subject pronoun).

4.4 Chapter Summary

In this chapter, we explored Korean-English bilingual children's development of Korean syntax. We looked specifically at two aspects of their Korean grammar that could potentially be difficult due to its divergence from English grammar. These are also areas that have been difficult for L2 Korean learners and adult heritage speakers of Korean, the two populations of learners we can draw on most from available research. These areas – word order and null pronominals – are also areas of syntax that would be expected to be high frequency in child grammar.

Overall, despite the expected difficulty with these areas, the bilingual children in this study showed proficiency with word order and prodrop in Korean. The fact that word order posed virtually no problems for all children speak to how well developed their overall language structure is. That these children had no trouble with word order even as they became older (as old as 7;11 for Sarah) also indicates that overall structure does not change or become 'lost' as some parents and educators may fear. It could be that large structural aspects of the language like word order are established early and not as susceptible to difference as compared to smaller, more nuanced areas, or internal structures. The backbone nature of canonical word order – established early on in the overall headedness and branching – perhaps makes it more resistant to change of crosslinguistic influence. Granted, that same argument cannot be made for all the studies that have shown influence of English to the heritage language. Alternatively, having learned the language from birth may be a contributing factor. Indeed, some preliminary work I have done with slightly older Korean heritage speakers, those aged 7–13, who were exposed to Korean from birth and English from early childhood all overwhelmingly showed excellent control of Korean SOV word order (Park-Johnson & Kim, 2021).

The prodrop study also revealed similar rates of success from all four of the children, who scored between 96.3% and 98.7% accuracy overall. Like word order, prodrop is an area of grammar that is frequent in the input; whether to drop the pronoun or provide it overtly is a decision that must occur in almost every utterance containing a verb. The four children had ample opportunities to hear it in the input and produce it in the output. Prodrop, however, is different from word order in that it is driven by pragmatics – residing at the syntax-pragmatics interface – and prodrop tends to have more of an acceptability gradient as opposed to a strict dichotomy. Dropping pronouns are especially common when the context is understood by the speaker and interlocutor; thus, in a parent–child interaction where we can assume more familiar and shared knowledge, prodrop would occur more frequently than among unfamiliar interlocutors or in more formal contexts. Thus, it is especially notable that heritage children are still able to negotiate the appropriate contexts for prodrop and non-prodrop utterances.

The question we have been grappling with in heritage language literature is whether adult and adolescent heritage speakers lose Korean syntactic features over time, or if speakers never acquire them in the first place (Benmamoun *et al.*, 2013; Polinksy, 2018). The most compelling answer to this question generally comes from child heritage speakers, to see if the features were present in early childhood. The data in this chapter suggest that Korean-English bilingual children do in fact develop target-like Korean word order and prodrop. If older learners do have difficulty with these areas of Korean grammar, the evidence from this chapter suggests it was not because they never acquired in the first place, but rather lost or changed over time. One of the reasons for this may be the increased use of English and the decreased use of the home language; from early childhood to young adulthood, the proportions of these languages in their input are likely to change. However, if the adolescents or adult heritage speakers are in a different proportional environment (e.g. increase the amount of exposure by going to Korea for a visit, attending Korean school, etc.) then this will help offset that steep mismatch of input. Although we cannot hypothesize based on the data collected here, what we can say with certainty is that at this stage of development the children do have excellent competence with Korean word order and Korean prodrop in early childhood.

The studies in this chapter also revealed that while children's Korean word order and prodrop are developing well, there may be some impact of Korean developing alongside another language, English. Indeed, it is perhaps oversimplistic – and inaccurate – to say that the children are developing these two languages separately as if they are two completely isolated processes. The impact of having Korean and English developing at the same time manifest in ways that we might not expect. For instance, in the prodrop study we would have expected that children would be more likely to use the overt pronoun more than they would drop the pronoun because English does not permit prodrop. However, it seems that the children in this study are far more likely to drop the pronoun and have higher success rates with prodrop than non-prodrop; while this is an unexpected pattern it may be that the children are very much aware that this is an area of difference between the two languages. One way to distinguish the two – or make Korean markedly different from English – is to drop the pronoun more frequently. In the word order study, results indicate that the children are actually quite successfully using SOV word order, an area of grammar that is saliently different between the two languages. As a way of marking the distinction between the two languages the children may be leaning into that canonical SOV word order far more than if they were monolingual. Indeed, their rates of canonical word order are actually higher than they are for native speakers who might occasionally use SVO word order in their Korean. The hypothesis here is that because of the marked difference between the two languages, one way the children distinguish them is to stay remarkably faithful to the canonical pattern in each of the languages. Going forward, we will compare with English syntactic development in similar areas of grammar to see if this hypothesis is borne out.

5 English Morphology

5.1 Introduction

Now that we have explored some of the morphological and syntactic patterns of Korean-English bilingual children's heritage language development, we shift to the other half of the equation: English. The goal with examining English is somewhat different given that (1) it is the societal language and (2) we know English will be the children's dominant language, as evidenced by the present studies and also the large body of heritage language research. As a result, we will not concern ourselves much with the question of 'are they learning English' so much as the question of 'what are some possible areas where Korean might influence the trajectory of their dominant language'.

The other ever-present goal of exploring the children's English is to address the notion of fear. A persistent concern among parents, educators and clinicians is that children who speak more than one language are going to fall behind in their English development. The implication is that their home language will interfere with English acquisition. While there is ample evidence demonstrating that this is not the case, the myth and the fear persist in the minds of many parents and educators (Jeon, 2008). With this research, we add to the body of evidence that shows bilingualism is not harmful. My goal – and one I implore the field to consider as well – is that this knowledge does not stay contained solely within the academic community, but that it can also be disseminated to society at large, especially parents of Korean-English bilingual children and other heritage language populations. In order to best support bilingual communities and bilingual children in schools, it is critical that we share facts about bilingualism and make them accessible to stakeholders. The belief that bilingualism is somehow harmful and somehow a threat to English may seem farfetched to the linguist; however, studies show this is not necessarily the mindset of parents, educators, medical professionals and bilingual communities themselves. The more we can disseminate information about bilingualism, the more we will be able to better address the notion of fear. This in turn supports students and children's heritage language maintenance, thereby maintaining close ties to their cultures and families, affirming their identities and boosting their overall well-being.

In this chapter, we examine the development of English morphology, especially in areas that are not supported by their Korean or are typically difficult for children learning English, such as articles and inflectional verb morphology. We look at the impact of beginning English development several years after the onset of Korean acquisition, and how – if any – the presence of the still-developing impacts English morphology acquisition.

5.2 English Articles

Although articles could be considered a syntactic element because articles in English are free morphemes, here we will investigate their use from a morphological and semantic perspective as opposed to its syntactic distribution. What tends to be difficult for learners is not necessarily where to place articles – there are very few errors across language acquisition where learners struggle with its syntactic positioning – but rather which article to use and when. Thus, articles for language learners fall more under the realm of morphology.

Articles are also highly complex because of the aforementioned interface complexities: articles are morphological spell outs that have syntactic properties and restrictions, but are driven by semantic features. This difficulty is documented not just for L2 or bilingual populations alone. In fact, there is a large body of literature on monolingual L1 English acquisition of articles by children (e.g. Maratsos, 1974; Schafer & de Villiers, 2000; Warden, 1976). These studies have shown that articles are challenging even for children learning only English. It appears that monolingual English-speaking children tend to make errors with articles until about age 4;0 (de Villiers & de Villiers, 1973), and some children still struggle with the nuanced use as late as 9 years of age (Maratsos, 1974, 1976; Warden, 1976, 1981). One typical pattern seen across various learner populations is the overuse of the definite article *the* in indefinite contexts. This is seen in monolingual L1 acquisition of English (Brown, 1973; Maratsos, 1974; Warden, 1976), adult L2 studies (Ionin *et al.*, 2004, 2008, 2021) and child L2 studies (Zdorenko & Paradis, 2012). Furthermore, in research of L2 acquisition of articles, the resounding trend for both adults and children seems to be that learners whose L1s do not have an article system – Korean, for example – tend to struggle more with acquisition of English articles than learners whose L1 does have an article system (Ionin *et al.*, 2004, 2021; Kang, 2002; Zdorenko & Paradis, 2008, 2012).

For Korean-English bilingual children, the odds seem to be stacked against them just based on prior research alone. Not only are English articles notoriously difficult for all learners of English, but for the children in the present study, there has been little input of English during the first several years of their lives. As such, it is especially interesting to see how they develop the acquisition of English articles over time. In this chapter, we first investigated whether children use them at all, when they start to appear and whether there are errors associated with the children's use of English articles that corroborate what is seen in the literature for other language learner groups. Formally, the research questions that drove this study are as follows:

(1) Do Korean-English bilingual children use English articles when speaking English?
(2) When is the earliest age that articles first appear?
(3) Do they use them in a target-like manner?
(4) If children make article errors, what are the sources of error?

To investigate the research questions above, every instance of articles *the* and *a(n)* in the children's productions was identified and coded. We also searched utterance by utterance for any instances when an article was correctly omitted (i.e. the null article Ø), instances when an article was omitted but should have been supplied and instances when an article was supplied but should have been omitted. These instances were coded by a native English-speaking research assistant and reviewed by me.

Results revealed that the children used all three types of English articles (*the*, *a/an*, Ø) throughout the study. Even the earliest data point of the youngest child, Dan at age 2;4, showed that he was using *the* and *a/an* correctly. Average accuracy for articles overall and for each article is reported in Table 5.1 below.

To address the first two research questions, (1) yes, Korean-English children do use English articles, and (2) they appear as early as 2;4. The third question inquired about the accuracy of the children's use of articles. Overall, children's accuracy with articles increases with age, where the older two children (Sandy 93.5% and Sarah 94.2%) outperformed the younger two (Dan 84.5% and Ben 87.0%). This is also the trend for *the* and *a* when tabulated separately. Findings also indicated increasing numbers of articles used as the children became older. This is certainly

Table 5.1 English article use accuracy overall

	the	*a/an*	Ø	Overall
Dan	84.4 (178/211)	82.4 (182/221)	87.3 (144/165)	84.5 (508/601)
Ben	84.5 (571/676)	83.0 (429/517)	92.9 (602/648)	87.0 (1602/1841)
Sandy	95.1 (1038/1092)	91.1 (848/931)	94.3 (827/877)	93.5 (2718/2908)
Sarah	97.4 (1628/1672)	91.3 (1019/1116)	92.8 (1113/1200)	94.2 (3895/4135)

Note: Percent correct (tokens correct/total).

expected for language acquisition, but it is important to note that this is also the case for Korean-English bilingual children who are not exposed to English from birth.

Next, we explored individual children's accuracy with articles across time. Accuracy for each article and articles overall with respect to age can be seen in Figures 5.1 through 5.4 for Dan, Ben, Sandy and Sarah, respectively. For Dan, the accuracy of articles varied substantially for the first several months of the study. His accuracy oscillated anywhere from 25% overall (at age 2;9) to 100% overall (2;10). What is interesting is how the path converges toward the last four sessions, from 3;8 to 4;3. By the time Dan is approaching age 4;0, his accuracy stabilizes overall and for each of the different types of articles. He does seem to struggle most with *a/an* and Ø toward the latter half of the study.

Ben is slightly older than Dan and picks up the age timeline at 3;4. Though we must use caution in directly comparing age points for one child versus another, Ben at 3;4 and Dan at 3;5 are remarkably similar in their use of articles (see Table 5.2). Ben has a similar overall pattern to Dan in that there is much more variation of accuracy in the beginning months, with *a/an* providing the most difficulty overall. He continues to have some variability of accuracy with *a/an* until around 5;5, but his overall success with articles remains 90% or above by the time he is 4;8. By the later data points, starting around 5;5, Ben regularly uses *the*

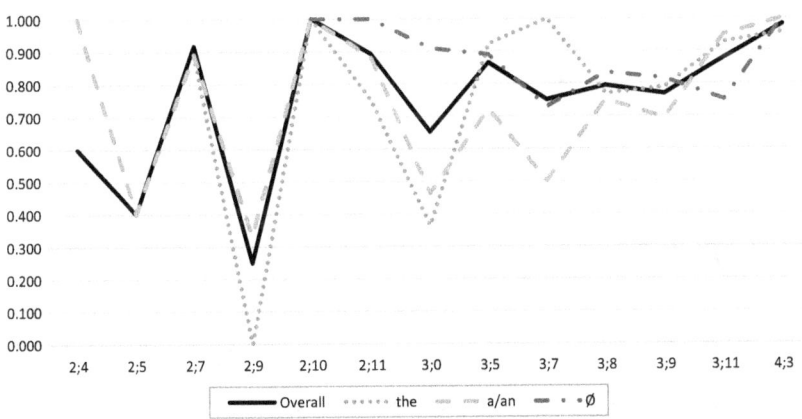

Figure 5.1 Percent correct for English article use by age: Dan

Table 5.2 English article use comparison of Dan and Ben

	the	*a/an*	Ø	Overall
Dan 3;5	91.1%	72.2%	88.9%	86.5%
Ben 3;4	75.0%	70.0%	100.0%	84.6%

64 Korean-English Bilingualism

and Ø with consistently high rates of accuracy (above 90%), as seen in Figure 5.2.

Sandy follows a similar pattern as the two previous children, but because she is older, we can observe that she tops out on article accuracy earlier in the study. For Sandy, around 5;1 her overall article accuracy reaches 90% or above and stays near that range throughout the rest of the sessions. By 5;11, her article accuracy overall and for each individual article is above 90% (with the exception of *the* at 6;11). See Figure 5.3 for Sandy's article use over time.

Finally, we examine the oldest child in the study, Sarah. Like the others, she starts out with much variability of accuracy early on, from 5;3 to about 6;2. Around 6;2, Sarah's accuracy with articles levels off close to 100% for the most part (with one exception; *the* at 7;7) (see Figure 5.4).

Overall, all four children start out with lower accuracy with articles, and all of them begin to show consistent high accuracy as time goes on.

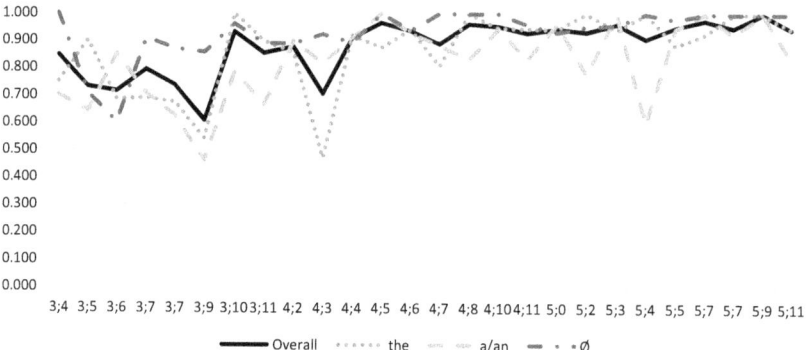

Figure 5.2 Percent correct for English article use by age: Ben

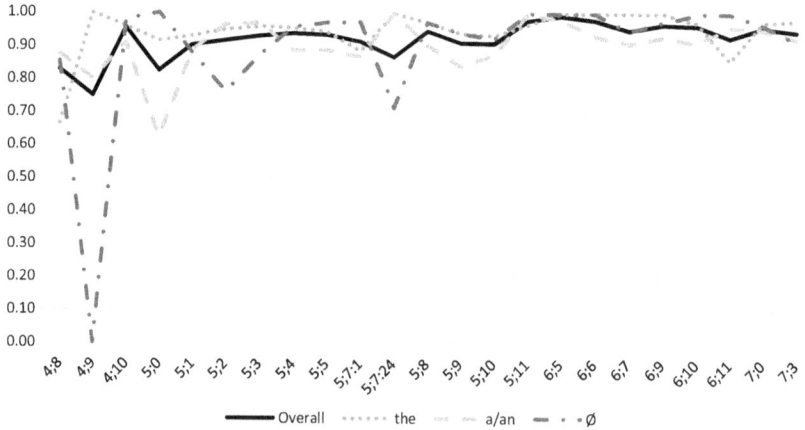

Figure 5.3 Percent correct for English article use by age: Sandy

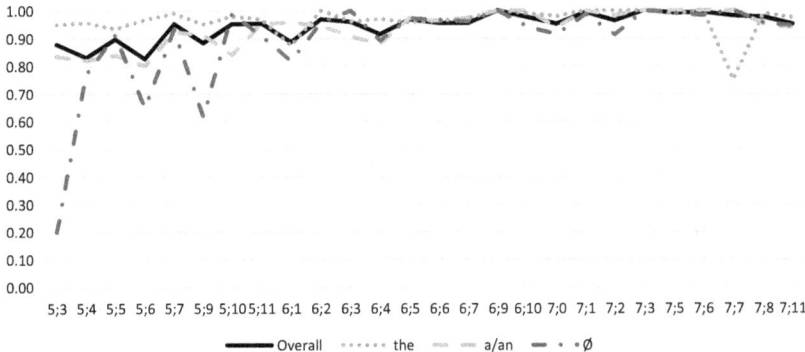

Figure 5.4 Percent correct for English article use by age: Sarah

Table 5.3 Proportion of English article errors by child

Child	the	a/an	Ø
Dan	0.355	0.419	0.226
Ben	0.439	0.368	0.192
Sandy	0.289	0.444	0.267
Sarah	0.193	0.425	0.382

It appears that mid to late 5s and going into 6;0 is around the time that Korean-English bilingual children exhibit adult-like English article use.

So far, we have focused on overall numbers and broad patterns across time. To look more specifically at the articles that children have difficulty with, let us examine the error patterns in further depth. In coding the article errors throughout the data, we noted which articles were causing the most difficulty overall for each child. Table 5.3 displays the proportion of errors by expected article for each child. Overall, the children tend to have more difficulty with supplying the article (*the*, *a*) as opposed to deleting the article (using Ø). Ben had the most errors with *the*, which comprised nearly half (43.9%) of his article errors. Interestingly, aside from Ben, the children had the most difficulty with the indefinite article *a*. This seems to follow the path found for other learners of English, both L1 and L2. For example, Zdorenko and Paradis (2012) reported that for L1, L2 child, and L2 adult learners of English, there is generally lower accuracy with *a*, and there appeared to be a year and a half during learner development when they did not find significant improvement. The findings from the present study with the Korean-English children corroborate that finding.

In order to investigate the nature of the article errors, we also coded the instances in which children used one article in place of another. Below is the coding schema used for this analysis:

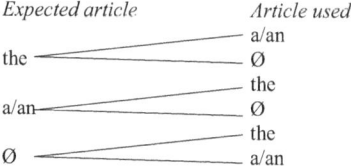

Put simply, we aimed to identify which article the child chose when a different article was expected. Figures 5.5 through 5.8 show article choice in place of expected article when children produced an error. These graphs allow for comparison of the proportions of incorrect articles used instead of the correct *the*, correct *a* and correct Ø.

The data reveal a convincing pattern: when children make errors with *the* and *a*, it is because they are overwhelmingly omitting the article (cf. rather than using the other overt article). This is notable for

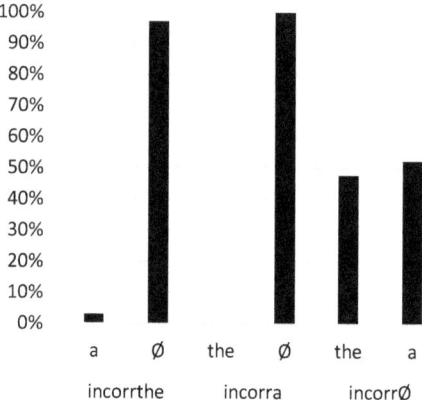

Figure 5.5 English article errors: Dan

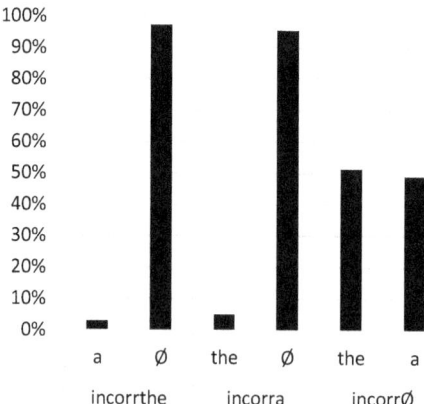

Figure 5.6 English article errors: Ben

English Morphology   67

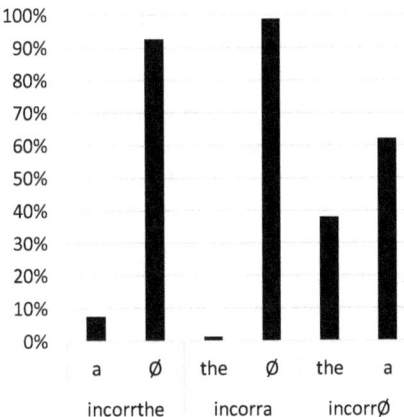

Figure 5.7 English article errors: Sandy

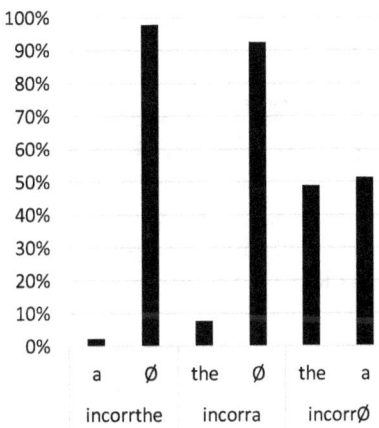

Figure 5.8 English article errors: Sarah

two reasons: first, it shows that children prefer to omit the article than oversupply with a clearly wrong overt article, a pattern of avoidance we often see from language learners. Second, this is different from L1 learners, who tend to oversupply *the*; in the case of Korean-English bilingual children, they prefer to omit the article altogether, perhaps defaulting to the null. Even when a null article is required, there is no strong preference for *the* versus *a* as we would expect from L1 children: the Korean-English bilingual children generally seem to have a slight preference for *a* when Ø is expected. Some examples of this can be seen in (1) below:

(1) (a) it's a breakfast (Ben, 3;7)
    (b) You mean yellow, kind of like a ketchup? (Sarah, 5;4)
    (c) here, I have a glue (Sandy, 5;3)

Thus, the findings show that while children acquire English articles and show a high accuracy rate, the types of errors we see from the bilingual children differ from what is expected for monolingual children. In short, bilingual and monolingual children develop differently and take different paths of acquisition, but both acquire articles.

A summary of the findings from the English article acquisition study are as follows:

(1) The earliest age that English articles appeared among these Korean-English bilingual children was at the earliest data point, 2;4, and presumably earlier.
(2) The children produced English articles at a high rate of accuracy: 84% to 94% accuracy overall.
(3) The accuracy increased over time with age.
(4) Children overall had the most difficulty with the indefinite article *a*.
(5) When children made errors with *the* or *a*, they overwhelmingly chose Ø rather than supplying an overt pronoun.

5.3 English Verb Morphology

Although English has an impoverished system of morphology as compared to Korean, it is worth exploring whether bilingual children are able to construct some of the aspects of English verbal morphology that other learner populations struggle with: past tense morphology (regular and irregular), copula *be* and third person singular (3sg) present -*s*.

Past tense morphology acquisition of L1 English is well-documented in the literature. Cazden (1968) posited the following stages of past tense acquisition by children learning English: (1) sporadic uses of irregular past tense forms and no regular past tense uses, (2) intermittent use of -*ed* on regular verb stems, (3) general use of -*ed* on both regular and irregular verb stems and (4) correct use of regular and irregular forms. The literature also suggests that monolingual children seem cautious about adding inflections and favor bare forms until they are sure they can get it right (Tomasello *et al.*, 1997). Most notably, irregular forms of past tense are typically the last stage of verb morphology development in monolingual English-speaking children (Cazden, 1968). In this study of English verb morphology for Korean-English bilingual children, we look at these regular and irregular forms for lexical verbs (including copula *be*) with the knowledge that this is difficult for all learners. Also, when examining bilingual children whose onset of English was several years after birth and who are also learning another language, it is important that we not place a direct age comparison between the bilingual children and monolingual children, but rather look more closely at the kinds of patterns that arise during the acquisition process. The research questions that drove this study are found below:

(1) For Korean-English bilingual children, what is the overall accuracy rate for English verb morphology?
(2) How does verb morphology use and accuracy change over time?
(3) What are the most frequent sources of error in English verb morphology?

In order to investigate these questions, all English utterances produced by the children that contained a verb were coded for the following: target-like accuracy, tense (past or present), regular versus irregular verb form, verb type and error type if any. Verb type was defined as the form of the verb in terms of infinitive, preterit, plain present, copula or 3sg. Error type provided a code for the source of error (e.g. null copula, missing 3sg -s, overregularization). In this study, I examined only utterances with declarative structure and only the main verbs; lexical verbs that followed auxiliaries were not included in this study, as they rarely inflect in English. The verbs *have*, *be* and *do* were only included when they were used as the main lexical verb.

To address Research Question 1, total accuracy rates are reported in Table 5.4. Here I report children's overall accuracy and accuracy for regular verbs, irregular verbs, past tense verbs and present tense verbs. The children scored between 62.5% and 92.2% overall, with irregular verbs and past tense verbs showing higher rates of accuracy over regular and present tense verbs, respectively.

Research Question 2 inquired about the changes across time. As children became older, they showed mild increase of accuracy, mostly the older two children, Sarah and Sandy. Sarah shows the steepest increase, from her overall accuracy in the 70–79% range earlier on, then increasing to the 90–100% range toward the end of the study (Figure 5.12). Sandy also shows a general increase in her accuracy; her initial accuracy at the start of the study is in the mid-80% range and increases to the mid-90% range toward the end (Figure 5.11). Interestingly, the two younger

Table 5.4 English verb morphology accuracy

Child	Overall	Regular verbs	Irregular verbs	Past tense	Present tense
Dan	82.4 (464/563)	63.2 (24/38)	84.3 (412/489)	86.5 (128/148)	80.4 (336/418)
Ben	62.5 (559/894)	40.5 (32/79)	66.4 (428/645)	84.8 (235/277)	52.5 (324/617)
Sandy	92.2 (3566/3867)	84.1 (482/573)	93.7 (3084/3292)	93.6 (1164/1244)	91.6 (2405/2626)
Sarah	86.1 (2827/3285)	62.5 (208/333)	89.2 (2239/2511)	93.3 (1030/1104)	82.4 (1797/2181)

Note: Percent correct (tokens correct/total).

children seem to hold steady in their overall accuracy over time, as shown in Figures 5.9 and 5.10. It may be that for these children, accuracy with English verb morphology does not make much improvement until children are older, in the 5–7 years age range.

Comparing types of verbs proves to be notable as well. For all four children, their irregular verb accuracy was higher than their regular verb accuracy (Figures 5.13 through 5.16). This is possibly due to two reasons: first, irregular verbs tend to be higher frequency (such as the verb *to be*)

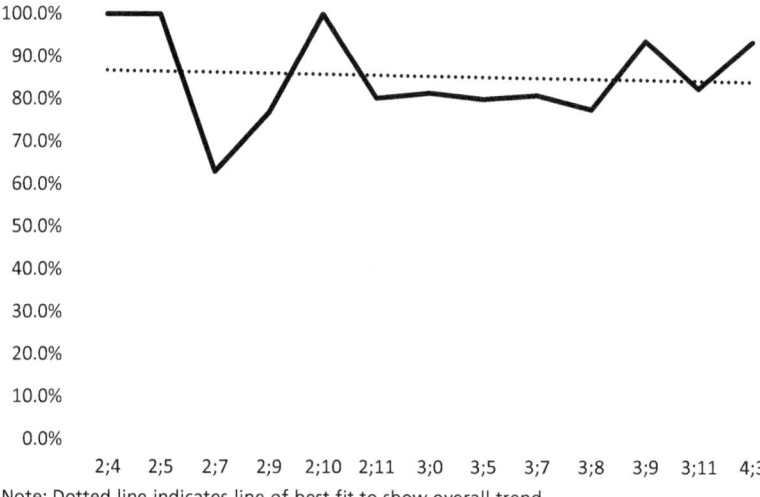

Note: Dotted line indicates line of best fit to show overall trend.

Figure 5.9 English verb morphology accuracy over time: Dan

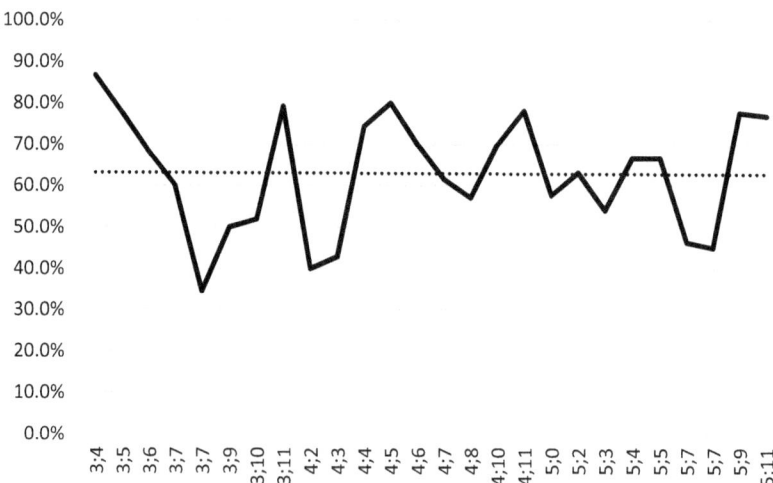

Figure 5.10 English verb morphology accuracy over time: Ben

English Morphology 71

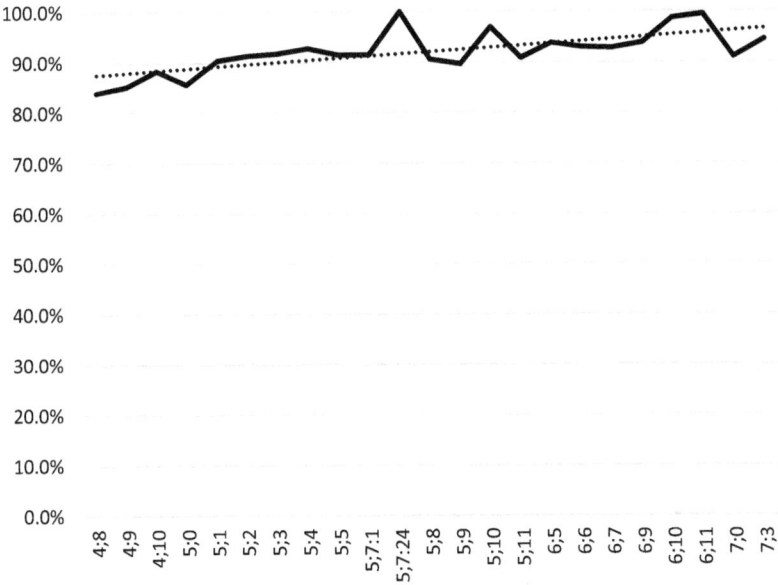

Figure 5.11 English verb morphology accuracy over time: Sandy

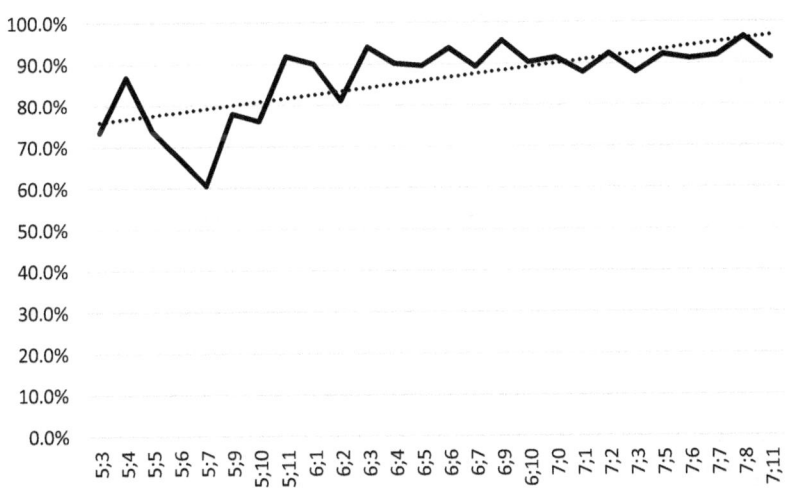

Figure 5.12 English verb morphology accuracy over time: Sarah

and thus there are more examples in their input. Second, irregular forms tend to be more salient than regular forms.

Additionally, the children in this study performed higher on past tense verbs than present tense verbs (Figures 5.17 through 5.20). Typically, English past tense verbs are either irregular or take past tense -*ed* for all persons and numbers, whereas present tense has both irregular

72 Korean-English Bilingualism

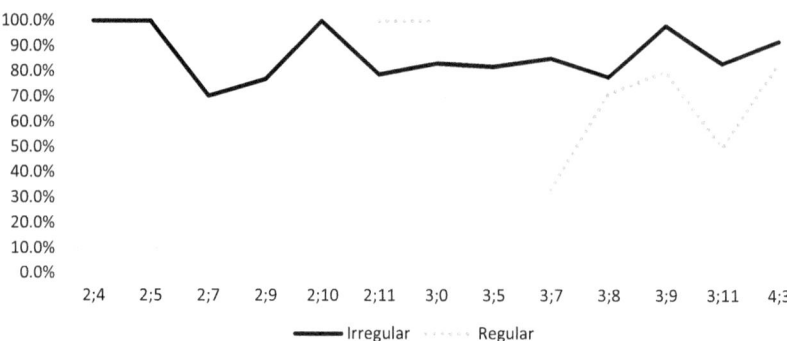

Figure 5.13 English regular and irregular verb accuracy over time: Dan

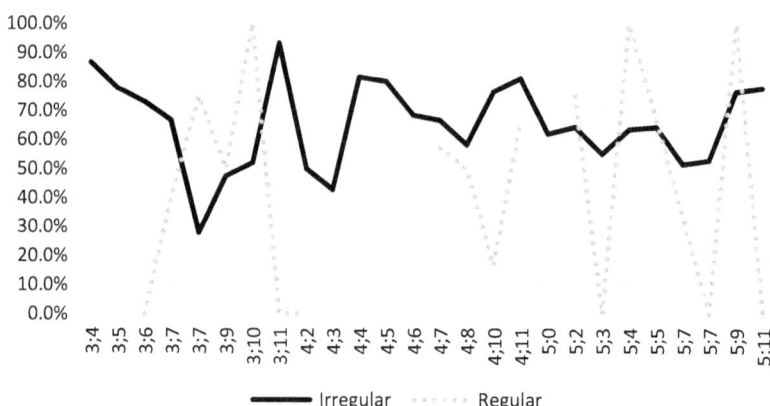

Figure 5.14 English regular and irregular verb accuracy over time: Ben

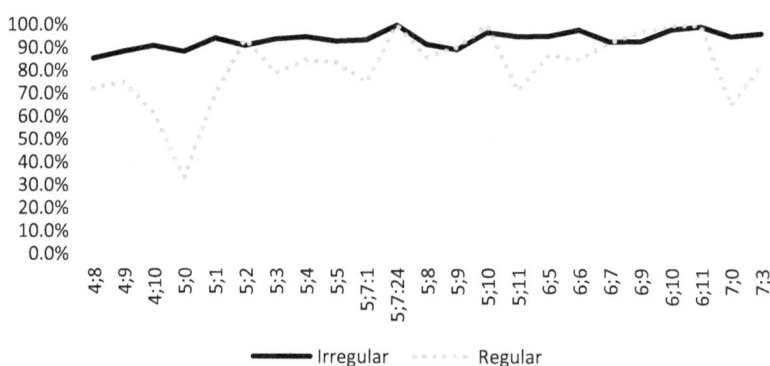

Figure 5.15 English regular and irregular verb accuracy over time: Sandy

English Morphology 73

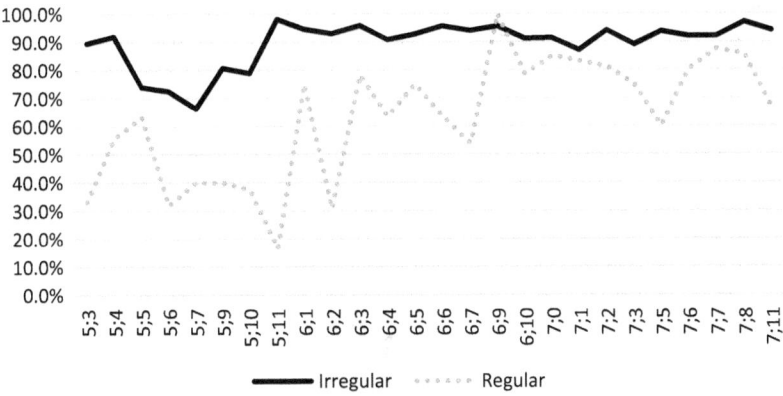

Figure 5.16 English regular and irregular verb accuracy over time: Sarah

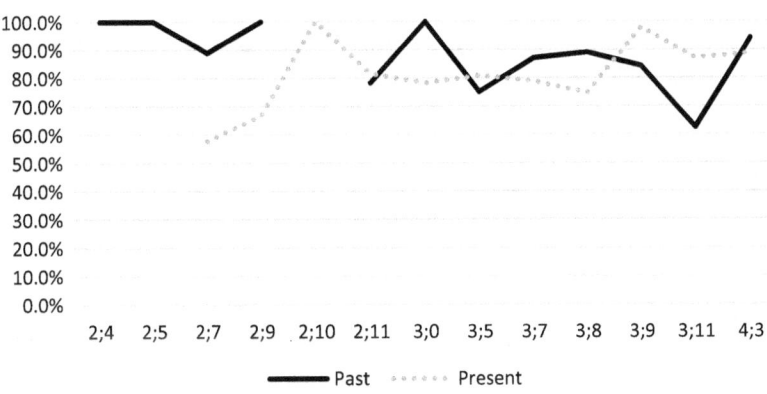

Figure 5.17 English past and present tense verb accuracy over time: Dan

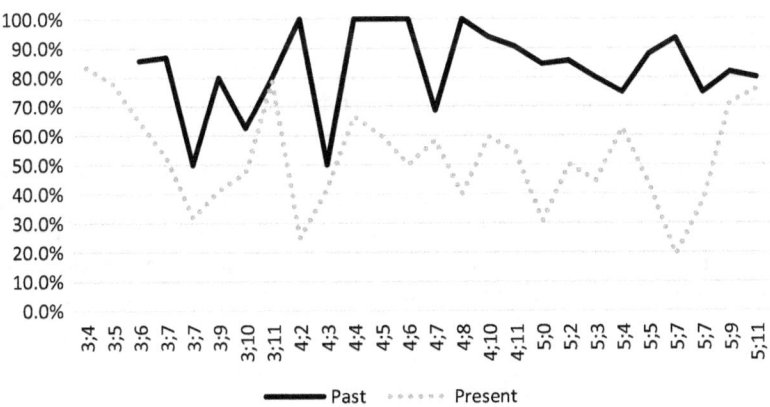

Figure 5.18 English past and present tense verb accuracy over time: Ben

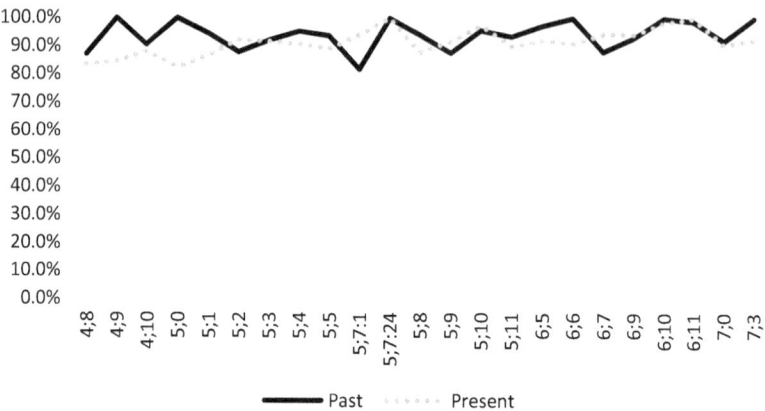

Figure 5.19 English past and present tense verb accuracy over time: Sandy

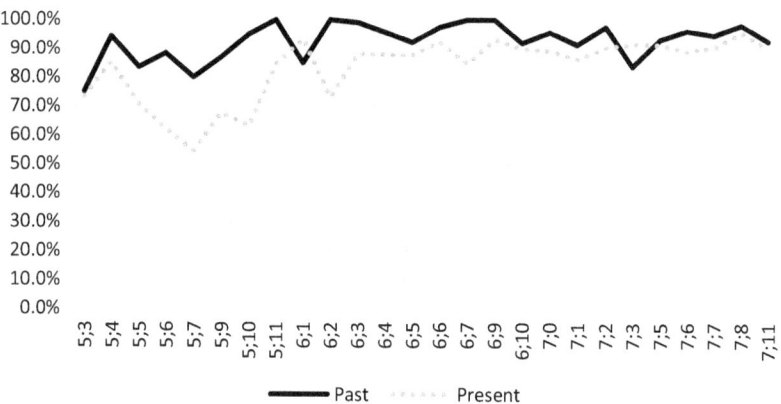

Figure 5.20 English past and present tense verb accuracy over time: Sarah

forms and a distinctly different 3sg form. This is an area of difficulty for many learners of English (e.g. Ionin & Wexler, 2002); it appears that Korean-English bilingual children may have that difficulty as well.

This segues us into the third research question, which explores the most frequent sources of error in English verb morphology for these Korean-English bilingual children. Throughout the data there were seven types of errors that were recurrent in the children's production of English verbs. These errors included the following: no copula, past tense errors, 3sg, number, no verb, double tensing and overregularization. The errors are defined as follows in (2):

(2) English verb morphology error types

null copula   the deletion of copula be in required contexts
past tense   the use of present tense when past tense was required

3sg	missing third singular present inflection -*s*
number	number agreement error, singular or plural
null verb	missing main verb when required
double tensing	the tensing of a lexical verb in the presence of another tensed verb
overregularization	the use of a regular form in place of an irregular form

Figures 5.21 through 5.24 show the proportions of error types for each child overall. For the two younger children, Ben and Dan, null copula was the error that occurred most frequently: Dan 43% and Ben 61%. For the two older children, Sarah and Sandy, the most common source of error was 3sg, omitting the 3sg -*s* morpheme: Sandy 29% and Sarah

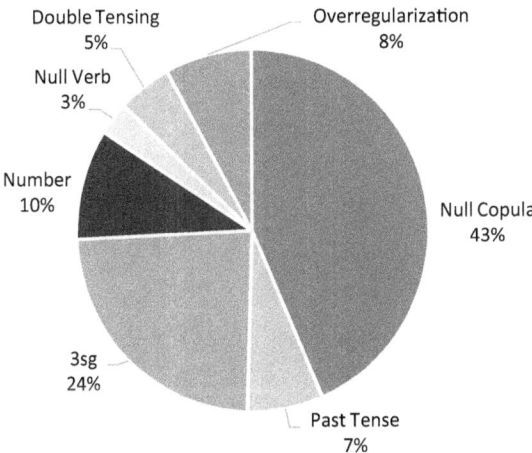

Figure 5.21 English verb morphology error types: Dan

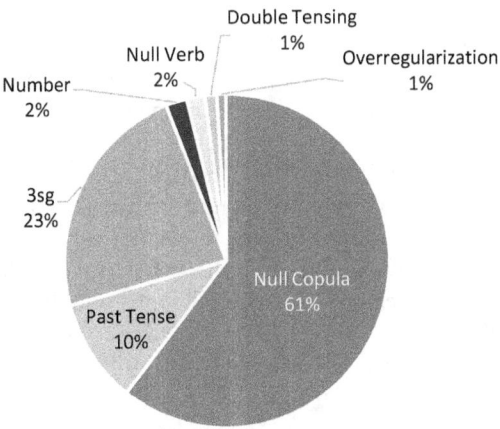

Figure 5.22 English verb morphology error types: Ben

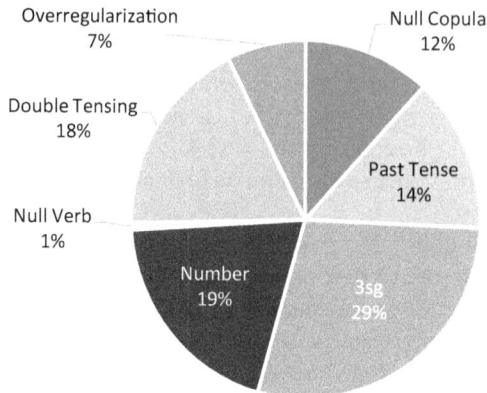

Figure 5.23 English verb morphology error types: Sandy

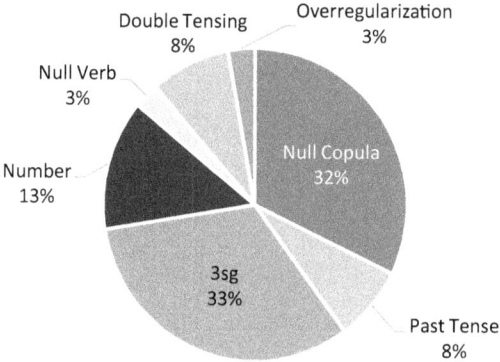

Figure 5.24 English verb morphology error types: Sarah

33%. Null copula still proved to be an area of difficulty for Sarah, comprising 32% of her errors, whereas for Sandy, number agreement (19%) is the next highest type of error. Number agreement is a special limited category because number agreement is only available in English in present tense, and the only time it does not appear as 3sg -s is for verbs *to be* (*is/are*) and *to have* (*has/have*). All other verbs that used, for instance, the plain present (e.g. *play, sing, talk*) instead of 3sg -s (e.g. *plays, sings, talks*) were marked as a 3sg error. Thus, although Sandy's error types seem to be more evenly distributed than for the other children, number errors are linked closely to 3sg. For the other three children the other types of errors – overregularization, null verb, double tensing and past tense – are fairly minimal.

Let us take a closer look at the two main types of errors: null copula and 3sg. Both types of errors are seen across different populations of English learners (Becker, 2001; Ionin & Wexler, 2002; Schutze, 2003; Song *et al.*, 2009; Sundara *et al.*, 2011; Theakston *et al.*, 2003). Although null

Table 5.5 Null copula errors by tense

Child	Present	Past
Dan	44	0
Ben	202	1
Sandy	35	0
Sarah	145	1

copula is not strictly a morphological issue, we discuss it here as part of the overall difficulty of the verb *to be* in English. One of the complexities of *to be* is that it is also used frequently as an auxiliary verb. Additionally, it is the only main verb in English that can function as an auxiliary, in that it can be raised to form a question without the insertion of a dummy *do* (e.g. She is tall → Is she tall?). This exceptional verb also carries no real meaning; the copula is essentially a placeholder for the verb. Because of this, dropping the copula has no bearing on the overall meaning of the clause. This is the case most especially when the verb *to be* is not indicating past tense. The data support this hypothesis: the children overwhelmingly drop the copula when it is present tense, but not past tense. Table 5.5 shows this comparison for each child. These explanations may point to why children are likely to drop the copula.

The verb morphology study revealed important trends in Korean-English bilingual children's development of English morphology. Namely, the following results were found:

(1) The children's overall accuracy with English verb morphology ranged from 62.5% to 92.2% correct.
(2) Children had higher accuracy rates with irregular verbs over regular verbs.
(3) Children had higher accuracy rates with past tense verbs over present tense verbs.
(4) The two older children showed gradual increase of accuracy over time, but the two younger children did not.
(5) For the two younger children, Ben and Dan, null copula was the error that occurred most frequently.
(6) For the two older children, Sarah and Sandy, the most common source of error was 3sg.

5.4 Chapter Summary

This chapter reported on studies of Korean-English bilingual children's acquisition of English morphology. The two areas of focus were English articles and English verb morphology, areas that either do not exist in Korean at all or differ significantly from Korean. The children showed some difficulty with English articles, especially with the indefinite article *a* and undersupplying an article when one was necessary.

The children also displayed challenges with English verb morphology, especially in the case of regular verbs and present tense verbs. In particular, they showed difficulty with third singular -s and undersupplying the copula when needed. In both the article study and the verb morphology study, the trend seemed to be that while the children were quite successful with English morphology, they struggled most with undersupplying the necessary morpheme. However, the longitudinal study affords us the ability to see progress over time. By the end of the study, the children were showing a range of 94% to 98% accuracy at their last data point for article acquisition, and 76.9% to 94.4% accuracy for verb morphology.

What is crucial to keep in mind is that we do not expect any children learning English, whether bilingually or monolingually, to have adult-like proficiency with articles and verb morphology. These are not areas of morphology that are expected to be adult-like at this age for any learner population, including English monolingual children. As reported above, monolingual English-speaking children still have difficulty with more subtle uses of articles as late as 9 years of age (Maratsos, 1974, 1976; Warden, 1976, 1981). English monolingual children also struggle with similar morphemes like 3sg -s until well after 3;0 (Hyams, 1986). Where the Korean-English bilingual children differ from other learner populations is that they overuse the Ø article, rather than overusing the definite article *the* as seen in child L1 and L2 studies (Brown, 1973; Maratsos, 1974; Warden, 1976; Zdorenko & Paradis, 2012). This is possibly either an avoidance strategy – avoid using the wrong article, better to omit it instead – or they are influenced by their other language, Korean, which does not have articles at all.

There are two main implications of these results. First, it is important to note that despite the presence of Korean as a first language – and initially dominant language – the children are developing English morphology in target-like ways. They are developing English morphemes that not only differ from Korean morphemes such as 3sg, irregular past tense and copula *be*, but they are also developing morphemes like English articles that do not exist in Korean. The comparison between these two aspects of their morphology development shows that while Korean may influence English and vice versa, the development of English is not hindered by the contents and structure of their heritage language. This finding is corroborated in other similar studies with bilingual children acquiring English verbal morphology (e.g. Kang & Uchikoshi, 2022). Models of bilingual language acquisition that speak to crosslinguistic influence or competition between languages suggest a negative impact of bilingualism for acquisition; however, it appears that children in this study are not hindered by the presence of another language. The children's grammars develop differently than that of children learning only English, but the different paths lead to the same outcome. In connecting back to the theoretical framework of generative grammar, it is predicted that bilingual development may take a differing path but the mechanisms available to all humans will allow them to generate the target language; this prediction is borne out in the data presented here.

The second implication connects the first point to the beginning of this chapter, in which we discussed the notion of fear among parents and educators of bilinguals. The fear is that young children acquiring two languages will become confused and overwhelmed, possibly delaying their development of English. (It is interesting how the question is rarely, 'will English harm the development of the child's home language?') The findings from this chapter show that this fear can be allayed, as the Korean-English bilingual children are still quite capable of developing two difficult aspects of English morphology with rates of accuracy upwards to 94% and 98% for verb morphology and articles, respectively. This is not at the risk of their Korean grammar, either, as we previously saw in Chapters 3 and 4 with Korean morphology and syntax. In the next chapter, we will continue to add to the overall picture of the children's language development with their English syntax.

6 English Syntax

6.1 Introduction

In this chapter, we examine the development of Korean-English bilingual children's English syntax as an analog to Chapter 4 where we investigated Korean syntax. Here we address a similar question that we posed in Chapter 5 with English morphology: how are Korean-English bilingual children developing English syntax, especially in areas that differ from their heritage language? Like English morphology, the question is not necessarily *whether* they develop English syntax but rather *how* they develop it. In other words, we pay special focus on what patterns children exhibit when they are developing English syntax. Again, I exercise caution here in comparing bilingual children to monolinguals, as we do not want to set the precedent that bilingualism is somehow a deviation from monolingualism. However, we do consider how it might differ from monolingual development since the greater goal is to inform stakeholders such as parents, teachers, policymakers and linguists of what bilingual children are capable of. Furthermore, the more we know about typical patterns of bilingual development, the more we can allay concerns about patterns that arise in bilinguals' English development that do not follow a trajectory that was based on monolingual children. Specifically, the chapter presents developmental patterns of wh-movement, subject auxiliary movement, word order and pronominal use in English by Korean-English bilingual children.

6.2 Wh-Movement

As we discussed in Chapter 2, English and Korean structure wh-questions quite differently. In Korean the wh-word stays in place – wh-in-situ – but in English there are two movements involved: wh-movement and subject auxiliary movement. Let us look first at wh-movement. Wh-movement is an operation in which the wh-word moves from within a clause to the frontmost position or highest projection in the clause. This movement is seen as a costly operation because of the movement itself, but also because the speaker must hold the trace in the position where the wh-word originated.

Wh-movement is expected to be difficult for Korean-English bilingual children because their first language does not have this movement operation. For children who speak one in-situ language such as Korean and one wh-movement language such as English, there is evidence of transfer from one language to another in previous research. For instance, Strik and Perez-Leroux (2011), Yip and Matthews (2000, 2007, 2009) and Soriente (2007) have all investigated bilingual children who speak one in-situ language and one movement language. All of the above studies have found evidence of crosslinguistic influence from the wh-in-situ language to the wh-movement language. That is, children would use the in-situ construction in a language that typically requires wh-movement, yielding information-seeking questions in English such as (1).

(1) They found what?

Although English does occasionally allow wh-in-situ, it only occurs in highly specific contexts: echo questions that express clarification or incredulity (Pires & Taylor, 2007). The studies above that have explored crosslinguistic influence of wh-in-situ all found instances of pragmatically inappropriate uses of wh-in-situ constructions in children's English productions (Soriente, 2007; Strick & Perez-Leroux, 2011; Yip & Matthews, 2000, 2007, 2009). In these cases, scholars argued that the crosslinguistic influence was triggered by either (a) language dominance or (b) structural complexity. The language dominance argument is that children will exhibit transfer in the direction of the dominant language to the non-dominant language, as seen in other studies of child bilingualism (e.g. Bernardini & Schlyter, 2004; Gawlitzek-Maiwald & Tracy, 1996; Jisa, 2000; Petersen, 1988). The structural complexity argument is that the less complex structure – in this case wh-in-situ – will be favored over the more complex structure – wh-movement. As a result, we would expect bilingual children to use wh-in-situ constructions even when wh-movement is typically necessary.

This leads us to the Korean-English bilingual population we are discussing in this book. In Park-Johnson (2017b), I investigated the question of whether Korean-English bilingual children would also exhibit wh-in-situ crosslinguistic influence in their English as a result of their Korean syntax. The structural complexity argument would also predict that Korean, as the in-situ language, would influence English, resulting in illicit wh-in-situ questions where wh-movement would be expected. The research questions I posed are as follows:

(1) Do Korean-English bilingual children produce more wh-in-situ questions in their English than mean length of utterance (MLU)-matched monolingual English-speaking children?
(2) If so, do these wh-in-situ questions appear in illicit constructions?

To investigate, all instances of children's English wh-questions were examined across the entirety of the data. Wh-questions not including verbs ('What sound?') and single word wh-questions ('Why?') were eliminated from the analysis as they do not allow us to discern whether or not movement had occurred. All remaining wh-questions were coded for placement of the wh-word.

Given the fact that the children learned Korean from birth and that wh-in-situ is less complex than wh-movement, I expected to see wh-in-situ questions in pragmatically inappropriate contexts. However, that prediction was not borne out. In fact, the Korean-English bilingual children at all ages and levels did not produce a single wh-in-situ utterance. Instead, all productive wh-utterances showed evidence of wh-movement. Example (2) shows some of these utterances:

(2) (a) What can he do? (Ben 3;6)
    (b) What this hand doing? (Dan 3;3)
    (c) Why's sunflowers on the shooting star? (Sandy 4;8)

In comparison, monolingual English-speaking children do seem to use wh-in-situ questions in their regular productions as early as 1;6 (Guasti, 2014). Post-hoc analysis of monolingual English-speaking children from the Bliss (1988), Garvey (1979) and Gathercole (1980) databases in the CHILDES corpus (MacWhinney, 2000) was conducted with children who matched in English proficiency (by MLU). The analysis showed that monolingual children did use wh-in-situ questions, predominantly for clarification or for requesting more information, consistent with adult-like usage of English echo questions as described in Pires and Taylor (2007).

Given that the Korean-English bilingual children in this study have been exposed to Korean from birth and thus been exposed to more Korean during their lifetime, the expectation is that their Korean wh-question structure would impact their English wh-question formation. Furthermore, it is predicted in the literature that because wh-in-situ is a less complex derivation than wh-movement, we would expect to see crosslinguistic influence in the direction of Korean to English – an increased use of wh-in-situ in English. However, the findings indicate that no such instances occurred in their productions throughout the entirety of the dataset.

This result is corroborated in Mishina-Mori (2005), who found a similar result with Japanese-English bilingual children living in the United States. She found no instances of wh-in-situ in the children's production of English questions despite the fact that they were also speakers of an in-situ language, Japanese. Mishina-Mori argued that because the children are living in the United States in an English-dominant environment, they had more evidence for wh-movement in their input. Yip and Matthews

(2009) also posited that because English and Japanese are not isomorphic in their surface strings – English is a subject-verb-object (SVO) language and Japanese is SOV – crosslinguistic influence of wh-in-situ is blocked. This is a possible explanation for why we did not see wh-in-situ for the children in this study.

The findings of the wh-movement study can be summarized as follows:

(1) Korean-English bilingual children did not produce any wh-in-situ utterances.
(2) All wh-utterances produced in English contained wh-movement.

Recall that in Chapter 4, the Korean word order and Korean prodrop studies showed that even when there are other options available within the language (e.g. noncanonical word orders or overt pronouns), children were more likely to maintain strict Korean-like word order and prodrop. Here, we see a similar pattern where children had the option of using wh-in-situ in their English, but chose to keep to strict wh-movement. It appears that again, children choose the option that is more canonical to the target language than exploring a range of options that may be more like the other language. This may be a strategy used to negotiate the different grammars in their minds, an innovative and functional way to sort those contrasting structures and keep those languages apart. We will return to this interesting comparison of findings in Chapter 9.

6.3 Subject Auxiliary Inversion

Closely related to the previous section, one of the more difficult movement operations involved in English questions is subject auxiliary inversion. Oftentimes language learners will successfully employ wh-movement but struggle to invert the auxiliary in English wh-questions. Historically, children do not have prolonged difficulty with subject auxiliary inversion in yes-no questions (Bellugi, 1971), but it is within wh-questions where this difficulty often surfaces. The complexity is furthered because subject auxiliary inversion in English is triggered only in the main clause of wh-questions and not in embedded wh-questions, as compared in (3).

(3) (a) What <u>can we</u> bring to the party?
 (b) I know [what <u>we can</u> bring to the party].

Therefore, in this study we looked specifically at wh-questions and the use of subject auxiliary inversion in main clause questions by the four children we have been investigating throughout this book. The research questions can be found below:

(1) Do Korean-English bilingual children employ subject auxiliary inversion in their wh-questions?
(2) How does the use of subject auxiliary inversion change over time?

The goal was to see if children are able to employ subject auxiliary inversion in their wh-questions. Like wh-movement, this is an operation that does not exist in Korean and would need to be acquired specifically for English syntax.

To investigate, all wh-questions produced by Sarah, Sandy, Ben and Dan were coded for subject auxiliary inversion. Questions that did not contain a verb were eliminated from this analysis. Additionally, here I narrowed the search to the inversion of two auxiliaries only: *do* and *be*. These two auxiliaries are two of the most high frequency auxiliaries that appear in child language (Rowland, 2007). Investigating *do* and *be* also allowed us to see whether there are any differences between auxiliaries that are present in questions only or in both questions and declaratives. Since *do* only appears when forming a question and does not appear in declaratives (4) and *be* appears in both questions and declaratives (5), observing children's use of both *do* and *be* allow us to discern differences there, if any.

(4) (a) The children play outside.   (declarative, no appearance of *do*)
    (b) Where *do* the children play?   (interrogative, appearance of *do*)
(5) (a) The children are playing outside. (declarative, appearance of *be*)
    (b) Where *are* the children playing? (interrogative, appearance of *be*)

Below I will provide an overview of each child's progression of subject auxiliary inversion use over time.

Dan

As the youngest child in our study, Dan's initial wh-questions were single-word utterances, or questions of identification (e.g. *What that?*). His wh-questions requiring auxiliary *be* always appeared with no overt auxiliary (6).

(6) (a) Where he going? (2;7)
    (b) What this hand doing? (2;9)

In the meantime, we saw similar patterns with wh-questions requiring *do*, with no overt *do* appearing (7).

(7) (a) What you wanna this play? (3;5)
    (b) Which you want? (3;5)

Dan lacked *do* overwhelmingly during this stage. There are a few exceptions to this, such as in (8) below where Dan produced two adjacent utterances at 2;9 with *do* present and inverted.

(8) What do you mean? What do you mean? (2;9)

However, the use of *do* for second person was sporadic, and it is more likely that this was an example of a memorized segment rather than productive uses of *do*. Indeed, as we followed Dan's progress from 3;5 to 4;3, we saw that his wh-questions requiring *do* and auxiliary *be* continually appeared without an auxiliary. This gives us some insight into the earliest stages of wh-question acquisition formation among the four children. We saw a strong and persistent stage characterized by questions without an overt auxiliary.

Ben

Next let us look at Ben's development of auxiliary inversion in wh-questions. Like Dan, Ben's early wh-utterances were either single word uses of wh-words, mostly *what* and *why*, or identification questions without the auxiliary *be*. However, although there are no examples of auxiliary *be*, copula *be* or any other auxiliary, we saw *do* appearing at this early stage, at least for utterances where the subject was in second person. In fact, as we will see shortly, *do* with third person utterances did not begin to appear until age 4;9. Before that point, all instances of *do* occur in utterances with the second person subject (9).

(9) Excuse me, what do you do that dinosaur I do? (3;10)

At age 4;0, we saw a stark change in Ben's most frequent wh-questions – *be* constructions of identification – which now occurred with a consistent appearance of *be* (10).

(10) (a) What's a duckling? (4;0)
     (b) Hm where's the classroom? (4;0)
     (c) What's a lasso? (4;3)

However, we saw that utterances requiring auxiliary *be* still did not appear with an overt auxiliary, regardless of person or tense, as in (11).

(11) (a) What you doing? (4;2)
     (b) So why you dressed up? (4;3)

Auxiliary *do* utterances appeared with the auxiliary in the appropriate inverted position if the subject is first or second person. However, utterances where the subject is in the third person appear without an overt *do* at this time. See (12).

(12) (a) Now where that thingy hide? (4;3)
 (b) Camping? What the camping mean? (4;5)
 (c) How the whale got, no died? (4;10)
 (d) Why they cover their mouth? (5;0)

As Ben turned 5, the sheer number and the variety of wh-utterances we see in these productions increased rapidly. Subject questions and modals (particularly *can*) occur frequently, as seen in (13) and (14) respectively.

(13) (a) Who put the pencil crayon over here, a water pencil? (5;3)
 (b) Who made it fall down? (5;4)

(14) (a) How the dinosaur can be the baby? (5;3)
 (b) Now what could we play? (5;4)
 (c) What will you eat today? (5;6)

We also saw auxiliary *be* appearing with second person (15).

(15) Why are you falling down for me crazy mom? (5;7)

Auxiliary *do* continued to have alternating patterns depending on person. While second person utterances that require *do* now exclusively appeared with an overt *do* in its moved position (16), third person utterances still lacked the dummy auxiliary altogether (17).

(16) (a) What do you want to eat? (5;6)
 (b) What do you say? (5;6)
 (c) What do you get when hungry? (5;6)
 (d) What do we do with the question how they gonna bump our head? (5;7)

(17) (a) What he do? (5;4)
 (b) What he did pull? (5;6)

Sandy

Sandy is older than the previous two children. When we first encountered Sandy at 4;8, she was already at the point where she is using a wide range of wh-words in both adjunct and argument positions. Sandy's use of copula *be* in wh-questions was seemingly target-like in terms of their movement, as seen in examples (18) and (19).

(18) Where's the camera? (4;8)
(19) Why's sunflowers on the shooting star? (4;8)

We also saw that Sandy had already acquired the use of *do* for at least first person, as seen in example (20) below.

(20) Oop, where did I drop it? (4;8)

However, as we have seen with the other two children thus far, her third person utterances requiring *do* appeared to have a special status in which they appear without the auxiliary, as in (21).

(21) (a) How this looks like? (4;9)
     (b) What this looks like? (4;9)
     (c) Why he have a short hair like this? (4;9)
     (d) Why, why he does that? (4;9)

The examples suggested that Sandy also seemed to undergo a stage in which third person wh-questions lack *do*, which is consistent with the evidence we had seen from the other children thus far.

At 5;4, we saw the first appearance of auxiliary *do* with third person, as in (22). We have here for the first time evidence that wh-questions of all three persons had auxiliary movement.

(22) What did he say when you make his_ when you were a baby? (5;4)

After 5;4, the presence of *do* for third person questions was consistent. In fact, most of her wh-questions after this point were structurally target-like. After Sandy reached the stage where *do* appears for all three persons, her wh-questions reached a level of sophistication in use of a range of auxiliaries, inflection and extraction. Some examples can be seen below in (23).

(23) (a) What sound does it make? (5;11)
     (b) Why does the camera's clock go very fast? (6;6)
     (c) What would I do without you? (6;7)

Sarah

With Sarah, we began at an even later stage than the previous children, but in turn it allowed us to see the later stages of wh-question development. When we first started looking at Sarah's productions at 5;4, her language was characterized by usage of a wide range of wh-words and types of wh-questions. However, this stage which roughly spans from 5;3 to 5;7 showed that her use of auxiliary *do* was still currently in development. More specifically, we saw dichotomous patterns between utterances with third person subjects and utterances with first and second person subjects, in which third person wh-questions never appeared without the required *do*. See example (24).

(24) (a) How that leave my neck? (5;3)
     (b) How they looks like? (5;4)

First and second person utterances seemed to be progressing toward target-like patterns earlier than third person. Sarah lacked *do* for some first and second person utterances in the first few months (25), but at 5;5 we see a curious pattern in which *do* is used – in an inverted position – with auxiliary *be* wh-questions. See the example in (26).

(25) How we do it? (5;3)
(26) (a) What do we're going to play? (5;5)
     (b) What do you're going to draw? (5;7)

What we notice here is that Sarah filled the inverted position with *do*, which would be filled with the auxiliary *are* in adult grammars.

The next stage of Sarah's auxiliary *do* acquisition showed the appearance of *do* in an inverted position but without any inflection for tense. See (27) below.

(27) (a) Why do you call me? (5;5)
     (b) Why do you mix the color with green and brown, because you make a mistake? (5;6)
     (c) How do you know I go to school today? (5;7)
     (d) How do you draw so many flower? (5;7)

Interestingly, during this stage where *do* was being used in its root form for second person utterances, third person questions never appeared with *do*, as in (28).

(28) What he drawed? (5;7)

Again, we see this curious pattern where the person value affects subject auxiliary inversion.

For Sarah, a critical point occurred at 5;10, at which we saw the first appearances of inflected *do* in her first and second person utterances (29). Third person utterances still do not show auxiliary *do* use (30).

(29) (a) What did I say? I forgot! (5;10)
     (b) How'd you make it? (5;11)
     (c) Why didn't you come and walk with me? (6;0)

(30) What he eat? (5;10)

This was precisely the pattern we observed from Ben from 5;4 to 5;7. This stage in which use and inversion of *do* appear for first and second but not for third is consistent with the patterns we had seen in the other children. This was also around the same time when we saw Ben productively using subject questions and modals, and we saw Sarah doing the same around this time, which can be seen in (31) and (32).

(31) (a) Who go up on the stage? (5;10)
    (b) Who has that crayon? (6;0)

(32) (a) Where should we make the door? (5;10)
    (b) What should we play? (5;11)

The first time we saw Sarah use *do* with third person utterances was at 6;2, as seen in (33).

(33) (a) Why don't they stop shotting me? (6;2)
    (b) What does she really like for dessert? (6;7)

This was later than what we saw for Sandy, who reached this stage at 5;4. However, although the timing of acquisition is different, the fact that the use of *do* for each person is treated differently in the children's grammars during their acquisition is similar across the other children we have seen thus far. From that point forward, Sarah's wh-questions requiring auxiliary *do* contained the auxiliary in the inverted position, complete with inflection. This gap between 5;5 and 6;2, in which first and second person utterances contain *do* (and appear with inflection starting at 5;10) while third person questions lacked the auxiliary altogether indicate a stepwise acquisition that is somehow linked to the person feature.

Only at 6;1, which is almost simultaneous with the point at which we see *do* for third person, Sarah used *be* in a target-like manner for third person and without contractions hindering movement. By the middle of Sarah's sixth year and certainly into her seventh, her wh-questions were essentially adult-like, showing sophistication in extraction (34), aspect (35) and inflection (36).

(34) So how do you think he would guess that? (7;1)
(35) Okay then why are you saying that that's too small? (7;1)
(36) What does that say there? (7;0)

Summary

The subject auxiliary inversion study set out to explore the use of subject auxiliary inversion in Dan, Ben, Sandy and Sarah. Because subject auxiliary inversion is not an operation that is in their Korean grammar, we were interested in seeing whether and how children acquire it in English. What we found was an interesting developmental process in which there are four discrete stages for both auxiliary *do* and *be*.

In Stage 1, children lack the presence of an overt auxiliary. In Stage 2, children show auxiliary movement for second person, but not for first and third person. In Stage 3, children show auxiliary movement for second and first person, then finally acquire inversion for all three person specifications by Stage 4. This is the same across both auxiliary *do* and *be*, with the exception that there is an intermediate stage, which I label as Stage 1b, in which overt auxiliary *be* appears in the structure but is not inverted.

Although the children in this study span different age ranges, we are able to see glimpses of each stage across the four Korean-English bilingual children observed in this longitudinal study. Table 6.1 lists the stages for auxiliary *do* and the children whose utterances show evidence for that particular stage, and Table 6.2 shows the same for auxiliary *be*.

Based on the findings from this study, an elicitation study was conducted in order to test the hypothesis that the person feature is linked to subject auxiliary inversion for Korean-English bilingual children. In Park-Johnson (2019a), the findings corroborated the results reported here; the person feature was found to be a significant predictive factor in subject auxiliary inversion for English wh-questions for Korean-English bilingual children.

Table 6.1 Stages of auxiliary *do* and supporting evidence

Stage	Stage description	Example	Supporting evidence from longitudinal data
1	Null auxiliary in C and T	*What you eat?*	Ben, Dan, Sarah
2	*Do* present in C for second person only, null T	*What did you eat?*	Ben, Sarah, Dan
3	*Do* present in C for first person also, null T	*What did I eat?*	Ben, Sandy, Sarah
4	*Do* present in C for third person also, null T	*What did she eat?*	Sandy, Sarah

Table 6.2 Stages of auxiliary *be* and supporting evidence

Stage	Stage description	Example	Supporting evidence from longitudinal data
1	Null auxiliary	*What you eating?*	Dan, Ben
1b	Auxiliary in T	*What you were eating?*	Sandy, Sarah, Dan
2	*Be* present in C for second person only, null T	*What were you eating?*	Dan, Sarah
3	*Be* present in C for first person also, null T	*What was I eating?*	Ben
4	*Be* present in C for third person also, null T	*What was she eating?*	Sarah

Why person? Although on the surface it seems an arbitrary factor in the licensing of subject auxiliary inversion, I posit in Park-Johnson (2019a) that because English is a language that specifically encodes person at the subject pronoun level (*I, you, he/she/it*), this person feature is connected to the licensing of the movement operation for the auxiliary. There is also evidence from L1 Korean monolingual development studies such as Cho (2004) that second person modals are most frequent and appear earliest, first person modals appear next, then finally third person modals appear last. This exact pattern seems to be reflected in the Korean-English bilingual children in the present study as well as the elicitation study in Park-Johnson (2019a), in which the rate of subject auxiliary inversion with second person is significantly higher than that of first person, which in turn is higher than that of third person. In short, person specification development in Korean seems to correlate with the frequency of subject auxiliary inversion in their English. Furthermore, it appears that for Korean-English bilingual children, while features for person may be available in their grammars, it is missing its specification and thus prevents it from surface appearance until the necessarily features are acquired.

For the purpose of documenting Korean-English bilingual development of morphology and syntax, the main implication from the subject auxiliary inversion study is that while the development pattern and path is not one that has been seen for monolingual learners, the eventual outcome is that children acquire subject auxiliary inversion for all three persons. Like we saw with articles in Chapter 5, the path may differ for bilinguals, but the eventual outcome is the same as non-bilingual learners. This is an important point that we will return to in Chapter 9.

6.4 Word Order

Word order in a language like English is critical due to its heavy reliance on positioning for meaning. Without the use of case markers like in Korean, the only way to discern the subject from the object is through context and word order. For bilingual children whose other language does not enforce this strict word order but does have case markers – which we have already seen they can use quite effectively – it is of special interest to see whether children are able to maintain canonical word order in English. We have evidence from adult learners of English whose L1 is Korean that word order is an area of difficulty (e.g. Son, 2020). Thus, it is interesting to see whether Korean-English bilingual children show this similar pattern when they are acquiring English syntax.

For this study, I focused investigation on declaratives and imperatives, as Sections 6.2 and 6.3 dealt with interrogative structures in the children's English. Declaratives in English typically follow an SVO canonical word order, as discussed in Chapter 2. Variations of this include SV for intransitive clauses and SVOO for ditransitive utterances. Imperatives in English typically do not appear with an overt subject (e.g. there is an implied second person pronoun) but the word order still follows the (S)V(O) structure.

The research questions that motivated this study are formalized as follows:

(1) Do Korean-English bilingual children maintain SVO English word order in declarative and imperative utterances?
(2) How does the children's English word order change over time?

In order to investigate these questions, all English declarative and imperative utterances spoken by the children across the entirety of the dataset were coded for word order. Utterances that did not contain a verb and single word utterances were omitted from this study, as canonical word order cannot be identified from these types of utterances. Interrogatives and exclamatives were also disregarded for this study.

Results indicated that all four children overwhelmingly used canonical English SV(O) word order for their declarative utterances, comprising 99.9% to 100% of their utterances. Table 6.3 shows total raw numbers and percentages of SVO, SV and SVOO structures used in children's declarative structures. Other noncanonical word orders used, such as SOV, VSO and OSV, are also included.

As can be seen in Table 6.3, the vast majority of declarative utterances were SVO word order (69.0% to 79.3%), and the remaining utterances were generally SV utterances with no object (intransitive) and a small number of SVOO utterances with two overt objects (ditransitive) for verbs like *give* and *put*. The children did use OSV, SOV and VSO on one occasion each, but as seen in the table, they make up a negligible percentage: 0.1% and below.

Turning now to the imperative utterances, which do not require a subject, the children were quite productive at using them and also maintaining expected word order of (S)V, (S)VO and (S)VOO, where the subject is an implied and elided second person pronoun. These data are seen in Table 6.4.

The imperatives follow a similar trend that the declarative utterances showed, with (S)VO comprising the largest group (68.4% to 76.6%), (S)V for approximately a quarter of the utterances (21.2% to 30.4%) and a small quantity of (S)VOO (1.3% to 3.5%). For imperatives, no other word orders were found.

What is notable here for the overall data is that canonical SV(O) word order was strictly followed with only three minor exceptions out of a total of 6721 utterances. The numbers quite convincingly demonstrate that the Korean-English bilingual children have no difficulty with English word order.

Table 6.3 Word order used in English declarative utterances

Child	SVO	SV	SVOO	Canonical total	OSV	SOV	VSO	Noncanonical total
Dan	490 (69.0%)	218 (30.7%)	1 (0.1%)	709/710 (99.9%)	–	1 (0.1%)	–	1/710 (0.1%)
Ben	939 (78.1%)	250 (20.8%)	13 (1.1%)	1202/1203 (99.9%)	1 (0.1%)	–	–	1/1203 (<0.1%)
Sandy	3142 (78.6%)	814 (20.4%)	40 (1.0%)	3996/3997 (>99.9%)	–	–	1 (<0.1%)	1/3997 (<0.1%)
Sarah	3207 (79.3%)	791 (19.6%)	44 (1.1%)	4042/4042 (100%)	–	–	–	0/4042 (0%)

Note: Tokens (percentage of total).

Table 6.4 Word order used in English imperative utterances

Child	(S)VO	(S)V	(S)VOO
Dan	108 (68.4%)	48 (30.4%)	2 (1.3%)
Ben	210 (76.6%)	58 (21.2%)	6 (2.2%)
Sandy	221 (73.7%)	74 (24.7%)	5 (1.7%)
Sarah	655 (73.9%)	200 (22.6%)	31 (3.5%)

Note: Tokens (percentage of total).

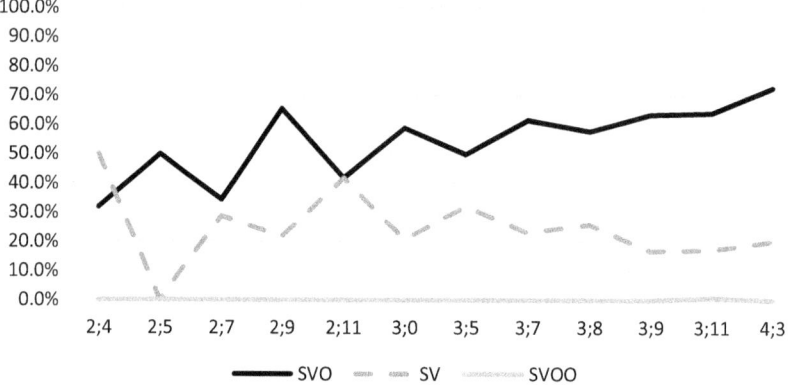

Figure 6.1 Rates of English word order over time: Dan

Over time, the rates of English word order for declaratives seem to be stable for the older children. There is a slight increase of SVO for Dan (Figure 6.1) starting at around 3;5, and an even more subtle increase for Ben (Figure 6.2). What this may indicate is that by the time children are 5;0, their rates of English word order have stabilized, and most of the changes occur between 2;4 and 4;11. By the time we begin working with Sandy and Sarah, this development may have already occurred, resulting in well-stabilized rates of English word order (Figures 6.3 and 6.4). This is a hypothesis that can be tested with more directed studies in future research.

Below is a summary of the results of the word order study:

(1) Korean-English bilingual children demonstrated excellent control of English word order, using canonical word order for declaratives 99.9% to 100% of the time.
(2) Although other word orders such as VSO, OSV and SOV structures did appear once each, the overwhelming majority of children's English utterances appeared in canonical English word order (S)V(O) (6718 out of 6721).
(3) Across time, the rates of each word order type remained consistent, with one possible trend: there was a slight increase of SVO for each of the younger two children, suggesting that word order stabilization occurs earlier in age, by about 5;0.

English Syntax 95

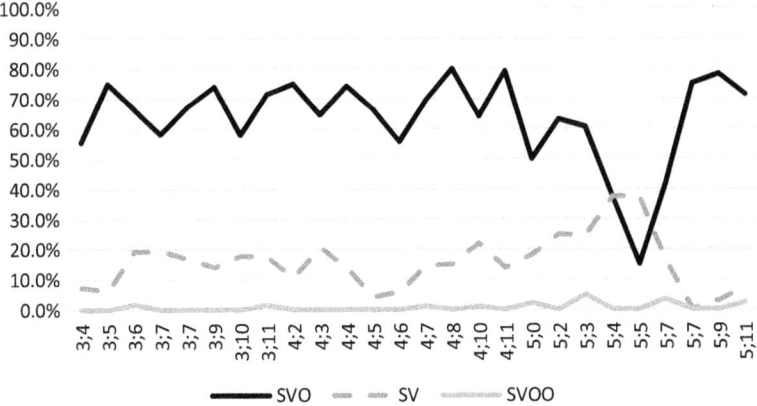

Figure 6.2 Rates of English word order over time: Ben

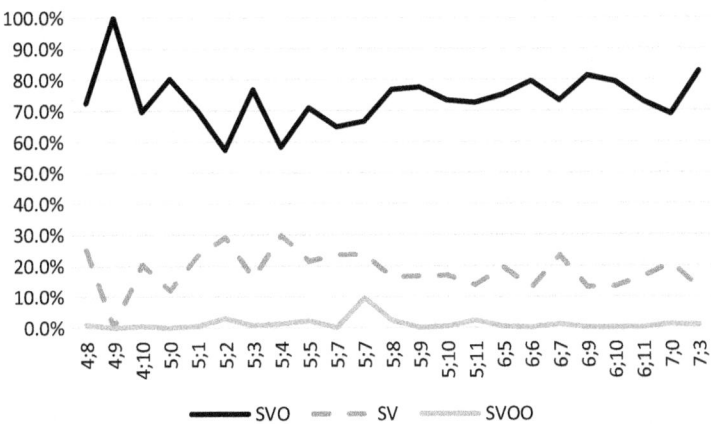

Figure 6.3 Rates of English word order over time: Sandy

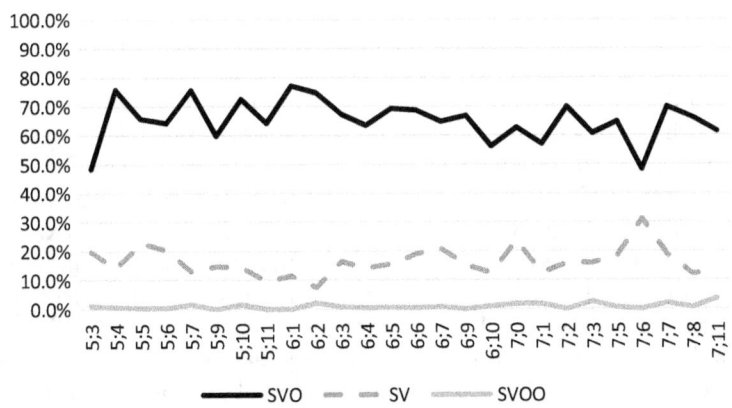

Figure 6.4 Rates of English word order over time: Sarah

6.5 Pronominal Use

Closely related to the topic of word order is the use of pronouns. English is a non-prodrop language that typically does not morphologically encode its verbs for subject person or plurality in its surface form, barring a few minor exceptions. Thus, subject pronouns are almost always required, and omitting these pronouns can lead to lowered acceptability. As we have seen from the word order study above, Korean-English bilingual children do not appear to be influenced by Korean grammar and are able to develop English canonical word order without apparent difficulty. Canonical word order, however, is an area that is regarded as pure syntax, whereas prodrop is an interface area, impacted not only by syntax but also pragmatics. Following interface hypotheses, it is predicted that pronominal use, an element that is impacted by context, previous mention and other discourse factors, would be an area of difficulty for acquisition by bilingual children. Indeed, there are many studies of bilingual acquisition where learners who speak one prodrop language and one non-prodrop language exhibit crosslinguistic influence, as discussed in Chapter 4. These studies are generally conducted with simultaneous bilinguals, and the trend is that children use null pronouns where overt pronouns are expected (e.g. Serratrice & Hervé, 2015). For instance, Yip and Matthews (2000) studied a Cantonese-English bilingual child who showed evidence of object pronoun omission in English utterances. In the present study we are interested in examining whether this pattern arises for Korean-English bilingual children. If so, the prediction would be that the children's English utterances would appear without overt subject or object pronouns in illicit contexts.

The research question that guided this study are as follows:

(1) Do Korean-English bilingual children appropriately supply subject and object pronouns in their English utterances?
(2) What types of subjects and objects do children use? If children drop pronouns, are they acceptable in English?
(3) How does the rate of prodrop change over time?

In order to investigate these research questions, all utterances spoken in English by Sarah, Sandy, Ben and Dan were examined. Utterances not containing a verb, single word utterances and interrogatives were omitted from this study. The remaining utterances, which were already coded for word order from the previous study in Section 6.4, were examined for the use and omission of subject and object pronouns. Subjects were coded for five different types: overt pronoun, dropped subject, overt non-pronoun subject (such as a determiner phrase (DP)), clausal subject or implied second person pronoun for imperatives. Objects were coded for five types as well: overt pronoun, dropped object, overt non-pronoun object (such as a DP), clausal object or no object needed (in the case of intransitives). These types are defined in Table 6.5.

Results indicated similar rates of accuracy as we found for the word order study above. Table 6.6 shows rates of accuracy overall for each child on their target-like subject and object use.

The results indicate that all four of the children performed at ceiling with their subject and object use in English across the age span. It also shows that children performed even higher on object use than subject use, though this difference is only a slight advantage given the overall high numbers. Also, despite the fact that Korean allows both subject and object drop, in English the children produced 606 examples where both the subject and object pronouns were supplied in the same utterance: 76 examples for Dan, 78 for Ben, 209 for Sandy and 243 for Sarah. Recall that we found zero instances of these in the children's Korean.

To address the second research question, we took a closer look at the types of subjects and objects used by the children, as defined in Table 6.5. Looking first at the subjects used by the children, the data revealed that children favored the use of overt pronouns (e.g. *I, you, she, they*) for two-thirds of their English subjects. The children also used DP subjects regularly, comprising 10.4% to 19.8% of their subjects overall, with a

Table 6.5 Types of subjects and objects coded in English prodrop study

Subjects	
Overt pronoun	Subject pronoun is supplied
Dropped subject	Subject pronoun is omitted
DP subject	Subject is determiner phrase
CP subject	Subject is a clause
Implied subject	Subject dropped but not necessary in imperative structure
Objects	
Overt pronoun	Object pronoun is supplied
Dropped object	Object pronoun is omitted
DP object	Object is determiner phrase
CP object	Object is a clause
No object needed	Object not necessary

Table 6.6 Rates of subject and object use accuracy in English overall

Child	Subjects	Objects
Dan	98.5% (929/943)	98.8% (848/858)
Ben	98.6% (1547/1569)	99.0% (1701/1718)
Sandy	99.5% (4470/4492)	99.9% (4771/4778)
Sarah	99.4% (5552/5586)	>99.9% (5586/5587)

slight increase for the older children. The values that are of special interest are the percentages that represent dropped subject pronouns, which we expected would be impacted by the children's Korean grammar. However, at 1.8% to 2.4% for dropped pronouns in non-imperative uses, this number is quite low. Further investigation shows that even among the utterances with dropped subjects, not all are ungrammatical, as in the examples below in (37) and (38). These utterances are common in casual, informal contexts in English and do not require an overt subject.

(37) Looks like a candy (Ben 5;2)
(38) Got the tissue! (Sandy 4;10)

In fact, when examining utterances with dropped subjects, the proportion of these that were ungrammatical decreased as children became older: 60.9% of Dan's dropped subjects were ungrammatical, 68.8% for Ben, 24.7% for Sandy and 34.0% for Sarah (Figure 6.5).

The study on object use reveals a different trend. For objects, children are far less likely to provide an overt pronoun (7.1% to 10.5%) and far more likely to use a DP object instead (53.9% to 62.4%). It also appears that as children become older, they use more complementizer phrase (CP) objects – objects that are clauses – as the number of dropped objects decreases. Unlike subjects, however, dropped objects are typically not as permissible in informal contexts; the proportion of dropped objects that were ungrammatical was higher overall than for subjects. The percentage of dropped objects that were ungrammatical was 76.9% for Dan, 77.3% for Ben, 70.0% for Sandy and 50.0% for Sarah (Figure 6.6)

When examining these utterances with object drop, most were utterances where the verb is ditransitive and the child supplies one of the objects but not the other. This occurs with verbs such as *put*, as in (39) below.

(39) Let's put in the middle (Sandy 4;10)

Now let us take a step back to look at overall results for subject and object use in English. In both the subject and object study, the rate of ungrammatical subject and object use was only approximately 1% overall for each child. This means that 99% of the time, children used subjects and objects grammatically in English. When looking at the 1% of ungrammatical uses, 100% of them was due to dropping the subject or object. There was never a case where children oversupplied the subject or object, or used one when unnecessary. This is notable in particular because it further demonstrates just how much control the children have with their English subject and object use, pronoun or otherwise.

The last research question posed whether there is change in prodrop over time. Given the ceiling rates of overt subjects and objects, there

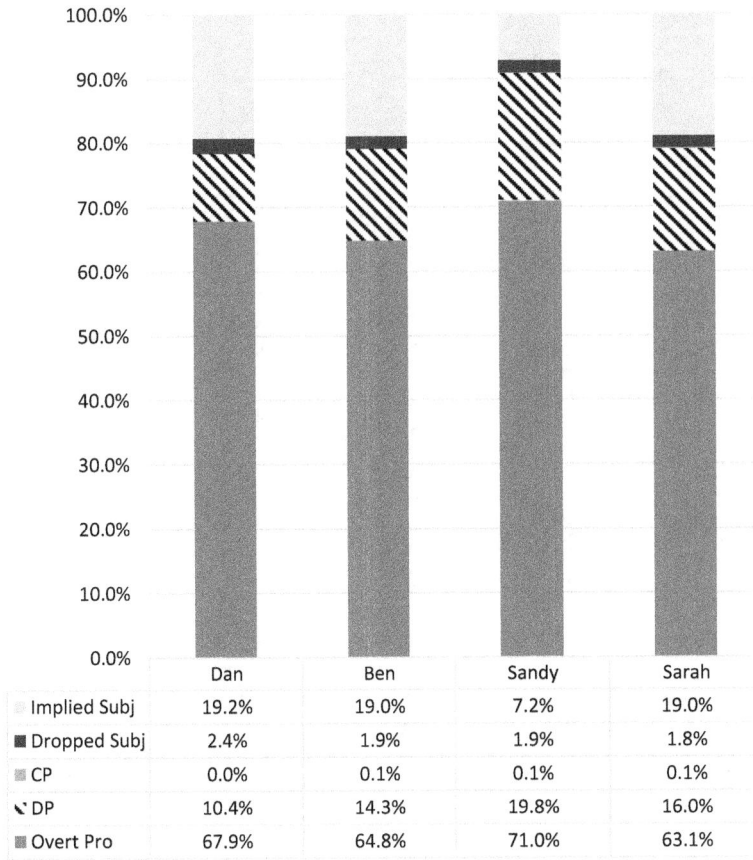

Figure 6.5 Types of English subjects used overall

was very little change over time for those rates. The rates of prodrop seemed to remain consistent throughout the duration of the study for all four children. In order to investigate longitudinal change further, we looked additionally at the types of subject (Figures 6.7 to 6.10) and object (Figures 6.11 to 6.14) used over time. The two most notable changes across time are as follows. First, types of non-pronoun subjects, particularly DP subjects, increase over time for the younger children, eventually ending at similar proportions of pronouns to DPs toward the latter end of the data collection period. Second, as children grow older, the proportion of CP objects – or clausal objects – increases; there are virtually none seen in the earlier sessions with Dan and Ben, and they make up a steady 10% to 15% of the latter sessions with Sarah and Sandy. This is an expected pattern: as children's grammars develop, they will accommodate more complex subjects and objects, some of them full clauses themselves, as in (39).

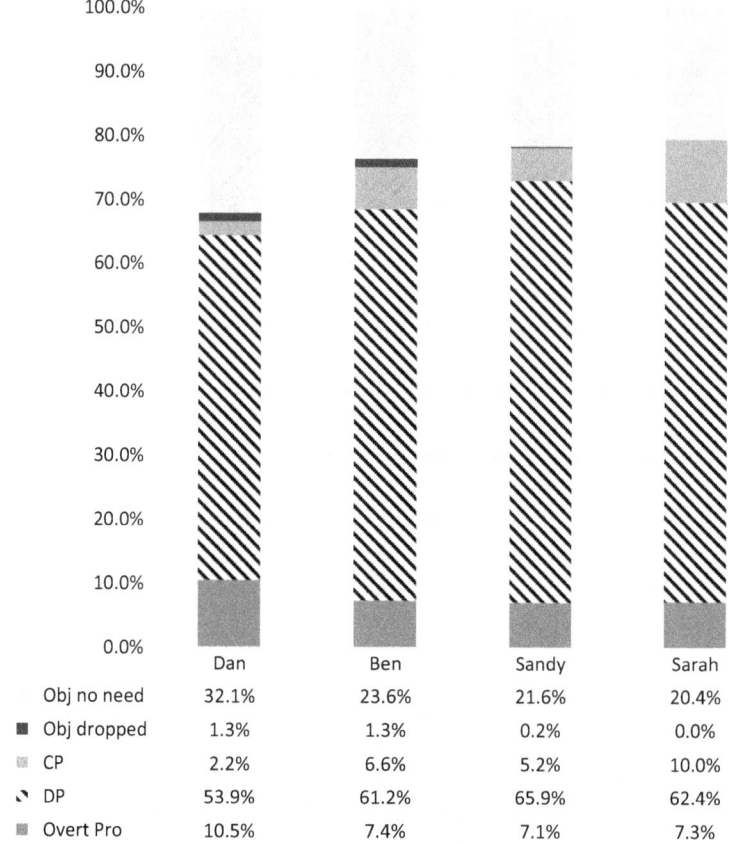

Figure 6.6 Types of English objects used overall

(39) (a) I want [you to see Simba] (Dan 3;5)
   (b) I going to [take a picture of a dinosaur] (Ben 4;7)
   (c) and then they found out [that they eat it] (Sandy 5;9)
   (d) well my mother said [when she was little she saw the same] (Sarah 6;3)

To summarize, the prodrop study investigated the use of subject and object pronouns in Korean-English bilingual children's English declarative and imperative utterances. The results can be summarized as follows:

(1) Korean-English bilingual children used English subjects at 98.5% to 99.5% accuracy and objects at 98.8% to 99.99%.
(2) Although it was expected that children would drop English pronouns more frequently due to Korean influence, their rate of prodrop was less than 2.4% for subjects and less than 1.3% for objects.

English Syntax 101

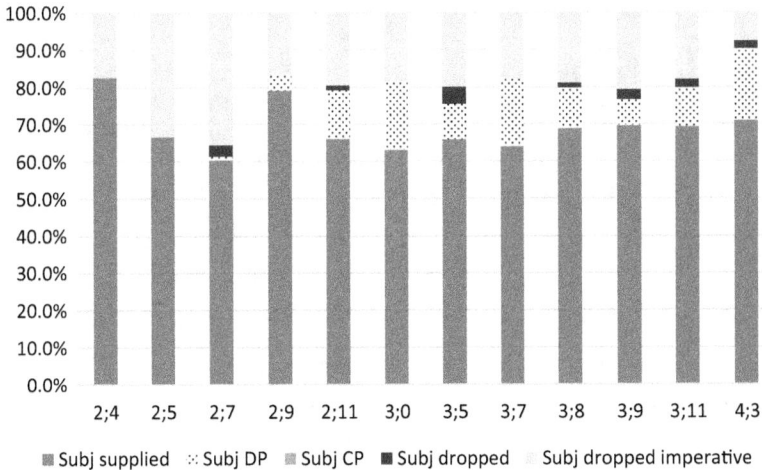

Figure 6.7 Types of English subjects overall: Dan

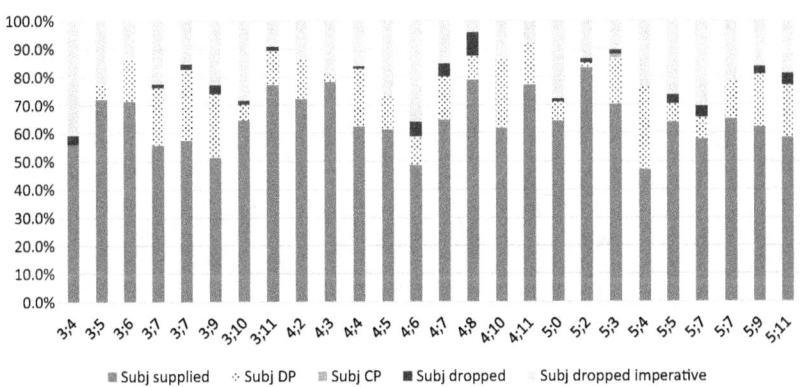

Figure 6.8 Types of English subjects overall: Ben

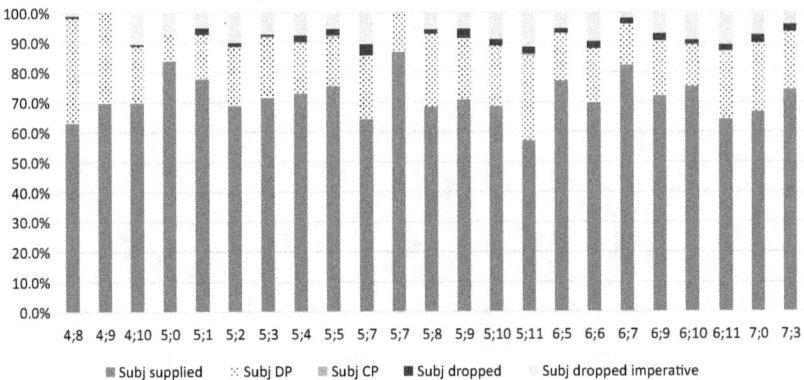

Figure 6.9 Types of English subjects overall: Sandy

102 Korean-English Bilingualism

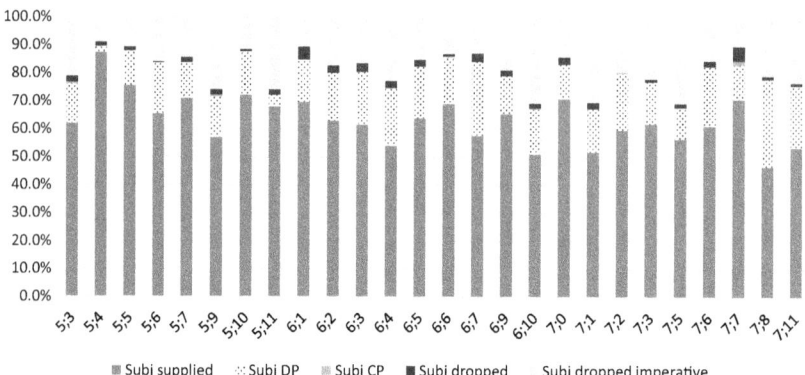

Figure 6.10 Types of English subjects overall: Sarah

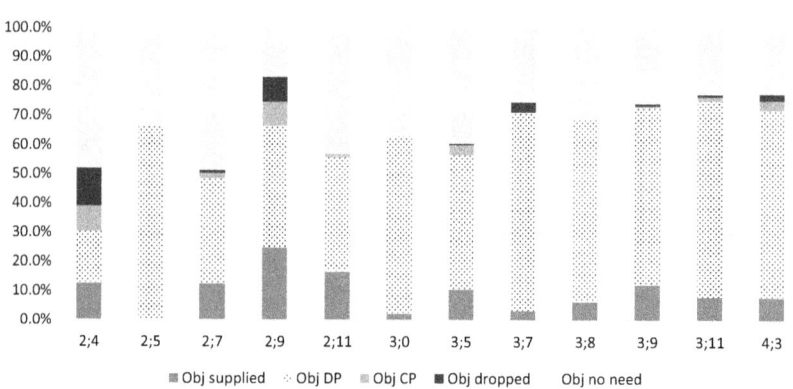

Figure 6.11 Types of English objects overall: Dan

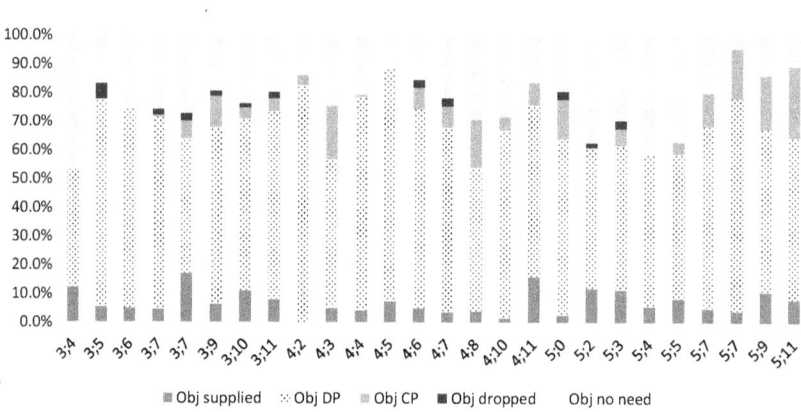

Figure 6.12 Types of English objects overall: Ben

English Syntax 103

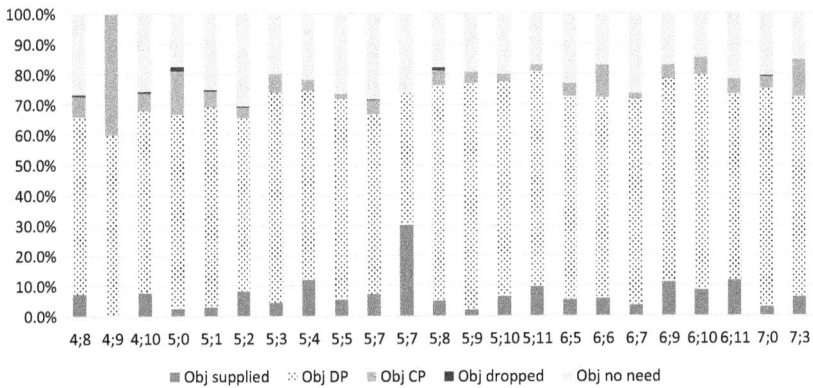

Figure 6.13 Types of English objects overall: Sandy

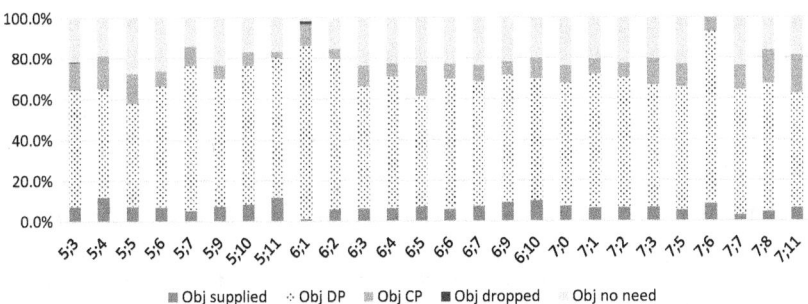

Figure 6.14 Types of English objects overall: Sarah

(3) Additionally, not all dropped subject and object pronouns were ungrammatical, especially in casual, informal contexts such as in relaxed play interactions with familiar adults in the home setting.
(4) Children used subject pronouns productively, comprising 63.1% to 73.0% of their subjects.
(5) Children used object pronouns productively, comprising 7.1% to 10.5% of their objects.
(6) Over time, rate of prodrop or accuracy of subject and object use did not change.
(7) Children used more DP subjects as they got older.
(8) Children used more CP objects as they got older.

6.6 Chapter Summary

In this chapter, we investigated the development of Korean-English bilingual children's English syntax development, particularly in the areas that are expected to be difficult for this population. The four areas explored include wh-movement, subject auxiliary inversion, word order and pronominal use. What the results revealed was surprising in how little the children's English is seemingly impacted by the presence of Korean. The Korean-English children had no difficulty with wh-movement: in fact, they moved the wh-word in every utterance in the entire corpus. The children had near ceiling or ceiling performance of target-like English word order and overt pronoun use for subjects and objects, despite the fact that Korean has markedly different word order and prodrop for both subjects and objects. The only area that potentially was impacted by Korean was with subject auxiliary inversion, which developed in a stepwise manner based on the person feature of the subject, a pattern that has never been seen for monolingual English speakers. However, the children acquired subject auxiliary inversion in English and reached target-like performance despite the different path of acquisition.

What are the implications of these results? A major takeaway is that if Korean impacts English development, its influence does not hinder or negatively impact English syntax acquisition. It seems that the children's English develops quite unimpacted by the presence of Korean, again in spite of the marked typological differences in the four areas investigated. Given that a primary concern that parents and early childhood educators have for bilingual children is that one language will negatively impact the other (especially in the direction of the home language interfering with English development), the results here can perhaps assuage some of those concerns. Chapter after chapter, we are discovering that the impact of bilingualism is not the detriment that society may fear. Even in the one area we found where the bilingual children develop differently from monolingual children – subject auxiliary inversion – the result was that children do acquire the structure and in a timely manner, even if the path getting there may differ from others. Put another way, if there are two different routes to reach the same destination and that will result in similar timing, what is to say one path is wrong and one is right? As we also saw, the 'unexpected path' to acquiring subject auxiliary inversion has a likely explanation – the acquisition order of person features in Korean – which further provides support for common underlying features between the two languages.

We now move from these chapters, where each language was examined separate from the other, and transition to the next chapter where we will look carefully at cases in which the two languages are mixed. This will allow us to put to the test again what sort of impact one language has on the other when they are in close proximity, for example, mixed within one utterance, since clearly their bilingualism does not seem to be significantly impacting the separate development of English or Korean.

7 Code-Switching

7.1 Introduction

Thus far we have focused primarily on the development of Korean and English separate from one another. However, bilingual language development is hardly a separate and parallel process but rather a complex intermingling of the two languages, their processes and their development. As we have long understood that bilingual children are not two monolingual children in one (Grosjean, 1989), this chapter serves an important role in looking at this interplay between the languages: code-switching.

The terms *code-switching* and *code-mixing* are sometimes used interchangeably; however, I use the terms very specifically here to discuss the level at which the switches occur. Code-switching is the general umbrella term for the use of two or more languages within discourse. Code-mixing, on the other hand, is a more specific term used to indicate the mixing of two or more languages within a single utterance, a phenomenon also called intrasentential code-switching. In this chapter, I use the term *code-switching* to refer to both the overall process and switches outside of the utterance boundary, and *code-mixing* for utterances containing both Korean and English.

It is also crucial when discussing code-switching and code-mixing to acknowledge how other related concepts and processes fit into this analysis. Such concepts include translingual practice (Canagarajah, 2013), code-meshing (Milson-Whyte, 2013) and most prominently, translanguaging, which is defined as 'the deployment of a speaker's full linguistic repertoire without regard for watchful adherence to the socially and politically defined boundaries of named (and usually national and state) languages' (Otheguy *et al.*, 2015: 281). In essence, translanguaging is regarded as a sense- and meaning-making communicative resource, as opposed to code-mixing, which is a narrower term used to define a linguistic strategy governed by grammatical rules (Canagarajah, 2013, 2017; García, 2009; Li, 2018; Otheguy *et al.*, 2015). Though translanguaging and code-mixing certainly have overlaps, the critical distinction is that translanguaging assumes an undifferentiated unitary system, an argument that discrete languages are irrelevant (MacSwan, 2017). Because the context of the present research focuses on the specific linguistic phenomenon of using two or more defined languages in one utterance and as a shared practice among groups of bilinguals, I chose to use the term *code-mixing* as the preferred concept for this investigation. I also use the term *code-mixing* because this present research examines the linguistic practices with the assumption that learners are drawing from two distinct linguistic repertoires.

Why is code-mixing of interest when investigating the morphosyntactic development of bilingual children? The investigation of code-mixing reveals a wealth of information about what children know: when two languages are as structurally divergent as English and Korean, the use of both languages in a single utterance can reveal much about the children's grammatical assumptions, knowledge and rules. Furthermore, it gives us an insight into how children come up with new strategies that do not exist in either language to negotiate the structural differences within one utterance. Studying the grammar of code-mixing is an opportunity to learn about the abilities of bilingual children, an important perspective precisely because of how mixing is perceived, by the general public, by stakeholders (e.g. educators) and by the bilinguals themselves. Although studies have shown overwhelming evidence that code-mixing is not an indication of language confusion (Genesee, 1989; Meisel, 1989, 2001) and that it is rule-based and systematic (Genesee & Nicoladis, 2008; Grosjean, 2012; Lanza, 1997; Myers-Scotton, 1993; Paradis *et al.*, 2000; Schieffelin, 1994; Shin, 2010b; Shin & Milroy, 2000), there are still lingering negative ideologies surrounding code-mixing in general society. Kang (2015b) found that while Korean parents in the United States have strongly positive views of bilingualism, 87.1% of parents reported that speaking English with Korean in the home was not helpful for their language development. In schools, children who code mix are sometimes labeled 'non-nons' or 'clinically disfluent' by clinicians (Valadez *et al.*, 2000). Teachers often believe code-mixing is harmful practice and is evidence of deficiency (Li, 2008; Park-Johnson, 2020b). These kinds of ideologies can impact teachers' attitudes toward their bilingual students and thereby impact students' learning (Lacorte & Canabal, 2005). For instance, Berthele (2012) reported that teachers rated code-mixing students significantly lower on fluency, correctness and even overall academic potential. Park-Johnson (2020b) revealed that while teachers tend to generally accept code-mixing as a practice, they tend to have negative views of code-mixing when it pertains specifically to student performance and academic potential. Furthermore, these negative ideologies are held by members of bilingual communities; Lee (2023) found in their study that language teachers in Korean heritage schools held strong monolingual ideologies, in which using English in the Korean classroom – and specifically mixing the two languages – was seen as confusing to learners and detrimental to their Korean development. To combat these harmful views of code-mixing, it is crucial to shed light on what code-mixing is, how it is used and why bilingual children use it.

In response to this need for better understanding of code-mixing, the goal of this chapter is to provide analyses of children's mixing in terms of the structure, content and use. Additionally, we explore and analyze the children's use of code-switching over time with special focus on frequency of code-mixed utterances as children are exposed to more English. Before reporting on these data, however, a crucial observation must be discussed. Because we collected data in two distinctly different contexts – English-speaking sessions with me and Korean-speaking sessions with a parent – the expectation was that code-switching would be observed in both types of sessions. What is surprising is that virtually no code-switching was observed in the English sessions. In other words, during the English sessions, the children did not use any Korean, even though they knew the adult interlocutor was a Korean-English bilingual speaker. A handful of times, they spoke metalinguistically about Korean ('do you know X') to ask me if I was familiar with a particular Korean word, but it was only in a focused context that they even used Korean words at all. A likely reason for this asymmetry is because the use of Korean in an otherwise English conversation is essentially never called for. Given that the children live in the United States, a context where most English speakers are not also Korean speakers, the occasion to speak in English with some Korean inserted is not a common experience. In their school, the English-speaking teachers and children do not have Korean proficiency; if the children were to mix Korean and English in the school context, they would not be understood. In comparison, almost all of the Korean speakers in the children's lives also have some English proficiency. Korean speakers living in the United States typically are also English bilinguals, and it is rare for them to encounter someone who is a Korean monolingual. Korean speakers, both in the United States and in Korea, also use quite a lot of English loan words, which adds to the perception for the children that English is permitted in Korean-speaking contexts. Thus, the entirety of the code-switching study is conducted in the children's Korean sessions with their mothers as no code-switching was observed in the English sessions.

7.2 Code-Mixing: Structure

The first areas we explore in children's code-switching are the structural aspects. In this study, children's code-mixing was investigated with special focus on their morphosyntactic characteristics. Because Korean and English have different base word orders and morphological processes, code-mixed utterances are of special interest to see how children manage the amalgamation of subject-object-verb (SOV) and SVO word orders with complex Korean verb and noun morphology.

Let us first explore children's word order used for their code-mixed utterances. Given that the two languages the children are mixing have different canonical word order, it raises the question of which word orders they would adopt for their mixed utterances. For this study, utterances without verbs were eliminated, as word order cannot easily be discerned without a predicate. The remaining 906 utterances containing both Korean and English were coded for word order.

The findings revealed that of these 906 utterances, 879 utterances (97.0%) maintained Korean (S)(O)V word order. Examples can be seen in (1).

(1) (a) strawberry *ettehkey sayngkyusse*? (Ben 3;7)
    Strawberry how   look-Q
    'what do strawberries look like?'
 (b) *ku-taum-ey* beaver-*ka tule-ka-sse* (Sarah 7;11)
    that-next-LOC beaver-NOM enter-go-PST
    'then the beaver entered'

Disaggregating the data by child, rates of (S)(O)V word order still largely outnumber non-Korean word orders. Korean-like word order also increases with age. See Table 7.1 for comparisons.

English word order accounted for only 1.6% to 11.1% of the code-mixed utterances per child, and only 3% overall. In other words, there is a marked asymmetry between Korean and English word orders in the children's code-mixing. This is unexpected given the hegemonic force of their societal language, which only increases its influence with age. Here, we see an inverse pattern where as children get older – thereby increasing English exposure – their code-mixing word order is increasingly more like Korean syntax.

Next, we looked more specifically at the word classes and phrase types of the English elements found in children's code-mixed utterances. The rationale for this study was to examine whether there are patterns for which English lexical items and phrases are more commonly mixed into a Korean frame. If there are trends, it may help us understand why

Table 7.1 Rates of Korean and English word order in code-mixed utterances

Child	Korean word order	English word order
Dan	8 (88.9%)	1 (11.1%)
Ben	131 (94.9%)	7 (5.1%)
Sandy	232 (95.5%)	11 (4.5%)
Sarah	508 (98.4%)	8 (1.6%)

those types of words or phrases are more likely candidates for mixing, telling us the intent behind the practice. For this study all utterances where English and Korean were found within a single utterance ('mixed') were coded for what type of English element was used. The coding schema can be found below in (2).

(2) Code-Mixing Structure Coding
Single word N – single English noun was inserted in Korean structure
Single word A – single English adjective
Single word V – single English verb
Single word C – single English complementizer
Single word D – single English determiner
Single word Adv – single English adverb
English VP – utterance starts in Korean, ended with English verb phrase
Korean VP – utterance starts in Korean, ended with Korean verb phrase
Wh – wh-word in English
Number – numerals
Filler – filler words that are distinctly English (e.g. like)
Single word affirmative – yes, yeah, yup
Single word negation – no, not, nah

Results indicated that the single word nouns, where a single English noun is found in an utterance otherwise entirely Korean, made up the largest category of code-mixing structure for all four children (Table 7.2). These comprised up to 63% of code-mixed utterances. Some examples of single word nouns can be seen in (3).

(3) Single Word Noun Examples
    (a) *kuliko*   pig *anhalkkeya* (Sandy 5;0)
         and   pig not-do-will-DECL
         'and I'm not doing the pig'

    (b) *kuntey*   *icey*   *ta*   square *ya* (Sarah 5;10)
         but then   now   all   square is-DECL
         'but then now it's all square'

Table 7.2 Structure of code-mixed utterances

Child	% single word nouns	% single word verbs	% Korean VP
Dan	63%	0%	25%
Ben	58%	9%	10%
Sandy	59%	8%	9%
Sarah	50%	10%	9%

(c) train *kace wasse*? (Ben 4;6)
    train bring-come-Q
    'did you bring the train?'

(d) *aniya na* chip cake *tto   meke* (Dan 3;0)
    no   I   chip cake again eat-DECL
    'no, I eat chip cake again'

In many cases, these single word English insertions also appeared with Korean case markers (see example (4)).

(4) Single Word Noun Examples with Case Markers
    (a) *emma*, second number-*un   mwe ya*? (Ben 5;11)
        Mom, second number-ACC what-is
        'Mom, what's the second number?'

    (b) *i*   pink-*nun   mwe ya*? (Sarah 5;10)
        This pink-TOP what-is
        'what's this pink one?'

    (c) *ku*   dress-*nun epse*? (Sandy 5;9)
        That dress-TOP not-exist
        'That dress isn't there?'

The fact that the majority of code-mixed utterances are single word nouns signifies that English is largely being used to fill vocabulary needs.

The next two most frequently used types of code-mixed structure were single word verbs, or utterances containing a single English verb, and Korean VP, utterances that start as English but end with a Korean verb phrase, often ending with object + verb. Table 7.2 shows percentages for each of these categories. Some examples of single word verbs and Korean VP can be found in (5) and (6), respectively.

(5) Single Word Verb Examples
    (a) *emma na-nun* pick *hay* (Ben 3;10)
        Mom I-TOP pick do
        'Mom, I pick'

    (b) *emma enni-nun*   drive *hal su isscanha* (Sandy 5;0)
        Mom, big sister-TOP drive do-can-CONFIRM
        'Mom, big sister can drive, can't she'

    (c) *mulkoki* jump *hanunkeya* (Sandy 6;9)
        Fish   jump do-thing-is
        'The fish is jumping'

(d) *na-nun yeki uyca-eyse* fishing *hako isse* (Sarah 6;4)
    I-TOP here chair-LOC fishing do-PROG
    'I'm here fishing from this chair'

(6) Korean VP Examples
    (a) a turkey *cohase* (Sandy 5;7)
        a turkey like-because
        'because I like turkey'

    (b) I think *ikey ilehkey ilehkey yeki tulekako* (Sarah 6;10)
        I think this-NOM like this like this here enter-go-CONJ
        'I think this goes in here like this like this'

    (c) No it's *chusek iya* (Ben 5;5)
        No, it's harvest festival is
        'no, it's the harvest festival'

The single word verb examples illustrate again that the children are using English verbs to supplement their vocabulary. What is interesting is that all English verbs used in this manner are nonfinite – usually plain form or present participle – and the Korean verb *hay* ('do') is attached to the English verb. The verb *hay* is a dummy verb in Korean that can be inserted without adding meaning, but serves an important morphosyntactic function: it allows Korean inflectional morphology to be added. Put another way, children know they cannot add Korean inflection to English verb roots, so rather they insert a dummy verb to indicate tense, aspect and mood. Examples can be seen in (7) below.

(7) *kurem ike i* seed-*lul* plant *hay-yaci* (Sarah 6;2)
    then this this -acc plant do-should
    'Then we should plant this seed'

For the Korean VP utterances, it is possible that when the predicate is in Korean, it triggers the overall word order of the mixed utterance. As we saw above, most code-mixed utterances maintained Korean SOV order; the Korean VP utterances may be linked to this finding.

The findings from the code-switching structure study revealed the following main trends:

(1) Code-mixed utterances predominantly followed Korean SOV word order (97.0% overall).
(2) Code-mixed utterances were largely the result of single word nouns (63% overall).
(3) Single word verbs and utterances that begin with English and end with Korean verb phrase were also frequent types of code-mixed utterances.

(4) All single English verbs used in otherwise Korean utterances appeared in nonfinite form with Korean light verb *hay* ('do') attached, which can then take Korean verb endings.

Overall, the findings show a strong preference for Korean-like structure and morphology despite the presence of English.

7.3 Code-Switching: Content

While the structure of code-mixing is certainly important to investigate, that is only part of the picture. The other side of the equation is the question of 'why': why do children code-switch? Research on code-switching has shown that even for young children, the use of code-switching is intentional and often has specific triggers. For instance, Chung (2006) found that code-switching is used by Korean-English bilingual children and adults to signal affection and solidarity with close members of their family or communities, lowering language barriers through inclusive language switching. Similarly, Shin (2010b) reported that Korean-English bilingual youth express their Korean identity through the use of code-switching. Using Korean with elders in the community shows deference and respect, as well as showing their Korean identity. In both studies, it is reported that young Korean-English bilinguals use code-switching intentionally for specific functions, expressions and communicative strategy as opposed to using it as a crutch (Chung, 2006; Shin, 2010b). Additionally, Kwon (2022b) found that parents' code-mixing is a helpful strategy to communicate with their children, especially when they are sharing a space that allows for the use of both meaning-making and connection.

Again, we look here only at the Korean sessions, as the English sessions did not include any code-switching. In the Korean sessions, we looked at the utterances that were mixed and utterances that were entirely in English. Rather than developing a coding schema prior to analyzing these utterances, I let the themes, functions and reasons for code-switching arise from the data itself. In coding the reason for code-mixing and code-switching, it was important to keep the researcher's assumptions at bay as much as possible, and coding in this manner allowed for the data to drive the research. What arose from the analysis were several key reasons for why code-mixed and all-English utterances appeared in the children's Korean interactions.

For the mixed utterances, the three most frequent reasons for code-mixing across the children were as follows: school vocabulary, specific verbs and low-frequency animal names. School vocabulary generally consisted of words that one would typically encounter in an academic setting, such as words for geometric shapes, math functions, scientific vocabulary and school-related concepts such as *recess*, *show-and-tell*, *flash cards*, *library* and *field trip*. These usually appeared as single word nouns or compound words, which as we saw in the previous section were the most common type of code-mixed utterance. Specific verbs are ones where the meaning of the verb is narrow and specific, such as *to twist*, *to crack* or *to melt*. While these words certainly have translations in English, the specific verb in English seemed to be one that children often chose instead. Finally, animal names – specifically low-frequency animal words – were another frequent reason children used English words in an otherwise Korean utterance. Words such as *octopus*, *giraffe*, *rhino* and names of various species of dinosaurs were all in English. These, like school vocabulary and specific verbs, are ones the children most likely hear in English rather than Korean. Although animals are certainly talked about in the home (e.g. dog, fish, bird), it is more likely that children will encounter words for less-commonly seen animals – like those that live on the savannah or are extinct – in school, especially in early childhood.

Other reasons for mixing English and Korean in a single utterance were identifying objects (e.g. that is an X), foods that are more part of American life (e.g. blueberries, turkey, fries) and the occasional filler word (e.g. 'like') that appeared in English, as in (8).

(8) *nuka*   like *keki tteleci-myun* (Sarah 6;4)
    Someone   like there fall-if
    'if someone, like, falls from there'

Next we look at utterances that were entirely in English. The reasons for the switch to English entirely were slightly different from the mixed utterances. The three most common reasons for using English utterances in a Korean session were as follows: complaint, defiance and talking to the sibling. Complaint was defined as any utterance where the child was expressing discontent. Sometimes, these were children asking their mother for something that they were not sure they were going to get or expressing a small injustice. Some of these examples can be seen in (9) below.

(9) Utterances Expressing Complaint in English
    (a) I want one (Dan 3;9)
    (b) <whining> *emma*, I never get a turn </whining> (Ben 5;5)
        mom
    (c) I can't see I can't see (Sandy 6;5)
    (d) then how come what, then how come I can't write it over there not fair (Sarah 7;7)

In each of these instances, the children were essentially complaining or whining to their mother, a communicative function that could have negative consequences, such as being rejected or scolded for complaining. To do this in English instead of Korean is interesting, because it does lessen the severity of the communicative function to use the mother's second language rather than the first. In essence, this softens the negativity. This is similar in the second reason for switching to all-English utterances, which is to express defiance. Utterances expressing defiance usually took on the sense of 'I'm going to do this whether you like it or not' which could also have negative consequences. It stands to reason why children might use English to express themselves in this way, as it sounds much harsher and disrespectful in Korean. To do this in English again softens the severity of the utterance, as in (10).

(10) Utterances Expressing Defiance in English
    (a) no I will I will do it first (Ben 5;2)
    (b) I wanna do it myself! (Sandy 5;7)
    (c) well I'm gonna do it this way (Sarah 5;10)

Finally, the children often switched to English to communicate with one another. Although both sibling pairs started out speaking Korean to one another primarily, they switched to using English with each other early on in the study.

A few other types that arose from the all-English code-switching included exclamations ('wow!' or 'oh no!'), self-talk ('where did I put that?' or 'Hm, I wonder how you do this') and utterances that were intended to be overheard by me. Although I generally sat in an adjacent room out of sight, I could overhear the conversation and the children appeared to be aware of that fact. When there were especially interesting things they wanted to share but knew they should stay with their mother, they would raise their voice and speak in English (but still in third person) in hopes that I would overhear. Other times, the children addressed me directly by raising their voices. A few examples can be seen in (11).

(11) Utterances For English-Speaking Overhearer
    (a) is it time for you to play with me? (Sandy 5;9)
    (b) <LOUDLY> I'm going make a flower (Sarah 5;9)
    (c) <LOUDLY> made this by myself (Ben 5;2)

The study on the content or the rationale for code-switching and code-mixing showed discernible patterns for why children use English. The results can be summarized as follows:

(1) Children were more likely to use English for vocabulary that one would encounter in English such as school vocabulary, animal names for more exotic animals and specific verbs with narrow meanings.
(2) All-English utterances were used:

(a) in order to soften the severity of a language function that could have negative consequences if the mother took it as a sign of disrespect;
(b) when the interlocutor or overhearer had a preference for English;
(c) when they were not directed at anyone in particular (such as exclamations or when they were talking to themselves).

The main takeaway from this study is that there is intent and specific communicative functions behind code-switched and code-mixed utterances. That is, mixing is not something that the children are doing randomly, and there are specific functions that appear to trigger the use of English in an otherwise Korean conversation.

7.4 Code-Mixing: Frequency Over Time

The final study for this chapter examines the number of code-mixed utterances that children produce over time. In Park-Johnson (2017a), I reported on the progression of the amount of code-mixing for each child as they increasingly become dominant in English. The motivation for this study came from theories of code-switching that view it from a deficit perspective. Many studies of young bilingual children offer explanations that point to lack of proficiency and language dominance shift as the primary reason for code-mixing. These dominance hypotheses posit that children code-mix when they are using their weaker language in order to support gaps in their proficiency (Bernardini & Schlyter, 2004; Gawlitzek-Maiwald & Tracy, 1996; Jisa, 2000; Petersen, 1988). The implication of this explanation is that children fill the grammatical gaps in their weaker language with elements of the stronger language, acting as a language crutch. For heritage speakers, this explanation is salient because elements of the societal language are often used when they speak their heritage language.

If it were the case that the children code-mix in order to support their weakening heritage language with the stronger societal language, then we would expect that as children become more English dominant and weaker in Korean, they would use more code-mixing to support their heritage Korean. It is widely attested that heritage speakers generally experience language attrition as they become dominant in the societal language (Chini, 2011; Portes & Schauffler, 1994; Smith, 2006). This shift in dominance occurs quickly within the first several years of life (Berman, 1979; Jisa, 2000; Lanza, 1992; Leopold, 1970; Olsson & Sullivan, 2005; Quay, 2001; Romaine, 1995). For the children in this study, we are in the fortunate position to observe this shift because they are at the prime age when this language dominance shift occurs. This study also affords us a longitudinal view that is often missing in these types of studies.

The research questions that were posed in Park-Johnson (2017a) are as follows:

(1) Does code-mixing correlate with language dominance shift?
(2) As bilingual children become more proficient and dominant in English, will there be increasing amounts of code-mixing in their Korean conversations?

To investigate these questions, the utterances from Korean sessions with the mothers were coded for language. The aforementioned utterances containing both Korean and English were coded as 'Mixed', utterances all in English were 'Eng' and utterances all in Korean were labeled 'Kor'. Any proper names and terms of address were not coded for language because they tend to stay in one language (e.g. they would always call their mother by the Korean term rather than in English). Nonlinguistic utterances, sound effects or unintelligible utterances where the language could not be determined were also omitted from analysis.

Measuring language dominance has eluded researchers for decades. Languages that are structurally similar can be measured using mean length of utterance (MLU) to make general comparisons between languages, but for pairings like Korean and English, the typological differences in morphology make MLU alone unreliable and misrepresentative of their complexity. In Park-Johnson (2017a), I adopted Yip and Matthews' (2006: 108) formula for MLU differentials, defined as 'the difference between MLU scores for a child's two languages at a given sampling point or over a period of development'. MLU differential calculates the proportion of English MLU over Korean MLU, then that value is followed over time for each child. This way, we can track relative complexity of children's Korean and English over time to give us some information on their language dominance shift.

To test the correlation between time and MLU differential, Pearson's product-moment correlations were conducted. Results revealed strong correlations between MLU differential and age for all four children, indicating that children were increasing in English dominance as they became older. Longitudinally, the children's amount of Korean was decreasing over time and English was increasing over time during their Korean sessions with their parents. However, in contrast, correlation tests showed that the amount of code-mixing was not significantly correlated with age for any of the children (Table 7.3).

If code-mixing was indeed used as a support for the weaker language, we would have seen a relationship between time and code-mixing as children undergo language dominance shift. However, this prediction was not borne out in the study; children's code-mixing remained consistent over time.

Table 7.3 Pearson correlations for age and percentage of language production

	Korean	English	Mixed
Ben	−.477*	.448	.043
Sarah	−.679**	.682**	−.467
Sandy	−.610*	.707**	.111
Dan	−.973	.997*	−.071

Source: Published in Park-Johnson (2017a).

Note: * = statistically significant at $p < .05$ level, ** = statistically significant at $p < .01$ level.

The results from the code-mixing frequency study can be summarized as follows:

(1) The Korean-English bilingual children became more English dominant over time as determined by MLU differential. This correlation was statistically significant.
(2) However, children's amount of intrasentential code-mixing did not change with age and time; their code-mixing frequency remained consistent across the entirety of the study.

7.5 Chapter Summary

This chapter brought together the two languages we have been investigating in this book thus far, with special emphasis on how those two languages are used within the same discourse. The investigation of code-switching revealed several trends. First, children's code-mixed utterances, where both languages are used within the same utterance, revealed structure that more closely resembled Korean syntax. We also found that code-mixing was generally single-word English inserted into an otherwise Korean utterance. Further investigation of the function of code-mixing revealed that these English words were often for academic vocabulary and specific verbs that are low frequency. When examining children's English utterances used in their Korean sessions, the findings presented an important trend: children use English when they need to soften their tone to appear less disrespectful when expressing complaint, defiance or pleading. Finally, the longitudinal study that investigated the amount of code-mixing over time revealed that although children are becoming more dominant in Korean, the amount they code-mix stayed consistent across the years of data.

Taken together, these findings point to five important implications. First, the fact that there are structural consistencies among the code-mixed utterances shows that children's code-mixing is not random, but rather systematic, driven by the rules that govern all human languages. What is most notable from this is not just that they are rule-governed, but that code-mixing followed Korean syntax and even took on Korean morphology, such as case markers. Instead of revealing evidence of gaps in their knowledge, the studies of code-switching actually added to the mounting evidence that Korean-English bilingual children have extensive and productive knowledge of Korean syntax and morphology. They are not only able to apply Korean structural rules in an all-Korean linguistic context, but they can also apply these to complex amalgamations of the two languages, an impressive feat for such young speakers.

Second, the study showed that there are specific and valid triggers for code-mixing and code-switching. Switches in conversation can signal solidarity – switch to the preferred language of interlocutor – or disagreement – switch to the less preferred language (Shin, 2004). Here, switching to English in a Korean conversation with their Korean-speaking parent may seem like an aberration or even an unintentional switch; however, investigation into the function of these switches shows children's keen awareness of what they can accomplish with their two languages. Indeed, it is far less disrespectful, rude and harsh to complain or defy their mother in English than it is to do this in Korean; the children show this nuanced knowledge very early on. Bilingual individuals often attest that certain phrases or communicative functions – such as profanity – are far more impactful or vigorous in one language versus the other. The children in this study seem to truly understand this at an early age, using English strategically to soften their tone and thereby reducing the chances that they will get rebuffed by their mother. Seeing these patterns arise directly from the data, it would be difficult to deny that the children know, at least subconsciously, precisely what they are accomplishing when they use English. Bolonyai (2005) reported similar findings, in which bilingual children switched from Hungarian into English; in this example, however, the switch to English was a signal of power and dominance over their peers. Had the Korean mothers in this study been English-dominant speakers, the switch may have had an entirely different meaning. Because they are Korean-dominant, the children's switch to English has a softer but still defiant sense that they were able to accomplish deftly.

With code-mixing within single utterances, the explanation is slightly different. We saw that the children tend to insert single English words in their otherwise Korean utterances, and the vast majority of these are academic words, animal names and verbs with specialized, narrow meanings. Because the children are educated almost entirely in English (apart from Korean school), it stands to reason that their academic vocabulary would be far more accessible in English than Korean. Generating vocabulary for scientific terms such as *asteroid belt* or school words such as *recess* is far more salient in the language in which the words are used. Low-frequency vocabulary such as exotic animal names and verbs with highly specific meanings (e.g. *to twist*) are also ones that are most likely to be used in school, where children spend five days a week prior to these sessions. Parents take this as evidence that children are losing their home language, and often worry why their child chooses to say *elephant, ruler* and *to add* instead of *khokkiri, ca* and *tehaki*. Here is the crucial link: vocabulary is not a measure of bilingual speakers' grammatical proficiency. Vocabulary is learned in context. When a student learns music in English, they will generate those music terms in English; when a student learns math in Korean, they will generate those math terms in Korean. Fully fledged monolingual native speakers of English who have excellent proficiency in their native language may struggle when faced with a new topic that has its own select vocabulary (e.g. plumbing, golf). There is a tendency to equate grammatical competence with lexical knowledge in academic settings – many assessments rely on vocabulary – and while this may have merit for some monolingual populations, lexical breadth and depth cannot be used as an indicator for syntactic or morphological development for multilingual individuals.

Fourth, the study on the rate of code-mixing indicated that even as the children receive more exposure to English and become more English dominant, their rate of Korean-English code-mixing stays consistent across the 2.5 years. Unlike what has been posited, this study showed that code-mixing is not an indicator of language dominance. Again, the results indicated that the children's Korean vocabulary may not be as well-developed or accessible as their English, so they choose English vocabulary instead. In the other two studies in this chapter, we saw that code-mixed utterances consistently follow Korean syntax and take on Korean morphology. There is no evidence here that the children are somehow resorting to English as a crutch for their weakening Korean; their Korean proficiency seems strong and highly productive, as seen both in this chapter and in Chapters 3 and 4. Thus we can conclude that code-mixing not an indication of decreased proficiency, but rather a rule-governed, systematic and complex process.

Finally, this was not treated as data because there was not a research question motivating it, but it is a crucial finding nonetheless: the children did not code-mix in the English sessions and only code-mixed in the Korean sessions. This is convincing evidence that there is intention behind code-mixing and that the children are keenly aware of the social dynamic of each language. Knowing that code-switching with Korean in an English setting does not work, but that mixing is absolutely permitted and quite common in Korean conversations tells us how tuned in children are on the linguistic landscape of their bilingualism.

8 Ten Years Later

8.1 Introduction

The benefit of researchers being members of the community in which they conduct research is the continued relationships that go beyond the scope of the original study. Generally, researchers work with children and families for a time, but too often there is little follow-through or opportunity for those same children to later reflect upon their own side of the experience. In this chapter, we have the unique and much-needed perspective of child language research and longitudinal study in which the children that were once participants of the study can return as adults. Here I had the opportunity for conversation with two of the children we have been learning about in this book, Sarah and Sandy. Both are now adult university students, and – delightfully – they are still bilingual in Korean and English. In our conversations, Sarah and Sandy each relayed to me their linguistic journey, their paths toward discovery of their identities, the hardships and victories of being minoritized language speakers and minoritized ethnicities in the United States and the impact of their bilingualism and biculturalism in their childhood, adolescence and now adulthood.

The methods involved in the case studies in this chapter are naturally different than those described in Chapter 2. For this study, I prepared 18 questions for a semi-structured interview and conducted the interviews over a video call. Sarah and Sandy were gracious in sharing their time and reflections. I was also able to play them videos of themselves as children over the call, and Sandy even called over her mother to watch those videos from so many years ago. Each interview lasted about 40 minutes.

The interviews were transcribed, then those transcriptions were coded for thematic analysis, a process adapted from Moustakas (1994). I read over the transcripts many times to familiarize myself with the data, then identified preliminary codes and tagged segments of the transcript with those codes. Next, the codes were combined into themes and subthemes. The result of that analysis is what I report in this chapter below. The analysis of the data in this chapter is conducted differently from those in Chapters 3 through 7 due to the nature of the data in this chapter. Despite the different nature of the data, this qualitative study provides insight that is not often seen in grammatical analyses; this view adds a depth and dimension of information that can be enriching and humanizing.

Both Sarah and Sandy remember our visits fondly. Sandy recalled how excited she used to be when I visited their home, and how it was simply a fun visit from an *unni* (big sister) rather than a formal research study. In our interview, we picked up right where we left off some 10 years ago.

8.2 Theme 1: Korean Language Proficiency and Identity, Belongingness and Family

Both Sarah and Sandy currently use Korean on a daily basis and have maintained excellent language proficiency in their heritage language. They both speak Korean to their parents still as the primary language. At the time of the interview, both Sarah and Sandy were living with other Korean roommates as well. When asked to rate their current Korean proficiency skills on a scale from 1 to 10 for listening, speaking, reading and writing, Sarah rated her receptive skills higher than her productive skills, while Sandy rated her oral language skills higher than her written language skills. Both reported that their writing was their weakest skill. This is consistent with how heritage speakers rate their heritage language skills, though this is often based on vocabulary and mechanics rather than grammar (Bermel & Kagan, 2000). Their self-assessment scores can be seen in Table 8.1.

With regard to their writing, Sarah confessed that she has not had much practice writing after Korean school was over.

> Honestly after I stopped doing the whole Korean school thing, there weren't many opportunities to write in Korean. So definitely, like spacing wise: absolute trash, SO trash! [both laugh] I cannot emphasize to you how bad my *ttuyessuki* is. (Sarah)

Sarah laughed about how her *ttuyessuki*, or Korean word spacing, was 'absolute trash'. However, she seems to know that this is more linked to opportunity to practice than personal deficiency. Sandy also had a similar reaction about writing:

Table 8.1 Sarah's and Sandy's self-assessment scores

	Listening	Speaking	Reading	Writing
Sarah	8	6.5	8	4
Sandy	9.5	8.5	5	3.5

> Writing? Okay, so basically, I'm very bad at grammar in all languages! [laugh] I took Spanish in high school: terrible at grammar. English? Terrible at grammar. Korean? Terrible at grammar [laugh] I can definitely write it, but it's more just grammatically having it make sense [that's hard]. And then the spelling, I'd say I'm not as good. (Sandy)

Sandy mentions that her grammar is poor across the board, which seems inconsistent with her strong grammatical abilities from early childhood. It is my impression that by 'grammar', she might actually be referring to writing conventions – like Sarah – which in academia is often conflated as being part of grammar.

Despite their self-assessment that writing was not their strong suit, both Sarah and Sandy felt their listening and speaking abilities were strong. Their high Korean language proficiency seemed to be a point of pride for Sarah and Sandy, a source of identity and familial belonging:

> I'm speaking to my mom and dad in their home language. I think that if I wasn't able to do that, my parents would also be like, 'who is this girl? We didn't raise her [like this]. What is going on?'. (Sarah)

They both informed me that while their parents did not enforce a formal Korean-only family language policy in the home, when they were younger their parents did encourage them to speak Korean exclusively. As they grew older, the home language became more of a mix, though it was still largely Korean. Sarah mentioned more than once the importance it held for her to speak in her parents' language rather than force her parents to accommodate to her. The fear of the language barrier is what drives her to make an additional effort to speak Korean to her parents:

> I'm so glad that I was at a point where I could listen to her in Korean, and then also hear her out in Korean as well. 'Cause I could not imagine if my parents had a language barrier with me. It almost hurts to think about how limiting that would be for them. (Sarah)

Sandy also expressed a similar sentiment, a certain gratefulness for being able to speak Korean to her family.

> I'd say I'm happy that we use Korean in our household…being able to really understand the language and understand conversations, and [understand] social cues too. (Sandy)

This ability to speak to their parents in their native language is an important part of Sarah's and Sandy's relationships with their parents.

Interestingly, both of them – as older sisters to younger brothers – indicated a certain sisterly responsibility toward their siblings, to demonstrate Korean and speak to them in Korean as much as possible:

> But if I wasn't speaking Korean at all, he would also have no motivation to keep it up in any way. (Sarah)

> I mostly speak Korean to him, but he always replies in English. I wanna better my Korean and wanna still make sure he remembers his Korean a bit. He's actually been improving and has increased his amount of [speaking] Korean back to me. (Sandy)

Both Sarah and Sandy made it clear that they are tremendously grateful to their parents for instilling this language in themselves and their families, a point that not many parents of heritage speakers get to hear until their children are older. Sarah and Sandy agreed emphatically when asked if they agreed with their parents' language choices and family language policy.

> Looking back now I'm very thankful for it because growing up as a Korean-American in America, I'm always gonna use English, especially because I go to a predominantly White school in a very White area. (Sandy)

Here, Sandy expresses that English is a given since she will have ample opportunity to speak it outside of the home, but is thankful she was able to develop Korean. Furthermore, being a Korean speaker and being bilingual was and is a source of pride for Sarah and Sandy. They both wear their bilingualism proudly:

> No, I was very proud about the fact that I could speak two languages. 'Cause at first it was more like a, 'oh I could speak two things' but later on it became like, I'm keeping up something that is part of my heritage. (Sarah)

They both use their Korean not only with their families and roommates, but also use it to enjoy Korean dramas, Korean music and even to chat with Korean restaurant owners.

Sarah and Sandy also both mentioned mixing the two languages. They both attend university in the United States where English is the medium of instruction, and they find themselves 'slipping' into English:

> Every time I go back home now, I kinda have to think [to myself] 'speak more Korean, speak more Korean', 'make sure not to like switch over to English'. It's almost a little bit of a conscious effort there. (Sarah)

While some of the time they use mixing to support the other language – usually using English to support their Korean – they both commented on how Korean words actually better describe certain tastes, emotions or situations.

> Because some jokes are better off in a certain language, and [you can] express the point better in that language. Like, my friends will use both chic and *toto*, which means the same thing but because it's used in English and Korean, it means different things in a way. (Sandy)

In this example, Sandy explains how the same word – English *chic* and Korean *toto* – expresses slightly different meanings, so her Korean-English friends use the two terms together to describe her. In the interviews, both participants mentioned how certain words just sound better in Korean, or how there are no translation equivalents for certain terms like *kosohata* (simultaneously salty, sweet and savory) and *sewunhay* (a mix of melancholy regret, disappointment and hurt). Much as they did as children, they use both languages to portray a wider range of meaning and purpose.

8.3 Theme 2: Shame

Although Sarah and Sandy both express immense pride in their Korean identity, their childhood and adolescence were not without pain, uncertainty and shame from their apparent and perceived differences. Both of them reported experiencing shame and wanting to hide their Koreanness. They shared about the burden of being minoritized and wearing that minoritized status plainly on their faces. Interestingly, both Sarah and Sandy have memories of shame and embarrassment associated with having Korean food in the lunchroom at school:

> I remember telling my mom 'don't ever make this again' or 'don't put this in my lunch box'...[other kids] being like 'oh that smells bad, what are you eating?'. (Sarah)

> I mean I didn't eat lunch because I was afraid of being made fun of for my lunches. Bringing rice and seaweed was like...I just didn't want to. (Sandy)

Both Sarah and Sandy brought up the food example as a tangible example of what made them feel different at school. They vividly remembered the stares from other students, the mocking and nose-plugging, and the way they were otherized for the culturally different lunches their mothers packed for them.

Sarah also found that teachers' expectations of her academic abilities were troubling:

> It's just the stereotype of being studious, academically, all that stuff. It's like almost a guaranteed thing. I did not like the fact that you can't really do anything. Even if you 'prove yourself', what are you proving? You're just reinforcing that stereotype! (Sarah)

Here, Sarah shares the futility of fighting stereotypes: if she performs poorly, she loses, but if she performs well, she also loses since it feeds the stereotype further. This double standard that Sarah perceived from her teachers is a prime example of the model minority myth, that Asian immigrants are expected to do well in school and conform to the societal language and culture. This myth creates standards that can be harmful (Kang, 2015a; Lee et al., 2017; Li, 2005; Museus & Kiang, 2009; Wing, 2007). Although Sarah did not let this change how she performed in school, it created a rift between herself and her classmates at school. Sandy noted the same, where she noticed teachers treating some students differently than her. Although she admitted she could not identify a direct link between race and teachers' behavior toward students, she commented that the constant question in her head was 'is it because I'm Korean?'. Ideology and discrimination played out in real time can be difficult to spot, especially in relationships of unbalanced power such as between teachers and students. What Sandy relays in her account seems to corroborate this.

School was not the only place they felt this sense of uncertainty. Sandy brought up examples where she felt alienated or embarrassed because she was not aware of some of the norms of dominant White culture. For instance, she shared how she was eating noodles with her White friend's family, and when she slurped her noodles – a perfectly normal and expected way to eat noodles in Korean culture – the family's father chastised her for the way she ate. Sandy commented that while these examples are far and few between, it was a recurring and constant reminder of her difference:

> Being Korean not only just changed my outward appearance but [also] my understanding what's normal and what's not. Even though being Korean didn't entirely separate me, everything in general would sometimes just go back to [my] being Korean. (Sandy)

Sandy's comment above points to a theme of deeper layers of shame, where it was not simply how she looked or how she spoke but rather a questioning of her core values. In other words, being chastised for breaking politeness norms – which differ largely from culture to culture – was a commentary on her character, her values and how she was raised. Being Korean then becomes linked to being sloppy, rude and coarse from the perspective of the majority gaze. This is certainly a heavy load to carry for a young person.

The questioning of one's belonging was a theme found in Sarah's responses as well. Though she expressed pride in her heritage, she often asked herself the question 'What if I were White? Would I blend in more?', a theme that captured much of Sarah's and Sandy's experience as an adolescent.

At the same time, Sarah and Sandy wished for more opportunities to be around other Koreans. There was sometimes rejection from other Koreans, and other times simply the lack of other Korean Americans in the geographical vicinity.

> Especially going to a predominantly White school, it was hard. I mean, I didn't have friends who I felt like I could be proud of my culture with. Also back then, people didn't even know the country of Korea. And if they did, they were like 'are you North Korean?'. (Sandy)

> I hear from other people that live in [town with large Korean presence], they talk in Korean with their friends, they go to Korean restaurants, they're around so many Korean people. That's something that I never got to do in [high] school. (Sarah)

The lack of opportunity to be with other Koreans and people who share that similar background seemed to be a source of regret for both Sarah and Sandy. Although it seems to contrast with their desire to blend in with the societally dominant culture, it speaks to a need to be accepted and among others that are like them, whether they change to be more like the White peers around them or they find others who are like them to be around.

Sarah in particular expressed opinions about how Korean people should act, and likewise opinions about mainstream White culture. She mentioned several times the connection between being Korean and speaking Korean:

> And it was almost like because I spoke Korean and because I still 'acted Asian' I was sometimes called out for that by those people.... They were either whitewashed or didn't speak Korean, so it was never that like vibe of having this connection to the school in terms of ethnicity and race. (Sarah)

In her view, Sarah felt that it was important for Koreans to have Korean language ability, and being able to speak the language was a source of belongingness and sense of ethnic identity, a theme found often in previous studies (e.g. Brown, 2009). Koreans that do not speak the language or 'act Korean' are, as Sarah noted, 'whitewashed'. As an adolescent, Sarah remembers feeling that Koreans that assimilated entirely into White culture set them apart from other Koreans and made them appear 'snotty' or stuck up. Perhaps it is this view that motivated Sarah to maintain her Korean language ability. This speaks to a tension between those who reject the heritage culture and those that reject the mainstream culture, which may cause resentment and scorn from one group to the other. On the one side, assimilating is perceived as abandoning your heritage (He,

2006), while on the other side, those that cling to their heritage are seen as unadjusted and cloistered (Shin, 2016). The balance is difficult to strike during adolescence especially, when identities feel rigid and alliances seem final (Ngo, 2008).

8.4 Theme 3: Finding Themselves

Although being different was a source of difficulty for both Sarah and Sandy, they also noted immense pride associated with their being Korean, especially now as adults. Looking back, they noted that there were key elements that helped them along the way: Korean school and peers that accepted and welcomed their culture.

For Sarah, attending Korean school was a large part of her childhood. She attended a Korean language and culture school held on Saturdays until she was in third grade. She mentions how much she valued the experience:

> I really liked [it] just 'cause you were able to do so many Korean traditional things like studying Korean dance. And I think it was only until Korean School I was able to actually learn about the history too. History was always really important to me and that's still something that I'm interested in. (Sarah)

She also noted how she was able to connect with other Korean children that she would not have otherwise known, and it was a great source of community. Many of those same children ended up at the same university as Sarah, and she commented on how joyful it was to reunite with childhood friends from that same experience.

Sandy attended a Korean language school through her church, and while she did not particularly appreciate it as a child, she did go on to become an assistant teacher at the school when she was in high school. With her high level of Korean, she ended up helping many of the students one-on-one, working with some students who were even older than she was:

> I also once taught someone who was two years older than me. I think she was a junior or senior at the time, and I helped her out. But then I also helped out other kids in the church who were kind of falling behind, so I sat next to them and taught them individually so they would be able to keep up with the pace. (Sandy)

Sandy joked that it was ironic that she ended up as the assistant teacher at a school she had disliked as a child, but also found it to be a way to connect with the children who expressed boredom and dislike as well.

In addition to Korean school, Sarah and Sandy both found that it was being with peers who accepted their culture, background and identity that allowed them to reclaim a sense of pride in their own identity as Koreans. During high school, Sandy found a diverse friend group that not only accepted her language and culture but actively embraced it:

> They'll come over to my house and be like 'Sandy, can I have your food?', or at lunch instead of me being ashamed of it, they'd be like, 'Sandy, can I have a bite?' and I'd be like 'Yeah! Sure!'. It's very new to me, but very different. I think it's the environment itself and who I surrounded myself with that changed how I view my identity. (Sandy)

The very thing that caused shame and embarrassment at a younger age – food – seems to have become a symbol of pride. These friends, who were not necessarily Korean themselves, watched Korean dramas together and Sandy would explain certain cultural references to them, and these friends themselves were from diverse backgrounds and had their own differences that Sandy embraced in turn.

Sarah had an experience in high school that was also an important turn in the way she viewed her own culture and identity. She attended a diversity dialogue program where high school students of diverse cultural backgrounds were brought together for mutual learning and discussion.

> I was the representative with four other kids from our district. It made me acknowledge even more how comfortable I was with [being Asian] and how proud I was with it. Because it's like you're representing the East Asian community from your district, talking to other different ethnicity groups, representatives from other districts. And it was cool 'cause everyone was so willing to learn about you, too. You realize like how much you know about yourself and how much you wanna share that as well. Having that energy from people of all different ethnicities, I think that's one of like my key experiences, a re-emphasis of how much I knew and how much I want to share it. (Sarah)

Like Sandy, being with others who did not necessarily share her specific background but welcomed and shared the experience of being culturally diverse helped her toward accepting and being proud of her own identity.

Of course, being with other Koreans that share even more background similarities, especially language, contributed as well. As mentioned above, both Sarah and Sandy currently live with roommates that are Korean-American, and they both reported comfort and connectedness being with other Koreans.

> I found comfort if I just ran into a random Korean. The initial conversations are easier, just 'cause you have like similar family background, similar lifestyle and stuff like that. You see people similar to you and just like the knowledge that they have. Some sort of genetic, traditional

similarity. Where it does become a little bit easier to talk initially, just 'cause you have so many baseline similarities. (Sarah)

Sandy also talked about having more Korean friends now in college as compared to when she was growing up. She is part of a Korean Student Association and most of her current friends are Korean-American. Like Sarah, Sandy reported feeling content and joyful being around others who share her background: the instant connection, the similar background and also the aforementioned mixing of Korean and English with friends who also speak both languages.

Interestingly, both Sarah and Sandy discuss how public and societal perception, tolerance and attitudes have changed throughout their lives with regard to cultural and linguistic differences. Sandy even noted the different experience between herself and her younger brother, Dan, who are only three years apart in age. As previously mentioned, she was ashamed of bringing Korean food for lunch, but her younger brother actually had the opposite experience, where his friends would beg for a bite of his food and he would have to ward them off. Sandy noted how strange it was to have distinctly opposite experiences with bringing Korean food, and sees this as a sign that things might be moving in a more accepting direction.

Sarah also mentioned that things are different now than they were when she was younger, and her perception is that people are becoming more tolerant of this change. Sarah and Sandy both expressed the theme of broader societal change, sensing that there is more tolerance and promotion of diversity.

8.5 Analysis

In many ways, the themes that arose from the interviews with Sarah and Sandy tell a similar story: both have immense pride in their language, culture and identity as Koreans; they went through difficulties as children and adolescents being part of a minoritized group, and they found communities and people and environments that allow them to be who they truly are; they both have strong Korean language skills and that contributes to their sense of belonging and identity as Koreans. A significant implication from these conversations with Sarah and Sandy is that they emerged from their childhood and adolescence as bilingual and bicultural individuals, and as thriving, self-assured members of their communities. They wear their Korean identity with pride, both in personal relationships but also in public. They are able to smoothly navigate a mainstream, majority culture as college students in the United States and also a proud vibrant subculture as Koreans raised in America.

The first theme, Korean Language Proficiency and Identity, Belongingness and Family, showcases just how important their language ability is in the way that they feel about themselves as Koreans and their belongingness in their family and communities. By being speakers of the language, they can carry on conversations not just with people they are familiar with, but with other Koreans they encounter in the community. Put simply, they are able to carve out a place for themselves with others that look and sound like them. With them averaging a 7 and an 8 in their oral language skills (based on their self-assessment), they truly are able to conduct a wide range of communicative tasks and speak to a wide variety of Korean speakers. They both expressed a connection between their Korean proficiency and connectedness with their Korean identity, a finding seen in many previous studies (e.g. Jo, 2001; Lee, 2002; Lee & Suarez, 2009; Phinney et al., 2001). Both of them also seem to have been encouraged (but not forced) to speak Korean at home. Had they been encouraged to speak English at home instead of Korean, they may not have this result, and their stories would certainly be very different than the one they shared in these interviews. Their parents chose to enroll them in Korean school, speak to them in Korean and expose them to Korean books and media. In many ways, parents sent direct and indirect messages to their children that Korean is important, which has evidently shaped the way that Sarah and Sandy think about language ability and bilingualism in general. This is consistent with themes found in the literature, where Korean parents view bilingualism and high proficiency in both Korean and English to be of the utmost importance (Jung, 2022), and parents' ideologies of bilingualism impact children's bilingualism (Leung et al., 2022). Additionally, Sarah and Sandy both took on responsibility for their younger siblings, modeling their bilingualism and supporting the siblings' linguistic growth. We see this in the literature, with older heritage speakers taking on the role of linguistic and cultural mediator (Kwon & Martínez-Álvarez, 2022), acting almost as a bridge or broker between the parents and younger siblings (Kwon, 2022).

The second theme of shame is one that was most expected. The findings from the interview indicated periods of wanting to assimilate and experiencing shame about their blatant differences. Both Sarah and Sandy experienced marginalization by their mainstream peers, teachers and sometimes even from other Koreans. Also, they both encountered difficulties managing their cultural differences, both internally and also unexpected situations with members of the mainstream culture (e.g. slurping noodles). This pressure to assimilate is not an uncommon experience (Tse, 2000). What is more surprising is that this was not a central theme in either of their interviews. They both commented on it and gave examples of shame and wanting to assimilate, but they both focused on overcoming these challenges. The challenges did not seem to dominate the way that they remembered their childhood and adolescence.

Another notable finding was that shame, embarrassment or marginalization was never really about language. Perhaps because Sarah and

Sandy have excellent English skills, as evidenced in Chapters 5 and 6, neither of them seemed to have faced major challenges as a result of their language. They also seemed quite adept at navigating the switch between Korean- and English-speaking contexts (evidenced in Chapter 7). If anything, heritage speakers often face ridicule by monolingual speakers of their heritage language (Goble, 2016); however, neither of them reported this. As mentioned above, their Korean language seems quite proficient, and thus neither their English nor Korean seemed to be a hindrance or source of shame for them. Sarah and Sandy spoke of their bilingualism in a positive way: opening opportunities for connection, belongingness and language play with other bilinguals (code-switching). The only time they disparaged their own language ability was regarding writing. This is to be expected since writing is not a large part of heritage language use.

For Sarah and Sandy, Korean school was a large presence during their youth; at the time it may have been a bother, but in retrospect they have lasting positive views of the experience. Indeed, Korean school allowed Sarah and Sandy to learn language and culture in an academic setting, but the crucial benefit seemed to be the opportunity to interact with other Korean children, something neither had in their mainstream school setting. Research on community language schools has shown that one of the main outcomes is that they instill positive views about the heritage language and culture, a chance to be a majority instead of a minority, and build camaraderie with other similar children going through the same experience (Beaudrie *et al.*, 2021; Chinen & Tucker, 2005; Kwon, 2022; Lo, 2009; You & Liu, 2011). This was certainly the case for our participants.

The last theme of finding themselves was one of hope and promise. A large part of their esteem seems to be linked to the lessons that their families instilled in them at a young age: that bilingualism is a source of pride, and that biculturalism is a value. They sought out ways to connect with people and communities that celebrate and invite their differences. In Sarah's case, she specifically engaged in opportunities to explore her heritage, participating in the diversity dialogue program during adolescence and Korean cultural groups once she attended university. Sandy sought out friend groups that celebrated and embraced diversity in many different facets, finding this important key message: that one does not have to be with people who are exactly alike in order to truly appreciate one's heritage.

Finally, the message that both Sarah and Sandy put forth was that society is changing for the better, and people are becoming more accepting of Korean culture. This is certainly seen in popular culture with the impact of *hallyu*, or the Korean wave, a world-wide popularity surge of Korean pop music (K-pop), Korean dramas (K-dramas) and Korean celebrities. Korean pop culture is now regularly consumed by people outside of Korea, which researchers have found motivates many young

Koreans to maintain their heritage language (You & Liu, 2011) and non-Koreans to learn Korean as a second language (Kim, 2022). Mainstream American music and television streaming services have entire sections on K-pop and K-dramas. Korean food has also become increasingly popular, components of Korean cuisine such as *kimchi* or *kalbi* appearing in non-Korean restaurants prepared by non-Korean chefs. There is also more awareness and social taboo associated with racial discrimination, mockery and marginalization. Sarah's and Sandy's reflections on their own personal journeys, compounded with these broader societal changes, hail an optimism for the future that raises a message of hope for newer generations.

8.6 Chapter Summary

Taken together, the interviews with Sarah and Sandy were an important opportunity to speak with the now-adult participants whose language data we have been studying throughout this book. Their experiences confirm what the theoretical framework of heteroglossia predicted: that bilingualism is a dynamic, ongoing process. Indeed, the best informants to report on this process are the speakers themselves, as they can reflect most accurately and report the details of their challenges, the ebb and flow of their bilingual experience and the way that their linguistic identities have shaped their lives from childhood to adolescence to adulthood. In this chapter, we had the unusual opportunity to hear from these participants themselves, giving them a platform to own their experiences and voice their perspective. It also allows for an interesting comparison between what their language was like in their early childhood and how it has moved and morphed across time. The framework of heteroglossia that undergirds the work in this book is reflected here in this chapter again, reaffirming that multilingualism is not unitary, static or even solely about language alone. Rather, it is 'social life and historical becoming' as described by Bakhtin (1992: 288). Their stories of coming of age, struggle and pride, and ownership of their bilingual bicultural experience extends and enriches the notion of heteroglossia further.

Additionally, to find that Sarah and Sandy are both still Korean speakers, consider their bilingualism to be a gift and are still proud of their Korean heritage and identity bring hope for others in their situation. Although Sarah and Sandy are but two stories among hundreds of thousands of others, their accounts of finding community and overcoming challenges, and their general message of pride and gratitude are important components that enliven the data we have explored in this book. They place a note of humanity behind the numbers and percentages, and offer a chance to make additional meaning from the data reported. What we find here is that these linguistic abilities have allowed two people to find belongingness, connectedness, familiarity, comfort and immense joy in their lives. We will continue to reflect on this as we bring everything together in the final chapter.

9 Conclusions and Implications

9.1 Introduction

In this book, we have taken a close look at the language of four Korean-English bilingual children during their early years, from as young as 2;4 up to 7;11. For each child, their language development has been investigated through monthly sessions that ranged across 2 to 2.5 years, capturing their linguistic journey in Korean, English and the intersection of the two. This book specifically explored their Korean and English morphology and syntax in Chapters 3 through 6, isolating each level and language and studying the areas that may give rise to unique patterns. In Chapter 7 we looked at the intersection of the two languages – code-switching – to see what its structure, content and frequency can reveal about children's linguistic and extralinguistic knowledge. Finally, in Chapter 8 we saw an epilogue of sorts, a rare opportunity to converse with the very children who were in the study and who are now young adults. In Table 9.1, I provide a summary of the empirical studies conducted throughout the book.

In Chapter 1, I posed the following question: So what? Why do we study heritage speakers in early childhood? What do these studies buy us in terms of linguistic knowledge or social impact? Why is it important to study these children who are not the 'ideal' bilingual, children who started learning the second language while the first language was still developing? I believe it is imperative to ask ourselves the 'so what' question as researchers, educators, policymakers, parents or bilinguals ourselves; knowledge for the sake of knowledge is interesting but it is the theoretical and practical implications that move us forward and directly impact the lives of the very people whose language we study. To that end, this final chapter will draw connections between the data we have seen and important implications for the following three areas: linguistic theory, identity and education. The chapter will conclude with next steps and directions for future research.

Table 9.1 Summary of results from book

Language	Domain	Topic	Main findings
Korean	Morphology	Case markers and case ellipsis	All children used subject and object case markers, and they displayed subject-object asymmetry. Case marker/ellipsis use did not change significantly over time. Case ellipsis followed predictable patterns based on word order for objects and demonstratives for subjects.
		Classifiers	Children produced Korean classifiers with 87–100% accuracy. They used 17 different types of Korean classifiers productively, but used the default classifier 46% of the time.
		Transitivity markers	Children used transitivity markers in Korean with 71–100% accuracy, with a wide range of verbs to express causative or agentive meanings.
		Sentence final markers	Children used sentence final markers in Korean with 98.1–99.8% accuracy, and used up to 447 types of markers. Children favored the use of -e (default declarative informal) and -iya (presentation declarative informal) markers.
	Syntax	Word order	Children produced Korean word orders at 99.9–100% accuracy, with strong preference for (S)(O)V orders. Structures did not change over time, but two older children showed slight increase of V type word order as they became older.
		Null pronominals	Children used Korean prodrop and non-prodrop with 96.3–98.7% accuracy, with higher success rates with prodrop over non-prodrop, and preference for omitting both subject and object pronouns.
English	Morphology	Articles	Children used English articles at a rate of 84–94% accuracy overall, and accuracy increased with age. Children had the most difficulty with indefinite *a*; errors of omission were far more common than insertion.
		Verb morphology	Children used English verb morphology with 62.5–92.2% accuracy. Children had higher accuracy with irregular verbs and past tense verbs, younger children had difficulty with null copula and older children had most difficulty with third person singular -s.

Syntax	Wh-movement	Children did not produce a single wh-in-situ question in the entirety of the dataset. All were wh-fronted/moved.
	Subject auxiliary inversion	Children acquire subject auxiliary inversion for English questions in a stepwise manner based on subject person: second person, first person, then third person.
	Word order	Children used English word order with 99.9–100% accuracy, with (S)V(O) comprising 99.9% of utterances. Word order type remained consistent overall, with slight increase of SVO for the two younger children over time.
	Pronominal use	Children used English subject pronouns at 98.5–99.5% accuracy and objects at 98.8–99.9% accuracy. Rate of accuracy did not change over time.
Mixed	Structure of mixing	Word order of code-mixed utterances was Korean (S)(O)V 97% of the time. Code-mixing generally occurred with a single English noun or verb in an otherwise Korean utterance, or utterances that started in English and ended with a Korean VP.
	Content of mixing	Code mixing only occurred in Korean sessions and never in English sessions. Code mixed (intrasentential) utterances were generally for school-related vocabulary, specific verbs and animal names. Code-switched utterances (utterances entirely in English) were usually to indicate a plea, complaint or defiance toward mother, or to speak to the sibling or English-speaking overhearer.
	Frequency of mixing over time	Children's rate of code-mixing did not change significantly over time and was not correlated with age or dominance.

9.2 Implications for Linguistic Theory

In Chapter 1, I introduced the two theoretical frameworks that pillar my work in this book: generative linguistics theory and heteroglossic perspective of bilingualism. Generative theory posits that all human language is rule-based and systematic, regardless of the language variety's status in society. This is true of all language, including that of language learners, and in this case the developing grammars of Korean-English bilingual children. Although heritage grammars do not always pattern like monolingual grammars, they are still governed by the rules of human language in a systematic way. This view of heritage language invites us to examine and analyze it in its own right, and opens our understanding of the possibilities of human language to a greater extent. In this book, we have seen evidence of this repeated throughout the data. For example, children used transitivity markers in Korean in a systematic way that mirrors how adult monolinguals of Korean use the markers, expressing causative or agentive meanings. In other examples, the Korean-English bilingual children developed language in ways that are not necessarily seen on the surface of Korean or English but have an underlying reason for each. In the example of subject auxiliary inversion in English as described in Chapter 6, the children acquired this movement for English questions in a stepwise manner based on subject person: second person, first person, then third person. This pattern has not been seen in children acquiring English only, and at first glance this might seem like an aberration. However, investigating Korean development of the person feature revealed that Korean learners develop person in Korean in the following order: second person, first person, third person (Cho, 2004). The underlying connection between acquisition of certain features in one language with the acquisition of auxiliary movement in another language is one that can only be made with linguistic theory that assumes a deeper structure beyond the surface. Generative theory allows us to see that the stepwise acquisition of subject auxiliary inversion has a logical, clear reason, thus allowing us to bestow a great amount of credit to the innovative and complex minds of these children. Another such example is in the code-mixing from Chapter 7, where children use a unique strategy to attach Korean verb morphology to English verb roots: they insert a Korean light verb *hay* after the English verb, then inflect the Korean light verb for tense, aspect, mood and other verbal information which could not have been attached to the English verb as is. This kind of innovation is another way that Korean-English bilingual children make use of the possibilities of human language to suit their particular linguistic needs.

The data from this book also reveal what happens in bilingual development when the two languages are structurally distinct. In some cases, the parameters of the language are in direct opposition, for example, English is head initial and Korean is head final. In other situations, features that are present in one language do not exist in the other language, such as case markers or classifiers in Korean or articles in English. Finally, there are situations where the structure or features are in opposition but there is slight overlap in some areas, such as in prodrop: English is non-prodrop and Korean is prodrop, but Korean also uses overt pronouns. Let us look at each of these cases in turn.

In the instance of oppositional parameters such as head final versus head initial structure, we had the opportunity to study word order in both Korean and English development. In Chapter 4, we studied the children's word order in Korean. Results indicated that children reached ceiling levels of accuracy for word order, at 99.9% to 100% overall. These results were impressive given their increasing use and exposure to English outside of the home. For 98% to 100% of their utterances, they used subject-object-verb (S)(O)V order, consistent with Korean canonical structure. In parallel, the study of English word order in Chapter 6 showed a similar finding in the head-initial direction: 99.9% to 100% of their utterances in English were in SV(O) order, all of which were grammatically acceptable. Only three utterances out of a total of 6721 English utterances were noncanonical. This contrast between children's Korean word order and English word order serves as convincing evidence that children are able to not only manage two distinct systems of grammar but also easily switch between the two with excellent, near perfect efficiency and accuracy. If their parametric switch was ever in question, the tidiness of these data would refute the notion quite convincingly.

For areas of grammar that exist in one language but not the other, the expectation is that given the limited amount of input in either language, the bilingual children would have some difficulty with the morphology or structure in question. In other words, with Korean input comprising just half (or less) of the child's input, one might expect their development of Korean-specific elements like case markers or classifiers to be an area of difficulty. Similarly, with English only heard outside of the home, the expectation may be that English-specific features like definite and indefinite articles pose a challenge for Korean heritage speakers. The data on Korean case markers and classifiers from Chapter 3 show that these predictions are not borne out. The children used Korean case markers productively, showing intentional case ellipsis based on predictable features (e.g. word order, deixis) and even showed subject-object asymmetry in their use of case markers, a pattern often found among adult monolingual Korean speakers. Children also used Korean classifiers productively, accuracy ranging from 87% to 100%. It was noted that while they used up to 17 different types of classifiers, children preferred the default classifier over more specific ones, a pattern commonly seen among heritage speakers (Jia & Paradis, 2015; Kan, 2019; Ming & Tao, 2008). In these examples, we might see patterning that may differ from monolingual speakers, but the children are still acquiring the features and using them productively. In their English development, the article study in Chapter 5 showed a similar result: although the children's home language does not have articles, they develop English articles and use them productively just the same. Their path was shown to be slightly different from that of monolingual children – they overused *a/an* in contexts where Ø was required, whereas monolingual children overuse *the* – but these paths eventually led to the same outcome. Children's overall accuracy ranged from 84.5% to 94.2% with English articles, with children increasing in accuracy over time as they got older, closing in on adult-like accuracy by the late 5s and into age 6. Given that their English development – particularly Sarah and Sandy – did not start until they were in preschool around age 2;6–3;0, this development of the notoriously challenging English articles is quick and efficient. In summary, the children in this study develop areas of both their grammars that are not supported or reinforced in the other. Despite the complexity of areas like Korean case markers or English articles, the children develop these areas even with reduced input in both languages. This has been attested in other bilingual studies and the data from this book add to this body of growing evidence that sheer amount of input is not proportional to speed or accuracy of grammatical development (e.g. Hauser-Grüdl *et al.*, 2010; Kwon & Uchikoshi, 2022).

Finally, the areas of slight structural overlap are opportunities to learn more about how the bilingual brain can discern nuance. Many studies with bilingual speakers have explored this in the overall discussion of interfaces (Cabo *et al.*, 2012; Cuza, 2013; Gondra, 2022; Grabitzky, 2014; Haznedar, 2003; Hulk & Müller, 2000; Ivanov, 2010; Müller & Hulk, 2001; Paradis & Navarro, 2003; Serratrice *et al.*, 2004). Partial structural overlap are cases in which one language offers two options but the other language only offers one. An example of this in Korean and English is wh-questions, where English allows for both wh-movement ('*What did you say?*') and wh-in-situ questions ('*You said what?!*') while Korean employs just wh-in-situ. Theories on crosslinguistic influence at interfaces, such as the syntax-pragmatics interface hypothesis (Hulk & Muller, 2000) may predict that because there is additional support for the wh-in-situ option – because it is available in both languages – that option will be reinforced in the language that allows two options. However, evidence from the study in Chapter 4 showed that contrary to prediction, Korean-English bilingual children did not use more wh-in-situ questions than pragmatically called for. In fact, they used none. Another such example is for the prodrop parameter, where Korean allows for two options (overt pronoun and dropped pronoun) and English allows only one option (overt pronoun). Again, the prediction would be that the language offering only one option, English, would influence the language offering two options, Korean, thereby increasing the number of overt pronouns in the children's Korean productions. However, the data from Chapter 4 suggest otherwise. Their overall success with Korean prodrop ranges from 96.3% to 98.7%, and the children were actually more likely to undersupply the pronoun in a context where one was necessary, contrary to expectation. At the same time, in Chapter 6 I found that the children's English pronoun use was target-like, with 98.5% to 99.9% accuracy, supplying subjects and objects productively in their English utterances from the youngest to oldest child and across all data points. Furthermore, even when they did drop the pronoun (1.8% to 2.4% of the time), not all of these were ungrammatical. The children also provided a total of 606 examples where they supplied both the subject pronoun and object pronoun in English; in stark contrast, the children produced zero examples in their Korean. In both the wh-in-situ and prodrop studies, we see evidence that theories of directionality of crosslinguistic influence and interface hypotheses are not borne out for this population.

It seems from the evidence here that observing heritage speakers in early childhood puts into question many theories about directionality and predicting crosslinguistic influence. Largely speaking, we should have seen more crosslinguistic influence – more wh-in-situ in English, more overt pronouns in Korean, more word order errors in either direction – and we simply do not find that data here. Why might this be? There are a few possibilities worth considering. First, the children in this study are considerably younger than the studies that are conducted on most bilingual populations. Many of the theories of interface, overlapping structures and directionality of crosslinguistic influence are based on research conducted on adult bilinguals (Cabo *et al.*, 2012; Cuza, 2013; Gondra, 2022; Grabitzky, 2014; Ivanov, 2010). There are obvious contrasts between those bilingual groups and the children in this study. Age is a powerful factor, which not only impacts learners' neurological processes and amount of input, but also the degree of life experience, metalinguistic awareness, external pressure to acquire language and the purpose for acquisition. Kwon and Uchikoshi (2022) found similar results when investigating Spanish-English and Cantonese-English bilingual children in the United States, wherein no crosslinguistic influence or L1 effects were found in their study of English tense and aspect. Children have not had as much experience learning as adults and have less metalinguistic awareness than most adults; at the same time, children have different societal pressures and purposes for language acquisition. Though these areas are beyond the scope of this book, this is a powerful factor nonetheless that can change how the theories impact learners' language.

The second possibility is that children are far more aware of the structural differences in their two languages than might be expected. In Chapter 4, it was noted that children tend to use Korean SOV word order overwhelmingly, even though other word orders like SVO, OSV or VSO are possibilities in Korean. In the Korean prodrop study in the same chapter, we saw this similar pattern: children have the option of prodrop – the canonical form – but also have the option of supplying an overt pronoun. However, the children adhered to the canonical form, even preferring to drop the pronoun than oversupply it. Similarly, in their English syntax studies, we found a parallel pattern in the opposite direction: children had the option of using both wh-movement and wh-in-situ in English. However, they did not produce a single example of wh-in-situ, a decidedly Korean-like structure. The children seem to be aware that Korean is a prodrop language and has SOV word order: instead of accidentally deviating into English-like syntax, they keep to what is canonically Korean. They do this for English as well: children show awareness that English is a wh-movement language, a feature directly opposite to Korean, and therefore they will adhere strictly to wh-movement. It is possible this is a method of keeping the two languages separate for these bilingual children. Rather than cross into murky territory (e.g. English can occasionally have Korean-like wh-in-situ, and Korean can occasionally use English-like word order), they keep the line clear of ambiguity and follow the most canonical pattern for each language. The overall thesis of this argument is that the children know far more of each language – both breadth and depth – than we might otherwise give them credit for, a theme that has resonated across the entire book.

9.3 Implications for Identity

Bilingualism is not skin deep. Beyond the language patterns, the work we do here serves more than linguists and linguistic theory. When we discussed the definition of bilingualism in Chapter 1, one crucial point was that language is intricately tied to one's identity. To speak Korean is to be Korean. To have pride in one's language is to have pride in one's identity, and as such that language serves as a banner for one's culture, background, ethnicity and community (Ortega, 2020). Thus, a negative comment about someone's language feels much more personal: a deep commentary on their family, upbringing or who they are as a person. At the same time, we look at the way heritage speakers and heritage grammars are treated: as deviations from the norm, as incomplete or attrited versions of 'the real thing' and as problems to be remedied. Pairing those two facts together is a recipe for linguistic insecurity. This inferiority complex could manifest in several ways. First, deficit perspectives on their language can become deficit perspectives of the speakers themselves, where they feel like they are missing or lacking in some way. I have borne witness to adult L1 speakers of Korean chuckling or even chastising heritage speakers of Korean for their 'funny grammar' or 'American pronunciation'. The resulting morale deflation is immediately evident. The second fallout can be the way the heritage speaker regards themselves with respect to the ethnic community. Feeling like they are 'not really bilingual' because they cannot speak Korean like monolingual Koreans can result in a crisis of belongingness. Even our participant Sarah commented that some of the Korean children in her grade who did not speak Korean were 'whitewashed' and did not '[have] this connection in terms of ethnicity and race', where linguistic proficiency is viewed as an important criterion for ethnic belongingness (Kwon, 2022).

However, careful investigation of heritage speakers like the studies in this book allows us to rewrite some of that narrative, shining light on what they can do and what they do know. Certainly, the young children in this study showed repeatedly just how much Korean they do know. In some cases, the grammatical elements are more salient and larger scale, such as word order, producing Korean canonical word order 99.9% to 100% of the time in their Korean utterances (Chapter 4). Even in their code-mixed utterances where English was inserted, their word order overall was 97% (S)(O)V. In other cases, the children are able to produce areas of grammar that are finely nuanced and quite challenging due to optionality or lack of salience. For instance, children used Korean transitivity marking to indicate causative meanings with 71% to 100% accuracy. They produced Korean sentence final markers with 98.1% to 99.8% accuracy and productively used 447 types of markers. They used Korean prodrop and non-prodrop with 96.3% to 98.7% accuracy. Their morphosyntactic knowledge of Korean, which is supposed to be the vulnerable area of heritage grammars, was very much intact.

Why, then, do heritage speakers experience linguistic insecurity? From previous research and from the work here in Chapters 7 and 8, I propose two hypotheses. One is that linguistic insecurity arises from heavy focus on academic, especially written, forms of language. Labov's (1972) seminal work on linguistic insecurity found a focus on academic skills among adult Spanish heritage speakers. Indeed, there is societal prestige, especially among education-focused communities, on academic language and formal written language, where the assumption is that this is a sign of language proficiency. Certainly, one must have certain levels of proficiency to accomplish academic or written tasks. However, heritage speakers do not grow up using the home language in an academic setting, nor are they expected to write formally. This is an impossible target when the nature of the heritage language is for informal, oral communication within families. For parents, educators or the bilingual individuals themselves to expect proficiency in a genre of language that is not part of their input or experience is a severe mismatch. However, the pressure is there: Preston (2013) demonstrated with the Index of Linguistic Insecurity how heritage speakers perceive linguistic inability of any sort as failure. Sarah talks about this when I asked her about her Korean writing ability in our interview:

> Honestly after I stopped doing the whole Korean school thing, there weren't many opportunities to write in Korean. So definitely, like spacing

> wise: absolute trash, SO trash! [both laugh] I cannot emphasize to you how bad my *ttuyessuki* [word spacing] is. (Sarah)

Although Sarah had immense pride in her language ability, she was rather self-deprecating about her writing ability. Sandy also confessed that her writing was her weakest skill, saying that she was 'terrible at grammar'; I suspect it is actually not grammar in the linguistic sense, but grammar in the sense of writing conventions and mechanics. This perspective does not come from a void; the ideology that writing is high prestige and – in some cases – a requirement of being bilingual is one that is learned, propagated and ingrained in heritage speakers' self-views (Ek *et al.*, 2013).

The second hypothesis for why heritage speakers who are linguistically proficient still experience linguistic insecurity is this: they are measured by their knowledge of specific vocabulary rather than their actual grammar knowledge. I discussed this briefly in Chapter 7, that vocabulary is not a measure of bilinguals' grammatical proficiency. There is a history of measuring speakers' grammar with vocabulary for monolingual children: some of the most prominent measures of language development are vocabulary based, such as the Peabody Picture Vocabulary Test (PPVT), the Expressive Vocabulary Test (EVT), and the British Picture Vocabulary Scale (BPVS). These may even be a reliable measure of monolingual grammatical proficiency, but I argue that using vocabulary to test bilingual students' grammar is not valid nor reliable. Vocabulary is context-driven and context-acquired. When a student learns math in Language A, they will draw from vocabulary in Language A rather than B to talk about math. Native speakers of English with high levels of English proficiency may stumble and have vocabulary gaps when asked to talk about something in which they have no background. For heritage speakers, because their heritage language vocabulary is acquired in the context of the home, familial relationships and/or religious communities, their vocabulary for food, emotions, household items and tasks are far more likely to be developed in Korean. In contrast, they rarely have the opportunity to learn Korean vocabulary pertaining to math, language arts and other school subjects. In our interview, Sandy expressed this sentiment perfectly:

> I definitely can speak it well, but there are some times where I'm just like, 'God what's that word again?', trying to figure out what I want to say in that language, because sometimes it's hard to say one way compared to the other language. (Sandy)

Even in the interview, Sandy admits that it is access to certain vocabulary that becomes her stumbling block rather than her grammar. Again, vocabulary is separate from grammatical knowledge. In Chapter 7, we showed that the code-mixed utterances were mostly English vocabulary that pertained to school, specific verbs and low frequency animal names, nouns and verbs that most likely were learned in school. However, the studies of the children's morphology and syntax showed time and time again evidence of development and sophistication.

The relationship between linguistic insecurity and identity is this: if a person feels that their language is not good enough, and if language is closely tied to one's identity, then the result is that in some part, the speaker feels like they are not good enough. While language is only part of the identity puzzle, for ethnic and heritage groups that are not part of the societal majority, language can serve as a symbol for unity and belongingness that runs as deep as familial relatedness. If this linguistic insecurity came entirely from factual representation of one's language, that is one story; however, if it comes from mismeasurement of language or misplaced prestige on improbable goals (academic writing), then it behooves linguists to set that record straight. Using empirical data from heritage language studies like the ones in this book can deemphasize vocabulary and provide examples of heritage proficiency. This is one practical implication that comes from heteroglossic perspectives.

9.4 Implications for Education

School is undoubtedly one of the most impactful, life-altering prolonged experiences of a young person's life, spending approximately 13,000 hours in total from Kindergarten through 12th grade in a typical US school system. The impact of teachers, administrators, peers, counselors and school staff is profound, just looking at contact time alone. In the United States, though some bilingual students go through a school system that teaches in a bilingual, heteroglossic framework, most multilingual speakers – especially if they are heritage speakers and are dominant in the societal language of English – are in mainstream educational settings with peers and teachers who speak only English. As such, a large percentage of teachers who will be working with linguistically diverse students are those without any special licensure, endorsement or training in bilingualism, second language acquisition or linguistics.

Studies have investigated how mainstream teachers perceive their linguistically diverse students, how it impacts their teaching and how open or receptive they are toward these multilingual students. The literature reveals that teachers generally have negative attitudes and beliefs about bilingual students, regardless of how long they have been teaching or their personal demographics (Walker *et al.*, 2004). Teachers may assume students are lazy, unwilling to learn, confused or even deficient in some way:

> Those poor kids come to school speaking a hodgepodge. They are all mixed up and don't know any language well. As a result, they can't even think clearly (teacher quoted in Walsh, 1991: 106)

Additionally, many teachers hold the belief that their bilingual students will be at a disadvantage because their home language interferes with their performance in English (Clair, 1995; Karabenick & Noda, 2004; Lee & Oxelson, 2006; Reeves, 2006). Although teachers believe having a different home language is not necessarily a problem, they feel that English development should be a priority and exposing students to more English in the home would lead to faster English acquisition (Lee & Oxelson, 2006). Walker *et al.* (2004) reported that teachers have a misunderstanding of the second language acquisition process, believing it should only take two years and that speaking only English at home will help this process. Furthermore, these myths and misunderstandings about bilingualism often contribute to the paradox in which bilingual children are encouraged to become English monolingual, while English monolingual students are lauded for learning a second language. Chen and Kang (2019) attribute the rapid heritage language loss – or the characterization of the United States as a 'linguistic graveyard' – largely to the US educational system and its ideologies of monolingualism. This is precisely the notion that Bakhtin actively rejects, the idea of a primary, national language that is prioritized over others (Bakhtin, 1992). Unfortunately, this has yet to be expunged from US educational culture and policy.

Where do these negative attitudes and ill-advised recommendations stem from? I would argue that part of it is from lack of information on bilingualism and second language acquisition in teacher preparation, a topic I discussed in Park-Johnson (2020b). However, a second source may be from a place of genuine concern mixed with fear and anxiety in a culture where comparison and competition permeate academia. Will my bilingual students be able to perform as well as monolingual students? If they speak another language at home, will they not fall behind with part of their attention drawn elsewhere? Will they learn like the English-speaking children? These are concerns not just held by teachers, but parents as well.

This is something we can address for bilingual children in early childhood using the research in this book. The overwhelming takeaway from all the chapters is that the children perform far better than they might be expected to do. This is the case in both directions: for Korean, which is just spoken in the home and not reinforced in school or dominant society, the children still develop incredibly nuanced morphology and syntax. As discussed above, they successfully acquired case marking and case ellipsis, transitivity markers, classifiers, sentence final markers, Korean word order and prodrop. Furthermore, their English development was at near-ceiling or ceiling for almost every category, developing English verb morphology, word order, overt pronouns, wh-movement and English articles. Even areas that did not follow typical patterns for English development like subject auxiliary inversion showed that despite the differing path of acquisition, children still acquire the target structure.

Additionally, the benefit of longitudinal observation provides further insight. First, in spite of the aforementioned fear of bilingual children falling behind monolingual children, we see here that the Korean-English bilingual children progress toward complex structures and rates of accuracy improve over time across various areas of grammar. Patterns of change over time reveal crucial information about stages (e.g. subject auxiliary inversion develops piecemeal by subject person), changes in complexity (e.g. children use more DP subjects and CP objects as they become older) and when certain features appear (e.g. Korean classifiers appear around 3;10). More importantly, however, we can learn about patterns that remain consistent across time. For example, in Chapter 7 we learned that the amount of code-mixing stays constant for each child across time, showing evidence that code-mixing is a characteristic of their language choices that is not influenced by the changes in their Korean or English. Knowing this may alleviate some concern from parents and educators who believe that code-mixing is interfering with their language development or evidence of confusion; it simply is not the case as evidenced by the empirical data.

Furthermore, in conducting these sessions with the children and interacting with them for years as the English-speaking adult, it is important to note that the children do not sound discernably different than monolingual English-speaking children. Already at the start of the study, in addition to the morphological and syntactic features we have explored in this book, the children have the phonetic and phonological characteristics of any English-speaking child. The older children at this point are already in full-day English-medium schools, and they participate seamlessly in school activities with other age-matched English monolingual peers. This furthers the evidence that they are not falling behind and they are able to function at age-level while at the same time developing a whole separate language at home.

The takeaway for educators is parallel to what was discussed about generative grammar: that heritage grammars may not always look like monolingual grammars, but they follow the rules of human language. In other words, even if there are differences during the language development process, it is not wrong. There is more than one way to arrive at a destination. The data in this book show that children develop both languages at complex levels of morphology and grammar.

How can educators best support heritage speakers? For supporting the heritage language, the most important change can come from ideological change: shifting from the deficit perspective that the heritage language is a problem or hindrance (Ek *et al.*, 2013) and moving toward the view that heritage language is an important resource and value. The child's home language can actually help with English development and be an important part of their overall development as well. Reversing the harmful myths surrounding bilingualism, gaining an understanding of second language acquisition and generating positive views toward multilingualism and multilingual students requires careful teacher preparation (Park-Johnson, 2020; Pettit, 2011). Requiring coursework that addresses these areas for all teachers – not just ones who will be working primarily with language learners – is a crucial next step in serving the growing population of linguistically diverse students. In these courses, studies like the ones we have examined in this book, which shed light on what bilingual learners can do and how they develop, can help demystify the process of bilingual acquisition and debunk longstanding myths that have subjugated students in the past. Additionally, in Jungmin Kwon's (2022) book on transnational Korean-American children, she calls upon educators to invite multilingual students to draw on their rich base of knowledge instead of stifling their agency and creativity:

> What if we encouraged immigrant children to draw on their multilingual repertoires instead of telling them that they have to speak English, Korean, or any other languages? What if we celebrated, respected, and honored all of the efforts that these children make to maintain their transnational connections and multilingual potentials? (Kwon, 2022: 98)

Reframing children's previously regarded 'deficiencies' as an asset is precisely what educators can implement in light of new and continued findings of the abilities, insights and lived experiences of bilingual children.

Community language schools also play an important part in supporting the heritage language, providing supplemental academic outlets for students of these communities to learn history and culture relevant to the ethnic community, and providing students the opportunity to develop academic proficiency in the heritage language. While certainly parental attitudes toward bilingualism and commitment to maintaining the heritage language are a crucial catalyst (DeHouwer, 2007; Kang, 2013, 2015b), community language schools play a significant role. These schools are a common way to increase opportunities for academic language development (Chinen & Tucker, 2005; Lee & Shin, 2008), and are often one of the only spaces where heritage speakers can share their transnational experiences and identities (Kwon, 2022). Korean school was mentioned as an important aspect of Sarah's and Sandy's childhood and adolescence during their interview, as they recalled their positive recollections and reflections of the experience. Researchers have shown that more important than the language itself is the positive cultural ethnic identity and sense of community gained by students, which can lead to a transformative experience for students (Lee & Bang, 2011; Song, 2019; You & Liu, 2011). For younger learners, it may even be their first experience being an ethnic majority in a classroom setting, and the first time they study Korean formally outside of the home. It may also be the first opportunity to learn Korean literacy. Realizing that school subjects like history, music or science can be learned in another language other than English can be an empowering experience for students whose heritage language had previously only been used in informal or social communication. Specifically, Korean schools can be opportunities for students to gain more Korean input to further grow their grammar, but also for introducing them to new vocabulary they would not otherwise get at home. In Chapter 7 we saw that children switch to English for school vocabulary, specific verbs and other vocabulary that is typically more accessible in English; this is a chance to support that vocabulary for Korean.

9.5 Next Steps

In this book I have provided a detailed picture of the morphological and syntactic development of Korean-English bilingual children in early childhood. We have looked specifically at areas of morphology and syntax that are predicted to be sources of difficulty given the nature of the two grammars. We also explored the blending of the two grammars in Chapter 7, studying code-switching and code-mixing structure, content and frequency over time. Finally, in Chapter 8 I provided an epilogue that allows for reflection and recollection by two of the participants in the study, now adult bilinguals. In this book, I have worked to provide a thorough account of Korean-English bilingual development in early childhood; however, there are certainly many more areas that need to be investigated for this dynamic, interesting population of heritage speakers. One goal going forward is to conduct this level of detailed longitudinal research with Korean-English bilingual children living in Korea. It is expected that the results would be similar in some ways (e.g. children acquire both languages and know more than we give them credit for) and quite different in other ways given the environmental language differences, amount of input and social expectations.

There is also the issue of what happens next in the children's development. By the end of this study, our oldest child is approaching 8 years of age, but it is at this point where we – as a field – have limited information about what happens in heritage language development and maintenance. We know that somewhere in the space between early childhood and early adulthood, heritage speakers undergo massive linguistic change; paired with this is change in their environment, the amount of language input they receive and interaction with peers, as well as the natural changes in one's identity development, cognitive development, maturity and life experience that comes with age. Further steps must be taken to investigate heritage language development in middle childhood and early adolescence to help bridge this gap and contribute to a fuller picture of the heritage language experience.

In looking at the heritage speakers in this study, however, I raise a philosophical question: are Korean-English bilingual children in early childhood really heritage speakers? Just as definitions of bilingualism can vary greatly, the definition of heritage speaker is put to the test here. I would argue that, yes, they are heritage speakers because they meet all the conditions for the criteria: they are 'individuals raised in homes where a language other than English is spoken and who are to some degree bilingual in English and the heritage language' (Valdés, 2000: 1). However, perhaps because they are still largely influenced by the home language, their grammars do not necessarily pattern like adult or adolescent heritage speakers. It may also be that given their age, they have not been exposed to English for as long as older learners. What we know of heritage grammars is that they exhibit challenges with morphology and syntax, the primary reason we focused on those categories in this book. In Chapter 1, I gave examples of difficulties that heritage speakers have with areas such as agreement particles, markers and features that are available in one language but not in the other language. However, the children in this book performed surprisingly well on many of the morphological or syntactic areas we have studied, sometimes reaching ceiling-like accuracy scores. They have indeed patterned like heritage speakers in that they had preferences for default forms – such as favoring the default classifier in Korean – or some paradigm leveling, as we saw with sentence final markers. However, these are also patterns that are expected in child Korean, so it is hard to say that this is necessarily as a result of their being heritage speakers. The crucial point is this: it is valuable to have this foundation of knowledge about heritage speakers in early childhood because (1) it shows us that these features were acquired and developing, even if these speakers experience change later in life, and (2) it allows us to capture the time in life before children start to reject the home language, if at all. By providing evidence to parents and educators that children ages 2 through 7 are fully developing both grammars, it may encourage them to continue educating and speaking to the children in both languages and ignore the myths about deficiency. I see this starting to change in the right direction already (Bohnacker, 2022; Jung, 2022; Kircher *et al.*, 2022; Leung *et al.*, 2022).

It is my hope that the combination of linguistic considerations and extralinguistic implications – such as identity, education and equity – continues to be explored in concert with one another, exploring the interconnectedness between these areas. It is also my hope that the topics raised in this book encourage scholars, practitioners, community members, parents and bilinguals themselves to enter into conversations that are interdisciplinary, collaborative and mutually informing to better the lives and experiences of heritage bilinguals.

References

Ahn, H.-D. and Cho, S.E. (2006) Layered nominal structures: Implications for caseless nominals. *Korean Journal of Linguistics* 31, 165–185.

Ahn, H.-D. and Cho, S.E. (2007) Subject-object asymmetries of morphological case realization. *Language and Information* 11 (1), 53–76.

Albirini, A., Benmamoun, E. and Saadah, E. (2011) Grammatical features of Egyptian and Palestinian Arabic heritage speakers' oral production. *Studies in Second Language Acquisition* 33 (2), 273–303.

Al-Kasey, T. and Perez-Leroux, A.T. (1998) Second language acquisition of Spanish null subjects. In S. Flynn, G. Martohardjono and W. O'Neil (eds) *The Generative Study of Second Language Acquisition* (pp. 161–185). Lawrence Erlbaum Associates.

Anderson, R.T. (2001) Lexical morphology and verb use in child first language loss: A preliminary case study investigation. *International Journal of Bilingualism* 5 (4), 377–401.

Argyri, E. and Sorace, A. (2007) Crosslinguistic influence and language dominance in older bilingual children. *Bilingualism: Language and Cognition* 10 (1), 79–99.

Artiles, A.J. and Ortiz, A.A. (2002) *English Language Learners with Special Education Needs*. Center for Applied Linguistics.

Au, T.K., Knightly, L.M., Jun, S.-A. and Oh, J.S. (2002) Overhearing a language during childhood. *Psychological Science* 13 (3), 238–243.

Bakhtin, M. (1992) *The Dialogic Imagination: Four Essays*. University of Texas Press.

Batalova, J. (2022) Korean Immigrants in the United States. migrationpolicy.org. See https://www.migrationpolicy.org/article/korean-immigrants-united-states (accessed 3 October 2023).

Beaudrie, S., Ducar, C. and Potowski, K. (2021) *Heritage Language Teaching: Research and Practice*. McGraw Hill.

Becker, M.K. (2001) The development of the copula in child English: The lightness of be. Dissertation, University of Pennsylvania.

Bellugi, U. (1971) Simplification in children's language. In R. Huxley and D. Ingram (eds) *Language Acquisition: Models and Methods*. Academic Press.

Benmamoun, E., Montrul, S. and Polinsky, M. (2013) Heritage languages and their speakers: Opportunities and challenges for linguistics. *Theoretical Linguistics* 39, 129–181.

Berman, R.A. (1979) The re-emergence of a bilingual: A case study of a Hebrew-English speaking child. *Working Papers on Bilingualism*, No. 19.

Bermel, N. and Kagan, O. (2000) The maintenance of written Russian in heritage speakers. In O. Kagan and B. Rifkin (eds) *The Learning And Teaching of Slavic Languages and Cultures*. Slavica Publishers.

Bernardini, P. and Schlyter, S. (2004) Growing syntactic structure and code-mixing in the weaker language: The Ivy hypothesis. *Bilingualism: Language and Cognition* 7 (1), 49–69.

Berthele, R. (2012) The influence of code-mixing and speaker information on perception and assessment of foreign language proficiency: An experimental study. *International Journal of Bilingualism* 16 (4), 453–466.

Bohnacker, U. (2022) Turkish heritage families in Sweden: Language practices and family language policy. *Journal of Multilingual and Multicultural Development* 43 (9), 861–873.

Bolonyai, A. (2005) 'Who was the best?' Power, knowledge and rationality in bilingual girls code choices. *Journal of Sociolinguistics* 9 (1), 3–27.

Bolonyai, A. (2007) (In)vulnerable agreement in incomplete bilingual L1 learners. *International Journal of Bilingualism* 11 (1), 3–23.

Brown, C.L. (2009) Heritage language and ethnic identity: A case study of Korean-American college students. *International Journal of Multicultural Education* 11 (1), 1–16.

Brown, R. (1973) *A First Language: The Early Stages*. Harvard University Press.

Cabo, D.P., Lingwall, A. and Rothman, J. (2012) Applying the interface hypothesis to heritage speaker acquisition: Evidence from Spanish mood. *Proceedings of the Annual Boston University Conference on Language Development* 36 (2), 437–448.

Caesar, L.G. and Kohler, P.D. (2007) The state of school-based bilingual assessment: Actual practice versus recommended guidelines. *Language, Speech, and Hearing Services in Schools* 38 (3), 190–200.

Canagarajah, S. (2013) *Translingual Practice* (1st edn). Routledge.

Canagarajah, S. (ed.) (2017) *The Routledge Handbook of Migration and Language* (1st edn). Routledge.

Cazden, C.B. (1968) The acquisition of noun and verb inflections. *Child Development* 39, 433–448.

Chang, S.-E. and Mandock, K. (2019) A phonetic study of Korean heritage learners production of Korean word-initial stops. *Heritage Language Journal* 16 (3), 273–295.

Chen, J.S. (2003) Pro-drop parameter, universal grammar and second language acquisition of Chinese and English. Dissertation, University of New South Wales.

Chen, J. and Kang, H.-S. (2019) Tiger moms or cat dads: Parental role in bilingualism among Asian and Latino Americans. *Social Science Quarterly* 100 (4), 1154–1170.

Cheng, L.-R. and Butler, K. (1989) Code-switching: A natural phenomenon vs language 'deficiency'. *World Englishes* 8 (3), 293–309.

Chinen, K. and Tucker, G.R. (2005) Heritage language development: Understanding the roles of ethnic identity and Saturday school participation. *Heritage Language Journal* 3 (1), 27–59.

Chini, M. (2011) New linguistic minorities: Repertoires, language maintenance and shift. *International Journal of the Sociology of Language* 2011 (210), 47–69.

Cho, S.W. (2004) Argument ellipsis in Korean -speaking children's early speech. Doctoral dissertation, Harvard University.

Choi, H.-W. (1997) Topic and focus in Korean: The information partition by phrase structure and morphology. In H. Sohn and J. Haig (eds) *Japanese/Korean Linguistics* (vol. 6, pp. 545–561). Center Study Language & Information.

Choi, H.-W. (2003) Paradigm leveling in American Korean. *Language Research* 39 (1), 183–204.

Chomsky, N. (1995) *The Minimalist Program*. MIT Press.

Choo, M. (2008) *Using Korean: A Guide to Contemporary Usage*. Cambridge University Press.

Chung, E.S. (2013) Exploring the degree of native-likeness in bilingual acquisition: Second and heritage language acquisition of Korean case-ellipsis. Dissertation, University of Illinois at Urbana-Champaign.

Chung, E.S. (2015) Challenging a single-factor analysis of case drop in Korean. *Language and Information* 19 (1), 1–18.

Chung, G.-H. (1994) Case and its acquisition in Korean. Doctoral Dissertation, University at Texas at Austin.

Chung, H.H. (2006) Code switching as a communicative strategy: A case study of Korean–English Bilinguals. *Bilingual Research Journal* 30 (2), 293–307.

Clair, N. (1995) Mainstream classroom teachers and ESL students. *TESOL Quarterly* 29 (1), 189–196.

Cuza, A. (2013) Crosslinguistic influence at the syntax proper: Interrogative subject-verb inversion in heritage Spanish. *The International Journal of Bilingualism* 17 (1), 71–96.

Davies, A. (1991) The notion of the native speaker. *Journal of Intercultural Studies* 12 (2), 35–45.

Ek, L.D., Sanchez, P. and Quijada Cerecer, P.D. (2013) Linguistic violence, insecurity, and work: Language ideologies of Latina/o Bilingual teacher candidates in Texas. *International Multilingual Research Journal* 7 (3), 197–219.

Forsythe, H., Greeson, D. and Schmitt, C.C. (2019) After the null subject parameter: Acquisition of the null-overt contrast in Spanish. *LingBuzz* 004882, August.

Fry, J.S. (2001) *Ellipsis and 'wa'-Marking in Japanese Conversation*. Stanford University Press.

Fry, R. (2007) Perspective shifts and a theoretical model relating to kaigaishijo and kikokushijo, or third culture kids in a Japanese context. *Journal of Research in International Education* 6 (2), 131–150.

García, O. (2009) *Bilingual Education in the 21st Century: A Global Perspective*. Wiley-Blackwell Publishing.

Garvey, C. (1979) An approach to the study of children's role play. *The Quarterly Newsletter of the Laboratory of Comparative Human Cognition* 12, 69–73.

Gathercole, V. (1980) Birdies like birdseed the bester than buns: A study of relational comparatives and their acquisition. Dissertation, University of Kansas.

Gawlitzek-Maiwald, I. and Tracy, R. (1996) Bilingual bootstrapping. *Linguistics* 34 (5), 901–926.

Genesee, F. (1989) Early bilingual development: One language or two? *Journal of Child Language* 16 (1), 161–179.

Genesee, F. and Nicoladis, E. (2008) Bilingual first language acquisition. In E. Hoff and M. Shatz (eds) *Blackwell Handbook of Language Development* (pp. 324–342). Blackwell Publishing Ltd.

Glass, W.R. and Perez-Leroux, A.T. (1998) A parametric interpretation of learners' errors: The acquisition of Spanish null subjects. *Estudios de Linguistica Aplicada* 16 (28), 27–46.

Goble, R. (2016) Linguistic insecurity and lack of entitlement to Spanish among third-generation Mexican Americans in narrative accounts. *Heritage Language Journal* 13 (1), 29–54.

Gondra, A. (2022) Testing the interface hypothesis: Heritage speakers' perception and production of Spanish subject position with unergative and unaccusative verbs. *International Journal of Bilingual Education and Bilingualism* 25 (5), 1730–1764.

Gottlieb, M. and Hamayan, E. (2006) Assessing oral and written language proficiency: A guide for psychologists and teachers. In G.B. Esquivel, E. Lopez, S. Nahiri and A. Brice (eds) *Handbook of Multicultural School Psychology* (pp. 245–263). Lawrence Erlbaum.

Grabitzky, V.K. (2014) Vulnerable language areas in attriting L1 German: Testing the interface hypothesis and structural overlap hypothesis. Dissertation, University of Iowa.

de Groot, C. (2005) The grammars of Hungarian outside Hungary from a linguistic-typological perspective. In A. Fenyvesi (ed.) *Hungarian Language Contact Outside Hungary: Studies on Hungarian as a Minority Language* (pp. 351–370). John Benjamins Publishing Company.

Grosjean, F. (1989) Neurolinguists, beware! The bilingual is not two monolinguals in one person. *Brain and Language* 36 (1), 3–15.

Grosjean, F. (2012) *Life with Two Languages*. Harvard University Press.

Guasti, M.T. (2014) An excursion into interrogatives in Early English and Italian. In M.-A. Friedemann and L. Rizzi (eds) *The Acquisition of Syntax* (pp. 105–128). Routledge.

Ha, K. and Choi, S. (2012) Adult second language learners' acquisition of word order and case markers in Korean. *The Korean Language in America* 17, 1–23.

Håkansson, G. (1995) Syntax and morphology in language attrition: A study of five bilingual expatriate Swedes. *International Journal of Applied Linguistics* 5 (2), 153–169.

Hakuta, K. (1976) A case study of a Japanese child learning English as a second language. *Language Learning* 26 (2), 321–351.

Hauser-Grüdl, N., Arencibia Guerra, L., Witzmann, F., Leray, E. and Müller, N. (2010) Cross-linguistic influence in bilingual children: Can input frequency account for it? *Lingua* 120 (11), 2638–2650.

Haznedar, B. (2003) The status of functional categories in child second language accquisition: Evidence from the acquisition of CP. *Second Language Research* 19 (1), 1–41.

He, A. (2006) Toward an identity theory of the development of chinese as a heritage language. *Heritage Language Journal* 4 (1), 1–28.

Hong, Y.-C. (1994) Incorporation theory and the distribution of case morphemes. *Studies in Generative Grammar* 4, 1–43.

de Houwer, A. (2007) Parental language input patterns and children's bilingual use. *Applied Psycholinguistics* 28 (3), 411–424.

de Houwer, A. (2009) *Bilingual First Language Acquisition*. Clevedon: Multilingual Matters.

Hulk, A. and Müller, N. (2000) Bilingual first language acquisition at the interface between syntax and pragmatics. *Bilingualism: Language and Cognition* 3 (3), 227–244.

Hyams, N. (1986) *Language Acquisition and the Theory of Parameters*. Dordrecht: Reidel.

Ionin, T. and Wexler, K. (2002) Why is 'is' easier than '-s'?: Acquisition of tense/agreement morphology by child second language learners of English. *Second Language Research* 18 (2), 95–136.

Ionin, T., Ko, H. and Wexler, K. (2004) Article semantics in L2 acquisition: The role of specificity. *Language Acquisition* 12 (1), 3–69.

Ionin, T., Zubizarreta, M.L. and Maldonado, S.B. (2008) Sources of linguistic knowledge in the second language acquisition of English articles. *Lingua* 118 (4), 554–576.

Ionin, T., Choi, S.H. and Liu, Q. (2021) Knowledge of indefinite articles in L2-English: Online vs. offline performance. *Second Language Research* 37 (1), 121–160.

Isabelli, C.A. (2004) The acquisition of the null subject parameter properties in SLA: Some effects of positive evidence in a naturalistic learning context. *Hispania* 87 (1), 150–162.

Ivanov, I.P. (2010) Second language acquisition of Bulgarian object clitics: A test case for the interface hypothesis. Dissertation, University of Iowa.

Jeon, A. (2022) Growing up (un)bounded: Globalization, mobility and belonging among Korean third culture kids. *International Multilingual Research Journal* 16 (1), 65–77.

Jeon, M. (2008) Korean heritage language maintenance and language ideology. *Heritage Language Journal* 6 (2), 206–223.

Jia, R. and Paradis, J. (2015) The use of referring expressions in narratives by Mandarin heritage language children and the role of language environment factors in predicting individual differences. *Bilingualism* 18 (4), 737–752.

Jisa, H. (2000) Language mixing in the weak language: Evidence from two children. *Journal of Pragmatics* 32 (9), 1363–1386.

Jo, H. (2001) 'Heritage' language learning and ethnic identity: Korean Americans' struggle with language authorities. *Language, Culture and Curriculum* 14 (1), 26–41.

Jung, C.D. (2022) Bilingual proficiency development and translanguaging practices of emergent Korean-English bilingual children in Korea. *Journal of Language Teaching and Research* 13 (6), 1156–1165.

Kan, R.T. (2019) Production of Cantonese classifiers in young heritage speakers and majority language speakers. *International Journal of Bilingualism* 23 (6), 1531–1548.

Kang, H.-S. (2002) What is missing in interlanguage? Acquisition of determiners by Korean learners of English. *Working Papers in Educational Linguistics* 18 (1), 51–65.

Kang, H.-S. (2013) Korean-immigrant parents' support of their American-Born children's development and maintenance of the home language. *Early Childhood Education Journal* 41 (6), 431–438.

Kang, H.-S. (2015a) Heritage language learning for contesting the model minority stereotype: The case of Korean American college students. In N.D. Hartlep (ed.) *Modern Societal Impacts of the Model Minority Stereotype* (pp. 185–204). IGI Global.

Kang, H.-S. (2015b) Korean families in America: Their family language policies and home-language maintenance. *Bilingual Research Journal* 38 (3), 275–291.

Kang, H.-S. (2016) Subject-object asymmetry in the second language acquisition of English relatives and embedded wh-questions. *Journal of Psycholinguistic Research* 45 (6), 1389–1406.

Kang, H.S. and Uchikoshi, Y. (2022) Child second language development of English tense and aspect: The role of narrative organization. *Applied Psycholinguistics* 43 (4), 785–804.

Karabenick, S.A. and Clemens Noda, P.A. (2004) Professional development implications of teachers' beliefs and attitudes toward English language learners. *Bilingual Research Journal* 28 (1), 55–75.

Kim, D. (1993) *The Specificity/Non-Specificity Distinction and Scrambling Theory*. Thaehaksa.

Kim, H. (2022) Learning in/through Korean pop culture fandom: A qualitative case study of Non-Korean US college students. Dissertation, University of Illinois at Chicago.

Kim, J.-H., Montrul, S. and Yoon, J. (2009) Binding interpretations of anaphors by Korean heritage speakers. *Language Acquisition* 16 (1), 3–35.

Kim, J.-H., Montrul, S. and Yoon, J. (2010) Dominant language influence in acquisition and attrition of binding: Interpretation of the Korean reflexive caki. *Bilingualism: Language and Cognition* 13 (1), 73–84.

Kim, S.-J. (2013) The syntax and acquisition of negative polarity items in heritage Korean. Dissertation, University of Kansas.

Kim, S.-Y. (2014) Errors in inflectional morphemes as an index of linguistic competence of Korean heritage language learners and American learners of Korean. Dissertation, University of Kansas .

Kim, T. (2008) Subject and object markings in conversational Korean. Ph.D. dissertation, State University of New York at Buffalo.

Kim, Y.-H. (1998) Overt case and covert case in Korean. *Studies in Generative Grammar* 8, 177–240.

Kircher, R., Quirk, E., Brouillard, M., Ahooja, A., Ballinger, S., Polka, L. and Byers-Heinlein, K. (2022) Quebec-based parents' attitudes towards childhood multilingualism: Evaluative dimensions and potential predictors. *Journal of Language and Social Psychology* 41 (5), 527–552.

Ko, E.-S. (2000) A discourse analysis of the realization of objects in Korean. *Japanese/Korean Linguistics* 9, 198–208.

Ko, H., Ionin, T. and Wexler, K. (2010) The role of presuppositionality in the second language acquisition of English articles. *Linguistic Inquiry* 41 (2), 213–254.

Kolb, N., Natalia, M. and Marit, W. (2022) Crosslinguistic influence in child L3 English: An empirical study on Russian-German heritage bilinguals. *The International Journal of Bilingualism* 26 (4), 476–501.

Kondo–Brown, K. (2005) Differences in language skills: Heritage language learner subgroups and foreign language learners. *The Modern Language Journal* 89 (4), 563–581.

Kwon, J. (2022a) *Understanding the Transnational Lives and Literacies of Immigrant Children*. Teachers College Press.

Kwon, J. (2022b) Parent–child translanguaging among transnational immigrant families in museums. *International Journal of Bilingual Education and Bilingualism* 25 (2), 436–451.

Kwon, S.-N. and Zribi-Hertz, A. (2008) Differential function marking, case, and information structure: Evidence from Korean. *Language* 84 (2), 258–299.

Kwon, J. and Martínez-Álvarez, P. (2022) A young linguistic and cultural mediator: A case of trilingual siblings' interaction. *International Multilingual Research Journal* 16 (1), 47–64.

Labov, W. (1966) *The Social Stratification of English in New York City*. Center for Applied Linguistics.

Labov, W. (1972) *Sociolinguistic Patterns*. University of Pennsylvania Press.

Lacorte, M. and Canabal, E. (2005) Teacher beliefs and practices in advanced Spanish classrooms. *Heritage Language Journal* 3 (1), 83–107.

Laleko, O. and Polinsky, M. (2016) Between syntax and discourse. *Linguistic Approaches to Bilingualism* 6 (4), 396–439.

Lanza, E. (1992) Can bilingual two-year-olds code-switch? *Journal of Child Language* 19 (3), 633–658.

Lanza, E. (1997) *Language Mixing in Infant Bilingualism: A Sociolinguistic Perspective*. Oxford University Press.

Lee, D.M., Duesbery, L., Han, P.P., Thupten, T., Her, C.S. and Pang, V.O. (2017) Academic needs and family factors in the education of Southeast Asian American students: Dismantling the model minority myth. *Journal of Southeast Asian American Education & Advancement* 12 (2), 1–31.

Lee, D.-Y. (2002a) The function of the zero particle with special reference to spoken Japanese. *Journal of Pragmatics* 34 (6), 645–682.

Lee, E. and Zaslansky, M. (2015) Nominal reference in Korean heritage language discourse. *Heritage Language Journal* 12 (2), 132.

Lee, E.H. (2018) L2 and heritage Korean tense morphology in discourse: Interplay between lexical and discursive meaning. *Heritage Language Journal* 15 (2), 173–202.

Lee, H. (2006a) Effects of focus and markedness hierarchies on object case ellipsis in Korean. *Discourse and Cognition* 13 (2), 205–231.

Lee, H. (2007) Case ellipsis at the grammar/pragmatics interface: A formal analysis from a typological perspective. *Journal of Pragmatics* 39 (9), 1465–1481.

Lee, H. (2008) Processing efficiency and object case ellipses in Korean. *Korean Journal of Linguistics* 33 (1), 159–179.

Lee, H. (2016) Usage probability and subject–object asymmetries in Korean case ellipsis: Experiments with subject case ellipsis. *Journal of Linguistics* 52 (1), 70–110.

Lee, H.S. and Thompson, S.A. (1989) A discourse account of the Korean accusative marker. *Studies in Language* 13 (1), 105–128.

Lee, J. (2005) The native speaker: An achievable model? *Asian EFL Journal* 7, 152–163.

Lee, J.S. (2002b) The Korean language in America: The role of cultural identity in heritage language learning. *Language, Culture and Curriculum* 15 (2), 117–133.

Lee, J.S. and Oxelson, E. (2006) 'It's not my job': K-12 teacher attitudes toward students' heritage language maintenance. *Bilingual Research Journal* 30 (2), 453–477.

Lee, J.S. and Shin, S.J. (2008) Korean heritage language education in the United States: The current state, opportunities, and possibilities. *Heritage Language Journal* 6 (2), 153–172.

Lee, J.S. and Suarez, D. (2009) A synthesis of the roles of heritage languages in the lives of children of immigrants: What educators need to know. In T.G. Wiley, J.S. Lee and R.W. Rumberger (eds) *The Education of Language Minority Immigrants in the United States* (pp. 136–171). Multilingual Matters.

Lee, N. (2019a) A pragmatic and sociolinguistic perspective to subject expression in spoken Korean: With focus on first and second person. PhD thesis, The Australian National University (Australia).

Lee, S. (2019b) Speaking Korean in America: An ethnographic study of a community-based Korean heritage language school. PhD thesis, University of Pennsylvania.

Lee, S. (2023) Bilingual youth identities contested through the use of K-12 language arts textbooks in a Korean heritage language classroom. *International Journal of Bilingual Education and Bilingualism* 1 (1), 1–14.

Lee, S. and Bang, Y.-S. (2011) Listening to teacher lore: The challenges and resources of Korean heritage language teachers. *Teaching and Teacher Education* 27 (2), 387–394.

Lee, S.K. (2006b) The Latino students' attitudes, perceptions, and views on bilingual education. *Bilingual Research Journal* 30 (1), 107–122.

Lee, W.R. (1995) 'Natives' and 'non-natives': Much ado about nothing-or something? *Praxis des neusprachlichen Unterrichts* 42 (2), 115–120.

Lee-Ellis, S. (2009) The development and validation of a Korean C-Test using rasch analysis. *Language Testing* 26 (2), 245–274.

Leopold, W.F. (1970) *Speech Development of a Bilingual Child; A Linguist's Record*. AMS Press.

Leung, G., Calcagno, S., Tong, R. and Uchikoshi, Y. (2022) 'I think my parents like me being bilingual': Cantonese–English DLBE upper elementary students mediating parental ideologies about multilingualism. *Journal of Multilingual and Multicultural Development* 43 (6), 518–533.

Li, D.C.S. (2008) Understanding mixed code and classroom code-switching: Myths and realities. *New Horizons in Education* 56 (3), 75–87.

Li, G. (2005) Other people's success: Impact of the 'model minority' myth on underachieving Asian students in North America. *KEDI Journal of Educational Policy* 2 (1), 69–86.

Li, W. (2018) Translanguaging as a practical theory of language. *Applied Linguistics* 39 (2), 261–261.

Lo, A. (2009) Evidentiality and morality in a Korean heritage language school. In A. Reyes and A. Lo (eds) *Beyond Yellow English: Toward a Linguistic Anthropology of Asian Pacific America* (pp. 175–194). Oxford University Press.

MacSwan, J. (2017) A multilingual perspective on translanguaging. *American Educational Research Journal* 54 (1), 167–201.

MacWhinney, B. (2000) *The CHILDES Project: Tools for Analyzing Talk* (3rd edn). Lawrence Erlbaum.

Maratsos, M.P. (1974) Preschool children's use of definite and indefinite articles. *Child Development* 45 (2), 446–455.

Maratsos, M.P. (1976) *The Use of Definite and Indefinite Reference in Young Children: An Experimental Study of Semantic Acquisition*. Cambridge University Press.

Meisel, J.M. (1989) Early differentiation of languages in bilingual children. In K. Hyltenstam and L. Obler (eds) *Bilingualism Across the Lifespan: Aspects of Acquisition, Maturity and Loss* (pp. 13–40). Cambridge University Press.

Meisel, J.M. (2001) The simultaneous acquisition of two first languages: Early differentiation and subsequent development of grammars. In J. Cenoz and F. Genesee (eds) *Trends in Bilingual Acquisition* (pp. 11–42). John Benjamins.

Meisel, J.M. (2011) *First and Second Language Acquisition*. Cambridge University Press.

Meyerhoff, M. (2016) *Introducing Sociolinguistics* (3rd edn). Routledge.

Milson-Whyte, V. (2013) Pedagogical and socio-political implications of code-meshing in classrooms: Some considerations for a translingual orientation to writing. In S. Canagarajah (ed.) *Literacy as Translingual Practice: Between Communities and Classrooms* (pp. 115–127). Routledge.

Ming, T. and Tao, H. (2008) Developing a Chinese heritage language corpus: Issues and a preliminary report. In A. He (ed.) *Chinese as a Heritage Language: Fostering Rooted World Citizenry* (pp. 167–188). University of Hawaii Press.

Mishina-Mori, S. (2005) Autonomous and interdependent development of two language systems in Japanese/English simultaneous bilinguals: Evidence from question formation. *First Language* 25 (3), 291–315.

Montrul, S. (2004) Subject and object expression in Spanish heritage speakers: A case of morphosyntactic convergence. *Bilingualism: Language and Cognition* 7 (2), 125–142.

Montrul, S. and Bowles, M. (2009) Back to basics: Incomplete knowledge of differential object marking in Spanish heritage speakers. *Bilingualism: Language and Cognition* 12 (3), 363–383.

Montrul, S. and Sanchez-Walker, N. (2013) Differential object marking in child and adult Spanish heritage speakers. *Language Acquisition* 20 (2), 109–132.

Montrul, S.A., Bhatt, R.M. and Bhatia, A. (2012) Erosion of case and agreement in Hindi heritage speakers. *Linguistic Approaches to Bilingualism* 2 (2), 141–176.

Montrul, S., Bhatt, R. and Girju, R. (2015) Differential object marking in Spanish, Hindi, and Romanian as heritage languages. *Language* 91 (3), 564–610.

Moustakas, C. (1994) *Phenomenological Research Methods*. SAGE Publications.

Müller, N. and Hulk, A. (2001) Crosslinguistic influence in bilingual language acquisition: Italian and French as recipient languages. *Bilingualism: Language and Cognition* 4 (1), 1–21.

Museus, S.D. and Kiang, P.N. (2009) Deconstructing the model minority myth and how it contributes to the invisible minority reality in higher education research. *New Directions for Institutional Research* 2009 (142), 5–15.

Myers-Scotton, C. (1993) *Duelling Languages: Grammatical Structure in Codeswitching*. Clarendon Press.

Nam, K. and Ko, Y. (2013) *Pyojun Kugo Munpomnon [Grammar of Standard Korean]* (3rd edn). Tap Chulpansa.

Ngo, B. (2008) Beyond 'culture clash' understandings of immigrant experiences. *Theory Into Practice* 47 (1), 4–11.

O'Grady, W., Lee, M. and Choo, M. (2003) A subject-object asymmetry in the acquisition of relative clauses in Korean as a second language. *Studies in Second Language Acquisition* 25 (3), 433–448.

Olsson, A. and Sullivan, K.P.H. (2005) Provoking dominance shift in a bilingual Swedish-American English 4-year-old child. In J. Cohen, K.T. McAlister, K. Rolstad and J. MacSwan (eds) *ISB4: Proceedings of the 4th International Symposium on Bilingualism* (pp. 1750–1764). Cascadilla Press.

Ortega, L. (2020) The study of heritage language development from a bilingualism and social justice perspective. *Language Learning* 70 (S1), 15–53.

Ortiz, A., García, S., Wheeler, D. and Maldonado-Colon, E. (1986) https://www.academia.edu/53810751/Characteristics_of_Limited_English_Proficient_Hispanic_Students_Served_in_Programs_for_the_Speech_and_Language_Handicapped_Implications_for_Policy_Practice_and_Research_Part_III (accessed 15 December 2022).

Otheguy, R., García, O. and Reid, W. (2015) Clarifying translanguaging and deconstructing named languages: A perspective from linguistics. *Applied Linguistics Review* 6, 281–307.

Paradis, J. and Navarro, S. (2003) Subject realization and crosslinguistic interference in the bilingual acquisition of Spanish and English: What is the role of the input? *Journal of Child Language* 30 (2), 371–393.

Paradis, J., Nicoladis, E. and Genesee, F. (2000) Early emergence of structural constraints on code-mixing: Evidence from French–English bilingual children. *Bilingualism: Language and Cognition* 3 (3), 245–261.

Park, C.H. (2012) Hankwukewa yengeuy saynglyak hyensangey tahan thongkyeycek cepkun: cwuewa mokcekeuy saynglyakul cwungsimulo [Statistical approach about ellipsis of Korean and English: Focused on ellipsis of subject and object]. *Emwunnoncip [Journal of the Society of Korean Language and Literature]* 66, 171–191.

Park-Johnson, S.K. (2017a) Code mixing as a window into language dominance: Evidence from Korean heritage speakers. *Heritage Language Journal* 14 (1), 49–69.

Park-Johnson, S.K. (2017b) Crosslinguistic influence of wh-in-situ questions by Korean-English bilingual children. *International Journal of Bilingualism* 21 (4), 419–432.
Park-Johnson, S.K. (2019a) The role of person in subject auxiliary inversion in English wh-questions: Evidence from Korean-English bilingual children. *International Journal of Bilingualism* 23 (1), 313–328.
Park-Johnson, S.K. (2019b) Case ellipsis: Acquisition of variability by young heritage speakers of Korean. *International Multilingual Research Journal* 13 (1), 15–31.
Park-Johnson, S.K. (2020a) Receptive knowledge of transitivity alternation by Korean Heritage speakers. *Heritage Language Journal* 17 (3), 355–376.
Park-Johnson, S.K. (2020b) Teachers' attitudes and beliefs about code-mixing by bilingual students. *Educational Studies* 56 (2), 125–144.
Park-Johnson, S.K. and Shin, S.J. (2020) *Linguistics for Language Teachers: Lessons for Classroom Practice*. Routledge.
Park-Johnson, S.K. and Kim, H. (2021) *Linguistic Distance for the Emergent Heritage Speaker: The Case of Korean Heritage Children*. University of North Carolina.
Pascual y Cabo, D. and Gómez Soler, I. (2015) Preposition stranding in Spanish as a heritage language. *Heritage Language Journal* 12 (2), 186–209.
Petersen, J. (1988) Word-internal code-switching constraints in a bilingual child's grammar. *Linguistics* 26 (3), 479–493.
Pettit, S.K. (2011) Teachers' beliefs about English language learners in the mainstream classroom: A review of the literature. *International Multilingual Research Journal* 5 (2), 123–147.
Phinney, J.S., Romero, I., Nava, M. and Huang, D. (2001) The role of language, parents, and peers in ethnic identity among adolescents in immigrant families. *Journal of Youth and Adolescence* 30 (2), 135–153.
Pires, A. and Taylor, H. (2007) The syntax of wh-in-situ and common ground. *Proceedings from the Annual Meeting of the Chicago Linguistic Society* 43 (2), 201–215.
Polinsky, M. (2008) Gender under incomplete acquisition: Heritage speakers' knowledge of noun categorization. *Heritage Language Journal* 6 (1), 40–71.
Polinsky, M. (2018) *Heritage Languages and their Speakers*. Cambridge University Press.
Polinsky, M. and Kagan, O. (2007) Heritage languages: In the 'wild' and in the classroom. *Language and Linguistics Compass* 1 (5), 368–395.
Pollock, D.C. and Van Reken, R. (2001) *Third Culture Kids: The Experience of Growing Up Among Worlds*. Nicholas Brealey/Intercultural Press.
Portes, A. and Schauffler, R. (1994) Language and the second generation: Bilingualism yesterday and today. *International Migration Review* 28 (4), 640–661.
Preston, D.R. (2013) Linguistic insecurity forty years later. *Journal of English Linguistics* 41 (4), 304–331.
Quay, S. (2001) Managing linguistic boundaries in early trilingual development. In J. Cenoz and F. Genesee (eds) *Trends in Bilingual Acquisition* (pp. 149–199). John Benjamins Publishing, ProQuest.
Reeves, J.R. (2006) Secondary teacher attitudes toward including English-language learners in mainstream classrooms. *The Journal of Educational Research* 99 (3), 131–142.
Rizzi, L. (1994) Early null subjects and root null subjects. In T. Hoekstra and B. Schwartz (eds) *Language Acquisition Studies in Generative Grammar* (pp. 151–176). John Benjamins Publishing Company.
Romaine, S. (1995) *Bilingualism* (2nd edn). Wiley-Blackwell Publishing.
Rowland, C.F. (2007) Explaining errors in children's questions. *Cognition* 104 (1), 106–134.
Rumbaut, R.G. (2009) A language graveyard? The evolution of language competencies, preferences and use among young adult children of immigrants. In T.G. Wiley, J.S. Lee and R.W. Rumberger (eds) *The Education of Language Minority Immigrants in the United States* (pp. 35–71). Multilingual Matters.

Rumbaut, R.G., Massey, D.S. and Bean, F. (2006) Linguistic life expectancies: Immigrant language retention in Southern California. *Population and Development Review* 32 (3), 447–460.

Schafer, R. and de Villiers, J. (2000) Imagining articles: What a and the can tell us about the emergence of DP. *Proceedings of the 24th Annual Boston University Conference on Language Development* 2. ScholarWorks, University of Massachusetts Amherst.

Schieffelin, B. (1994) Code-switching and language socialization: Some probable relationships. In L. Hewett, R. Sonnenmeier and J. Duchan (eds) *Pragmatics: From Theory to Practice* (pp. 20–42). Prentice Hall.

Schutze, C. (2003) The non-omission of nonfinite be. *Nordlyd* 31 (3).

Serratrice, L. (2008) Null and overt subjects at the syntax-discourse interface: Evidence from monolingual and bilingual acquisition. *LOT Occasional Series* 8, 181–200.

Serratrice, L. and Sorace, A. (2003) Overt and null subjects in monolingual and bilingual italian acquisition. *Proceedings of the Annual Boston University Conference on Language Development* 27 (2), 739–750.

Serratrice, L. and Hervé, C. (2015) Referential expressions in bilingual acquisition. In L. Serratrice and S.E.M. Allen (eds) *The Acquisition of Reference* (pp. 311–333). John Benjamins.

Shin, J. (2016) Hyphenated identities of Korean heritage language learners: Marginalization, colonial discourses and internalized whiteness. *Journal of Language, Identity, and Education* 15 (1), 32.

Shin, K.Y. (2010a) Auxiliary selection and the role of transitivity in grammaticalisation. *Journal of Historical Pragmatics* 11 (1), 96–121.

Shin, S.J. (2004) *Developing in Two Languages: Korean Children in America*. Multilingual Matters.

Shin, S.J. (2018) *Bilingualism in Schools and Society: Language, Identity, and Policy* (2nd edn). Routledge.

Shin, S.J. and Milroy, L. (2000) Conversational codeswitching among Korean-English bilingual children. *International Journal of Bilingualism* 4 (3), 351–383.

Shin, S.-Y. (2010b) The functions of code-switching in a Korean Sunday school. *Heritage Language Journal* 7 (1), 91–116.

Shin Kim, M. (2013) The mental lexicon of low-proficiency Korean heritage learners. *Heritage Language Journal* 10 (1), 17–35.

Silva-Corvalán, C. (1994) *Language Contact and Change: Spanish in Los Angeles*. Oxford University Press.

Smith, D.J. (2006) Thresholds leading to shift: Spanish/English codeswitching and convergence in Georgia, U.S.A. *International Journal of Bilingualism* 10 (2), 207–240.

Sohn, H. (1994) *Korean* (1st edn). Routledge.

Son, M. (2020) Cross-linguistic syntactic priming in Korean learners of English. *Applied Psycholinguistics* 41 (5), 1223–1247.

Song, J. (2019) Wuli and stance in a Korean heritage language classroom: A language socialization perspective. *Linguistics and Education* 51, 12.

Song, J.Y., Sundara, M. and Demuth, K. (2009) Phonological constraints on children's production of English third person singular -s. *Journal of Speech, Language, and Hearing Research* 52 (3), 623–642.

Song, M., O'Grady, W., Cho, S. and Lee, M. (1997) The learning and teaching of Korean in community schools. *The Korean Language in America* 2, 111–127.

Sopata, A., Długosz, K., Brehmer, B. and Gielge, R. (2021) Cross-linguistic influence in simultaneous and early sequential acquisition: Null subjects and null objects in Polish-German bilingualism. *The International Journal of Bilingualism* 25 (3), 687–707.

Soriente, A. (2007) Cross-linguistic and cognitive structures in the acquisition of wh-questions in an Indonesian-Italian bilingual child. In I. Kecskes and L. Albertazzi (eds) *Cognitive Aspects of Bilingualism* (pp. 325–362). Springer Netherlands.

Strik, N. and Pérez-Leroux, A.T. (2011) Jij doe wat girafe? Wh-movement and inversion in Dutch-French bilingual children. *Linguistic Approaches to Bilingualism* 1 (2), 175–205.
Sundara, M., Demuth, K. and Kuhl, P.K. (2011) Sentence-position effects on children's perception and production of English third person singular -s. *Journal of Speech, Language and Hearing Research (Online)* 54 (1), 55–71A.
Theakston, A.L., Lieven, E.V.M. and Tomasello, M. (2003) The role of the input in the acquisition of third person singular verbs in English. *Journal of Speech, Language, and Hearing Research* 46 (4), 863–877.
Tomasello, M., Call, J. and Gluckman, A. (1997) Comprehension of novel communicative signs by apes and human children. *Child Development* 68 (6), 1067–1080.
Tse, L. (2000) The effects of ethnic identity formation on bilingual maintenance and development: An analysis of Asian American narratives. *International Journal of Bilingual Education and Bilingualism* 3 (3), 185–200.
Useem, J., Useem, R.H. and Donoghue, J.D. (1963) Men in the middle of the third culture: The roles of American and non-western people in cross-cultural administration. *Human Organization* 22 (3), 169–179.
Valadez, C.M., MacSwan, J. and Martinez, C. (2000) Toward a new view of low-achieving bilinguals: A study of linguistic competence in designated 'semilinguals'. *The Bilingual Review/La revista bilingue* 25 (3), 238–248.
Valdés, G. (2000) Introduction. In T.G. Wiley, J.K. Peyton, D. Christian, S.C.K. Moore and N. Liu (eds) *Spanish for Native Speakers: AATSP Professional Development Handbook* (vol. 1, pp. 1–29). Harcourt College.
Valdés, G. (2005) Bilingualism, heritage language learners, and SLA research: Opportunities lost or seized? *The Modern Language Journal* 89 (3), 410–426.
Valdés, G. (2014) Heritage languages students: Profiles and possibilities. In T.G. Wiley, J.K. Peyton, D. Christian, S.C.K. Moore and N. Liu (eds) *Handbook of Heritage, Community, and Native American Languages in the United States: Research, Policy, and Educational Practice* (pp. 27–35). Routledge and Center for Applied Linguistics.
de Villiers, J.G. and de Villiers, P.A. (1973) A cross-sectional study of the acquisition of grammatical morphemes in child speech. *Journal of Psycholinguistic Research* 2 (3), 267–278.
Walker, A., Shafer, J. and Iiams, M. (2004) 'Not in my classroom': Teacher attitudes towards English language learners in the mainstream classroom. *NABE Journal of Research and Practice* 2 (1), 130–160.
Wang, Q., Lillo-Martin, D., Best, C.T. and Levitt, A. (1992) Null subject versus null object: Some evidence from the acquisition of Chinese and English. *Language Acquisition* 2 (3), 221–254.
Warden, D.A. (1976) The influence of context on children's use of identifying expressions and references. *British Journal of Psychology* 67 (1), 101–112.
Warden, D. (1981) Learning to identify referents. *British Journal of Psychology* 72 (1), 93–99.
Westergaard, M. (2003) Unlearning V2: Transfer, markedness, and the importance of input cues in the acquisition of word order in English by Norwegian Children. *EUROSLA Yearbook* 3, 77–101.
Wing, J.Y. (2007) Beyond Black and White: The model minority myth and the invisibility of Asian American students. *The Urban Review* 39 (4), 455–487.
Wolfram, W. and Schilling-Estes, N. (2005) *American English: Dialects and Variation* (2nd edn). Blackwell Publishing Ltd.
Yeon, J. (2001) Transitivity alternation and neutral-verbs in Korean. *Bulletin of the School of Oriental and African Studies* 64 (3), 381–391.
Yip, V. and Matthews, S. (2000) Syntactic transfer in a Cantonese–English bilingual child. *Bilingualism: Language and Cognition* 3 (3), 193–208.

Yip, V. and Matthews, S. (2006) Assessing language dominance in bilingual acquisition: A case for mean length utterance differentials. *Language Assessment Quarterly* 3 (2), 97–116.

Yip, V. and Matthews, S. (2007) *The Bilingual Child: Early Development and Language Contact*. Cambridge University Press.

Yip, V. and Matthews, S. (2009) Conditions on cross-linguistic influence in bilingual acquisition: The case of wh-interrogatives. Paper presented at the 7th International Symposium on Bilingualism, Utrecht, The Netherlands.

You, B. and Liu, N. (2011) Stakeholder views on the roles, challenges, and future prospects of Korean and Chinese heritage language-community language schools in the phoenix metropolitan area: A comparative study. *Heritage Language Journal* 8 (3), 67–92.

Zdorenko, T. and Paradis, J. (2008) The acquisition of articles in child second language English: Fluctuation, transfer or both? *Second Language Research* 24 (2), 227–250.

Zdorenko, T. and Paradis, J. (2012) Articles in child L2 English: When L1 and L2 acquisition meet at the interface. *First Language* 32 (1–2), 38–62.

Zentella, A.C. (1997) *Growing up Bilingual: Puerto Rican Children in New York*. Wiley-Blackwell Publishing.

Index

acceptability 31, 50, 54, 58, 96
agglutinative 14, 16, 25, 40
articles 27, 29, 61-68, 77-79, 91, 134, 137-138
aspect 25, 28, 43, 89, 111, 136, 139

Bilingual Education Act 6

case ellipsis 14, 25, 30-36, 134, 137, 144
case marker 14, 25-26, 30-37, 46, 91, 110, 118, 134, 137-138
classifier 10, 14, 25-30, 37-41, 45-47, 134, 137, 144-145, 162
code-mixing 7, 17, 21, 33, 104, 113, 115-118, 123, 129, 136, 141-145
    definition 105-106
    function 106, 112, 114-115
    perception 106-107, 145
    structure 16, 107-113, 117, 119, 135, 141, 147
code-switching 3, 14, 16-17, 105, 107, 111-112, 114-115, 117-119, 131, 133, 135, 147
community language school, see also Korean school 131, 146
crosslinguistic influence 15-16, 49, 57, 78, 81-83, 96, 138-139

declarative 25
    English 29, 69, 84, 91-94, 100
    sentence final marker 26, 45-46, 134
default 28, 67
    classifier 10, 27, 37-40, 134, 137, 148
    sentence final marker 45-46, 134
    double tensing 74-76

education 7, 9, 13, 133, 141, 143, 148
    parents 18
    policy 3-4, 133, 144
    special education 17
educator 4, 6, 16-17, 57, 60, 79, 104, 106, 133, 141, 145-146, 148

family language policy 13, 122-123

generative linguistic theory 2-4, 47, 78, 136, 145

heteroglossia (heteroglossic) 2-4, 132, 136, 143
honorific 14, 25, 27

identity 4-5, 8, 17, 133, 146-148
    affirming 61
    language 6, 126, 129-130, 132, 140, 143
    Korean 12-13, 112, 120-122, 124, 126-130, 132, 146
imperative 25, 91-92, 94, 96-98, 100, 133
inflectional morphology 30, 43, 111
input 3, 15, 47, 58, 137-139, 141
    English 18-21, 62, 71, 82
    heritage language 10-11, 18, 32, 37-38, 46, 58, 137, 147
interface 14-15, 58, 61, 96, 138-139
interrogatives see also wh-questions 25, 29, 84, 91-92, 96
intransitive 25, 40-42, 54-55, 92, 97
intrasentential code-switching see also code-mixing 105, 117, 135
irregular verbs 43, 68-70, 72-73, 77, 134
isolating 14, 16, 28

Korean community school, see Korean school
Korean school 13, 21-22, 58, 118, 121, 127, 130-131, 141, 146-147

language dominance (dominant) 1, 7, 9-10, 13-15, 19, 22, 41, 53, 60, 78, 81-82, 115-119, 135-143
linguistic insecurity 12, 140-143
listening 11, 121-122

mean length of utterance (MLU) 81-82, 116-117
modal (modality) 25, 28, 43, 86, 89, 91

null copula 69, 74-77, 134
null pronominals see also prodrop 48-49, 52, 57, 96, 134

object drop see also prodrop 48, 53, 55-57, 97-98
object use see also pronominal use 54-56, 97-98, 103
overregularization 69, 74-76

parents 13-14, 16-24, 35, 56-58, 60, 79-80, 96, 104, 106-107, 112, 116, 118, 121-124, 130, 133, 141, 144-146, 148
person feature 31, 89-91, 104, 136
pragmatics 25, 30-32, 35, 49, 53, 58, 81-82, 96, 138
pride 122-125, 127-129, 131-132, 140, 142
prodrop 14-15, 26, 29, 48, 52-59, 83, 96-100, 103-104, 134, 137-141, 144
pronominal (pronoun) use 53-54, 80, 96, 104, 135, 139

reading 11, 121
regular verbs 68-70, 72-73, 77-78

semantics 2, 25, 27, 29, 31-32, 37, 61
sentence final markers 30, 43-47, 134, 141, 144, 148
sequential bilingual(ism) 1-2, 4, 7-9
shame 124, 125, 128-131

sibling 19, 24, 39, 113-114, 122, 130, 135
simultaneous bilingual(ism) 1, 4, 7-8, 14, 16, 96
speaking 11, 121-122
subject auxiliary inversion 29, 83-84, 88-91, 103-104, 135-136, 144-145
subject drop see also prodrop 48, 54-57, 97
subject use see also pronominal use 36, 55-56, 97-98, 103
subject-object asymmetry 33-36, 134, 137

teacher preparation see also educator 144, 146
tense 25, 28-29, 43, 69, 85, 88, 111, 136, 139
    past 28, 68-69, 71, 74-78, 134
    present 69, 71, 73-74, 76-78
third person singular (3sg) 28, 68-69, 74-78, 134
transfer see also crosslinguistic influence 15, 49, 81
transitivity (transitive) 14, 25, 28, 30, 40-43, 46-47, 134, 136, 141, 144
translanguaging, see also code-switching 13, 105-106

voice 25, 28

wh-questions 15, 26, 80, 82-90, 138
    wh-in-situ 14, 26, 80-83, 135, 138-140
    wh-movement 14, 29, 80-84, 103-104, 135, 138, 140, 144
word order 14-15, 25, 48-50, 52, 57-59, 80, 91-92, 94, 96-97, 107-108, 134-135, 137, 139
    canonical 15, 26, 34-36, 48-50, 52-53, 57, 59, 83, 91-94, 96, 108, 137, 140-141
    English 14, 29, 49, 80, 91-97, 104, 108, 135, 137, 139-140
    Korean 14, 26, 31-32, 48-52, 57-59, 83, 108, 111, 134, 137, 139-141, 144
writing 121-122, 131, 141-143

For Product Safety Concerns and Information please contact our EU Authorised Representative:

Easy Access System Europe

Mustamäe tee 50

10621 Tallinn

Estonia

gpsr.requests@easproject.com

www.ingramcontent.com/pod-product-compliance
Lightning Source LLC
Chambersburg PA
CBHW070617300426
44113CB00010B/1560